"*Waiting to Inhale* shows the sparks that fly when the people pass initiatives the politicians don't like."

— John Stossel, *ABC News*

"An incredibly comprehensive and thorough history of the medical marijuana dispute as well as a sophisticated analysis of the medical marijuana issue in general. It deserves wide readership.

"It is impossible to read this book without feeling indignation about the behavior of officialdom both statewide and federal. It is incredible how strong myths and the status quo can be.

"A splendid and powerful book."

— Milton Friedman, Nobel Prize winner for economics, 1976. Senior Research Fellow, Hoover Institute, Stanford University

"This is an important book with far-reaching policy implications. Alan Bock carefully documents the irrational governmental controls on the use of marijuana for medicinal purposes. More importantly, Bock systematically constructs a compelling argument for legalizing the use of medical marijuana."

— Jim Doti, President of Chapman University and Donald Bren Distinguished Professor of Business and Economics

"A balanced account by a veteran journalist detailing the political treachery and cowardice that kept the will of the California voters from being implemented on medical marijuana.

— Joe McNamara, former police chief of San Jose, California, and Kansas City, Missouri

"Medical marijuana may sound like a narrow issue, but it touches on large topics such as the role of doctors in easing pain and saving lives, states' rights and popular sovereignty, and the right of individuals to make their own decisions about their lives. *Waiting to Inhale* is a comprehensive book about this important subject—the only book you'll need on the growing political movement to give individuals access to marijuana for medical purposes."

— David Boaz, Cato Institute

"Alan bock provides the history and political analysis behind one of the most important political, medical, criminal, and social issues of our time. The fight over medical marijuana is the first test in post–World War II America of the fundamental question of governance: the individual versus the state. Bock captures the importance of the fight as no other author has, sees its implications for broader issues throughout our society, and makes fascinating predictions for how this titanic struggle will be resolved. It is essential reading for students of government in the United States and lovers of liberty everywhere."

— Congressman Tom Campbell

"Alan Bock's coverage of the politics of medical marijuana has been candid and compelling, casting a bright light on those who would suppress the voters' wishes in passing Proposition 215 to justify their failed drug policies. It takes journalists like Bock to put the will of the people first, to ensure the integrity of our electoral process is maintained in the face of even the most virulent and unprincipled opposition."

— State Senator John Vasconcellos
(D-Silicon Valley, CA)

"This important book provides what you need to know to understand the great battle for state regulation to allow use of medical marijuana, which is not only consistent with Constitutional limitations on federal reach into the states, but moves us toward the founders' vision of a government that leaves individual Americans free to choose their own medicines. Whose body is it anyway?"

> — Durk Pearson and Sand Shaw, authors of
> *Life Extension: A Practical Scientific*
> *Approach*

"*Waiting to Inhale: The Politics of Medical Marijuana* by Alan Bock goes far beyond the sound bite simplisms of other documentaries on medicinal cannabis. Instead of settling for a compilation of contradictory utterances by contemporary authorities, the author methodically sets the stage historically. He properly reminds us that cannabis was once available for prescription and how it was taken away sixty years ago. With this added perspective, his interviews materially add to his review of scientific, medical, and political sources. Bock gives the reader an in-depth appreciation of the complex issues raised by recent changes in marijuana law enforcement policy and the underreported stories of the cultural creatives and their salutary roles in the ambiguous and changing worlds."

> — Tod H. Mikuriya, M.D.

"With a journalist's keen eye and clear voice, Alan Bock has written the important—and continuing—chronicle of California's Compassionate Use Act, Proposition 215. *Waiting to Inhale* should be read by all who consider themselves compassionate. Count among them Women of Reform Judaism, an organization that has taken a strong position in favor of changing legislation to permit medicinal use of marijuana and to enable research on its effectiveness.

> — Jane Marcus, Ph.D., Beth Am Women, Beth Am Congregation, Los Altos Hills, California

Waiting to Inhale

The Politics of Medical Marijuana

ALAN W. BOCK

SEVEN LOCKS PRESS

Santa Ana, California
Minneapolis, Minnesota
Washington, D.C.

Seven Locks Press
P.O. Box 25689
Santa Ana, CA 92799
(800) 354-5348

Individual Sales. This book is available through most bookstores or can be ordered directly from Seven Locks Press at the address above.

Quantity Sales. Special discounts are available on quantity purchases by corporations, associations, and others. For details, contact the "Special Sales Department" at the publisher's address above.

Printed in the United States of America

Library of Congress Cataloging-in-Publication Data
is available from the publisher
ISBN 0-929765-82-6

Cover and Interior Design by Sparrow Advertising & Design
Editorial Services by Peoplespeak

To dozens of patients I have met, and to thousands I haven't, who are contending with uncertainty on the front lines with pitifully little help from anybody—and also, of course, to Jennifer and Stephen.

Contents

Preface

As an editorial writer and columnist for the *Orange County Register,* I write about what is in the news—and sometimes about subjects *Register* writers and editors think should be in the news—on a given day. The *Register*'s editorial board does formulate an editorial agenda each year, highlighting issues we members think will be important or that should be important to our readers and to our overall mission of building the intellectual underpinnings of a free society. For the most part, however, journalists are driven by events and only on occasion will have the opportunity to step back and see patterns or a larger picture.

Therefore, as the story of the implementation of Proposition 215, the medical marijuana initiative California voters passed in 1996, unfolded, I covered it firsthand, getting to know many of the principals—some face to face, some as voices on the telephone. But I also wrote about local zoning and planning disputes; tussles in Sacramento and Washington; taxes; regulation; economic issues; environmental issues; political developments; the latest twists and turns in the Middle East, northern Ireland, Bosnia, Kosovo, and elsewhere; and cultural developments.

Insofar as there are patterns in the passage of medical marijuana initiatives and efforts to implement them, it took time for reflection and review to see them and to place them in some kind of context. By the time I began writing this book, I had compiled so much information on the issues I had to leave out more than I could include here. But if this book helps patients, doctors and other health-care workers, law enforcement personnel, and government officials to make more informed decisions about whether the medical use of marijuana is indicated, how medical marijuana can be obtained safely and affordably, and under what conditions it should be used, it will have served its main purpose.

Most journalism—or media coverage, if you will—on this topic (as on most) lacks context, and it's not hard to see why. Reporters cover the news events of the day, and since most reporters have to cover a multitude of topics in a career (and often in a week), they use the information most readily available, often official statements plus a check of previous clippings on the topic. Even if a reporter knows some context or history, the constant editorial demand for brevity often dictates that important information has to be left out. Most newspapers subscribe to several wire services but use stories as they choose, based on their own news judgment; thus, a 15-inch wire story packed with context may appear in the paper as a 3-inch item under "Nation Briefly" or some such heading. In addition, few American journalists or headline writers, when the topic is medical marijuana, can resist the urge to insert in a few sixties-style countercultural references or puns of varying degrees of cleverness, which tends (unintentionally in most cases, I believe) to trivialize the subject or treat it like a joke.

I have written four or five Sunday Commentary section cover pieces on various aspects of medical marijuana since 1996, pieces that offer the luxury of 1,500 to 2,200 words with which to explore a subject or event. Each time I have found myself cutting material, abbreviating explanations, eliminating subtopics, and the like to make the piece fit in the space available. The editorial process pushes writers to simplify and think about the reader's attention span; usually clarity is gained but a bit of color and context is lost.

Journalists rely on a wide array of tools to ply their trade. We plow through reams of press releases from people and organizations with different political and commercial agendas, scan the wire services for topics of interest, consult standard reference sources, and sometimes actually read books. Most journalists use the Internet extensively these days. We talk on the phone, ideally with people who really know something about the topic and will lay out the case for all sides of an issue, often enough with people who we know from experience will give us good sound bites and get the basic facts right. Interviews of varying degrees of formality contribute to the process, from a formal editorial board meeting where politicians or representatives of some group with an interest in a current issue meet in a relatively formal setting with every syllable on the record, to brief questions asked of those who were witnesses to some notable event, to personal reporting that includes witnessing an event and getting impressions from other witnesses and observers, to the long and wide-ranging interview with a public figure or person in the news that might yield an in-depth or feature article, to a private talk with a participant who promises to explain what's really behind a current controversy so long as you don't use the participant's name and find other sources for the information imparted.

This process sometimes leads to abbreviated or unbalanced stories without much context, but most journalists develop enough skill to get the verifiable public facts right, even when they miss the real story in the process. The fact that if you quote somebody he or she will be able to read the quote in the paper the next day and that a certain coterie of readers takes delight in finding errors in newspapers and pointing them out can catch your attention quickly after a few embarrassing mistakes.

Good journalists like to think they serve readers best when they write about a topic on which they have done personal reporting, often through seeing events themselves and questioning the participants, as compared to interviewing a couple of experts about an event in

Afghanistan none of you has actually seen. That way one's own skills—as an observer, as an interrogator, as a seeker for what lies beyond or beneath the surface of events, as an organizer and synthesizer of information, and finally as a writer—come most actively into play. Even the best reporters miss things, but when they concentrate their skills and their attention on an event or topic they are observing personally, they can give a reader particularly valuable information. At least we hope so.

I have done more personal reporting and gotten to know more of the principals on the topic of medical marijuana than on almost any other topic I have covered in my 20 years at the *Register*. In part this has been happenstance. For a writer in Orange County, California, who is not a foreign correspondent, it is easier and more practical to cover a trial in Santa Ana than a genocide in Rwanda. In addition, the modern medical marijuana movement began in California, at least in terms of getting a measure on the ballot and passed.

Having written my first column on the industrial uses of hemp in 1988 and attended the 1992 National Organization for Reform of Marijuana Laws (NORML) convention in San Francisco, I already knew many of the people involved in the issue. Many of the politicians and officials involved in various aspects of the issue have visited the *Register* for meetings with the editorial board, on which I sit, and have been generous with their time and candor in other venues as well. During the time I was a media fellow with the Hoover Institution at Stanford University I was able to visit with a number of people involved in this issue in Northern California, some of whom I had previously known only as voices on the telephone, as well as give a talk on the subject. California Attorney General Bill Lockyer has been gracious enough to meet and discuss the issue with me at length on several occasions. District attorneys and candidates for DA positions, sheriffs, and police officers on the street have been generous with their time, giving me their perspectives and describing the problems they face in their work.

Patients, operators of cannabis dispensaries, doctors, and caretakers have spent hours explaining to me how marijuana used medically has helped them to cope with medical conditions, as well as the difficulties they face in obtaining their medicine reliably and legally, even after the laws were changed. Several, including Marvin Chavez and Steve Kubby, have opened their complete medical records to me so I could better understand the role of cannabis in their therapy.

Simply by following trials and court actions I have gotten to know many of the defense attorneys who have worked on behalf of medical marijuana patients facing various charges. They, along with a few judges, have been extremely helpful as I have tried to sort through some of the legal issues involved. Durk Pearson and Sandy Shaw, principals in one of the lawsuits concerning the scope of federal power over medical marijuana, have hosted me in their home in Nevada and were more than generous with their time and attention whenever I called wanting clarification on some legal or scientific issue.

Rand Martin of state Senator John Vasconcellos's office and Dave DeAlba of Attorney General Bill Lockyer's office have always been available or returned telephone calls promptly and have been especially helpful in finding information on the few occasions they didn't know the answer right away. Jack Herer seems to know everybody and everything and has always been willing to generously share what he knows. Richard Cowan, former executive director of NORML who now runs the Web site MarijuanaNews.com, has been very generous with information, leads, and encouragement, as have Kevin Zeese and Allen St. Pierre. Tom Umberg, formerly with the Office of National Drug Control Policy (ONDCP, the "drug czar's" office), has spent considerable time fielding my queries and challenges, maintaining a cheerful and professional attitude even (or especially?) when he knew we were bound to disagree. ONDCP director General Barry McCaffrey shared some of his valuable time with me on one of his trips to California.

My wife, Jennifer, and my son, Stephen, have been extremely

patient and understanding about the late hours tapping on the computer and the trips away from home. It would not have been possible to gather the information that has made this book possible if publishers Dave Threshie and Chris Anderson, along with Commentary Directors Ken Grubbs and Cathy Taylor, of the *Orange County Register*, had not been willing, over a period of several years, to risk possible ridicule and allow me to keep reporting and writing on a topic many would prefer to ignore. The *Register*'s editorial page continues to do something almost unique in American journalism: to stand for a set of principles embracing human liberty and dignity rather than splitting the difference with an acceptable compromise, reflecting some pollster's version of what readers want to see, or serving as cheerleaders for local officials and civic organizations. Even so, management could have passed the word quietly but firmly that we had written enough on medical marijuana that some people thought we were a bit obsessed with the topic and that it might be a good idea to focus on some of the other multifarious threats to human liberty abroad in the world for the time being. Nobody in management did.

After focusing on this topic for a while, I think it can become tempting to want to shout at people on all sides of the issue: "It's only a plant. Reasonably intelligent human beings should be able sit down and figure out how to use it for its beneficial properties and avoid any harms associated with it without all this rancor." But for a number of reasons, marijuana is more than a plant in modern America. It is something of a cultural signifier, a totem laden with assumptions and attitudes about what constitutes a good life, how people can live well and responsibly, and to what extent one person's opinion on such matters can or should determine how another person acts. Perhaps this book can help to clarify and demystify some of these issues.

CHAPTER ONE

The Voters Speak

On election day 1996, voters in California and Arizona endorsed initiatives that would make it easier for people under the treatment of a physician to have legal access to drugs that had before been illicit. As of spring 2000, voters in Arizona (for a second time; the legislature tried to void the 1996 vote), Alaska, Oregon, Nevada, Washington, Maine, and the District of Columbia, representing about 20 percent of the U.S. population, have passed similar measures to authorize qualified patients to use marijuana (and in the case of Arizona, other illicit drugs). In April 2000 the state legislature of Hawaii passed and the governor signed a similar law, making Hawaii the first state in this most recent round of legislation to change its laws through legislative action (rather than through the initiative process) to permit certified patients to use marijuana medically. Connecticut, Louisiana, New Hampshire, Ohio, Vermont, Virginia, and Wisconsin also have laws, passed in the 1970s or early 1980s, that either permit physicians to prescribe marijuana for medical purposes, set up a legal regime to make it possible for physicians to do so when and if the federal government changes the legal status of marijuana, or authorize a medical-necessity defense against marijuana possession, use, and/or cultivation statutes.[1]

Although principals of the drug war proclaimed after the California and Arizona votes that the people had been duped, persuaded by sympathetic images of sick and dying people—put forward in a sophisticated campaign that took opponents by surprise—to endorse a medical policy that would be a "cruel hoax" for patients, it is increasingly difficult to defend such a position four years later. Voters in every part of the country, despite opposition from almost all elected officials, have supported medical marijuana by increasingly large margins. The strict prohibitionists have made their case and the people have considered it and rejected it. Only a minority of Americans favors legalizing marijuana for recreational use. But every poll shows that 60 to 70 percent of them favor allowing it to be used medicinally, under some sort of supervision by a doctor. In every state where a medical marijuana initiative has made it to the ballot, that initiative has been successful. Despite opposition and foot-dragging from officialdom at all levels, the American people clearly favor this modest reform.

Yet almost four years after voters changed the law, patients in most of California had little expectation that a safe, reliable, and legal source of marijuana would be available to them through aboveboard methods and without hassle. Indeed, dozens were in the throes of prosecution, and many had had their medicine seized with no conviction having been declared and in some cases with no charges being filed. The California Narcotics Officers' Association continued to proclaim on its Web site that "Marijuana is not Medicine." The federal drug enforcement establishment continued to do everything in its power—which was less than it had hoped it would be able to do under the law, which did nothing to tone down the rhetoric—to emphasize that federal law still made marijuana illegal for medical purposes and states and voters who tried to decide otherwise did so at their peril.

In California an attorney general elected in 1998 as an enthusiastic supporter of medical marijuana and Proposition 215, part of a near-complete Democratic sweep of statewide offices, had been able to do almost nothing to facilitate orderly and reasonably uniform implementation of the new law. In early 2000 some district attorneys were still following something close to a "zero tolerance" policy—arresting patients, even after being shown a written recommendation from a physician, seizing their medicine, and forcing patients into expensive court battles in order to "let the courts sort it out." Patients who wished to travel from one part of the state to another, in a state where people love their cars and love to travel, often faced the risk of being arrested simply by carrying their medicine from one county to another. More people with credible medical reasons for smoking marijuana were being arrested in 2000 than in 1996. Thousands of patients were wondering: They told us to change the law if we wanted to use marijuana medicinally, so we did. But if we can't get officials to obey the law, what was the point?

Before I explain how this situation came about, it might be useful to define a few terms and clarify just what the law says. To define the terms, I'll use the March 1999 publication *Marijuana and Medicine: Assessing the Science Base,* assembled by the Institute of Medicine (IOM), a quasi-governmental body chartered in 1970 by the National Academy of Sciences (NAS) "to enlist distinguished members of the appropriate professions in the examination of policy matters pertaining to the health of the public."[2] This particular study was requested and paid for by the Executive Office of the President, Office of National Drug Control Policy (the "drug czar's" office) after California and Arizona passed their initiatives in 1996. I use it not necessarily because it is the best of the many government studies on marijuana's risks and benefits but because it is the most recent, so it incorporates information not available to scientists who prepared earlier reports, and reflects a conscientious effort to assess all the most recent scientific studies, not only in the United States but in other countries.

In the introduction to the book, the research team describes the object of its study this way:

> Marijuana is the common name for *Cannabis sativa,* a hemp plant that grows throughout temperate and tropical

climates. The most recent review of the constituents of marijuana lists 66 cannabinoids. But that does not mean there are 66 different cannabinoid effects or interactions. Most of the cannabinoids are closely related; they fall into only 10 groups of closely related cannabinoids, many of which differ by only a single chemical moiety and might be midpoints along biochemical pathways—that is, degradation products, precursors, or byproducts.

Delta 9-tetrahydrocannabinol (Ä9-THC) is the primary psychoactive ingredient; depending on the particular plant, either THC or cannabidiol is the most abundant cannabinoid in marijuana. Throughout this report, THC is used to indicate Ä9-THC. In a few cases where variants of THC are discussed, the full names are used. All the cannabinoids are lipophilic—they are highly soluble in fatty fluids but not in water. Indeed, THC is so lipophilic that it is aptly described as "greasy."

Throughout this report, *marijuana* refers to unpurified plant extracts, including leaves and flower tops, regardless of how they are consumed—whether by ingestion or smoking. References to the effects of marijuana should be understood to include the composite effects of its various components; that is, the effects of THC are included among the effects of marijuana, but not all the effects of marijuana are necessarily due to THC. Discussions concerning *cannabinoids* refer only to those particular compounds and not to the plant extract. This distinction is important; it is often blurred or exaggerated.

Cannabinoids are produced in epidermal glands on the leaves (especially the upper ones), stems, and the bracts that support the flowers of the marijuana plant. Although the flower itself has no epidermal glands, it has the highest cannabinoid content anywhere on the plant, probably

because of the accumulation of resin secreted by the supporting bracteole (the small leaf-like part below the flower).
The amounts of cannabinoids and their relative abundance
in a marijuana plant vary with growing conditions, including
humidity, temperature, and soil nutrients (reviewed in Pate,
1994). The chemical stability of cannabinoids in harvested
plant material is also affected by moisture, temperature, sun-
light, and storage. They degrade under any storage
condition.[3]

As the IOM report notes, cannabis, marijuana, and hemp are all the
same plant. There are different varieties that produce more or less THC
content (although growing conditions seem to play almost as important
a role in THC content as genetic qualities). When the hemp plant is
grown for fiber it is usually harvested when the stalk is relatively slen-
der—as the fiber is thought to be most useful and versatile then, which
is before many blossoms or buds have had a chance to develop—and the
plants are sown closely together. A field planted with hemp to be used for
fiber, therefore, will be of little interest to somebody seeking psychoactive
substances, but if the plants were allowed to mature fully they would
have THC-laden buds. A field planted with the idea of harvesting the
seeds, which are used for birdseed, oil extraction, and even food (much
of the cereal and "gruel" eaten by peasants in the Middle Ages was made
from hempseed),[4] of course, will also feature buds or flowers, which must
mature to produce seeds.

In essence, then, the terms *marijuana, cannabis,* and *hemp* all refer to
the same plant, and they will be used virtually interchangeably in this
book, although *hemp* will be used mainly to refer to industrial or fiber-
related uses of nonflower parts of the plant. If one of the terms occurs in
quoted material in a sense that differs from this rule, I'll try to explain
the differences in brackets. In some older material the spelling *marihuana*
is used, and that spelling will be retained in direct quotations or where it
is part of a proper name.

The IOM report's introduction notes that "Marijuana plants have been used since antiquity for both herbal medication and intoxication. The current debate over the medical use of marijuana is essentially a debate over the value of its medicinal properties relative to the risk posed by its use." It goes on to assert that "modern medicine adheres to different standards from those used in the past. The question is not whether marijuana can be used as an herbal remedy but rather how well this remedy meets today's standards of efficacy and safety. We understand much more than previous generations about medical risks. Our society generally expects its licensed medications to be safe, reliable, and of proven efficacy; contaminants and inconsistent ingredients in our health treatments are not tolerated."[5] Whether that statement is true of all people who seek either medical treatment or therapies to make them feel better—the popularity of low-tech "alternative" therapies suggests that some prefer a different approach, although most herbal medications do come in standardized dosages—the respect for science and the scientific method that permeates most of the IOM report is welcome. The scientific approach has its limitations. Arriving at something close to the scientific truth about a question doesn't necessarily tell you what the proper public policy toward that phenomenon should be; different societies whose members have different beliefs or values may well approach the same phenomenon quite differently. But without some respect for the kind of answers the scientific method can produce, those making public policy will be largely groping in the dark.

Having discussed some of the properties of marijuana from a biological or medical perspective, let's look at the language of Proposition 215, the initiative passed by California voters in November 1996:

> SECTION 1. Section 11362.5 is added to the Health and Safety Code, to read:
>
> *11362.5 (a) This section shall be known and may be cited as the Compassionate Use Act of 1996:*

(b)(1) The people of the State of California hereby find and declare that the purposes of the Compassionate Use Act of 1996 are as follows:

To ensure that seriously ill Californians have the right to obtain and use marijuana for medical purposes where that medical use is deemed appropriate and has been recommended by a physician who has determined that the person's health would benefit from the use of marijuana in the treatment of cancer, anorexia, AIDS, chronic pain, spasticity, glaucoma, arthritis, migraine, or any other illness for which marijuana provides relief.

To ensure that patients and their primary caregivers who obtain and use marijuana for medical purposes upon the recommendation of a physician are not subject to criminal prosecution or sanction.

To encourage the federal and state governments to implement a plan to provide for the safe and affordable distribution of marijuana to all patients in medical need of marijuana.

(2) Nothing in this section shall be construed to supersede legislation prohibiting persons from engaging in conduct that endangers others, nor to condone the diversion of marijuana for nonmedical purposes.

(c) Notwithstanding any other provision of law, no physician in this state shall be punished, or denied any right or privilege, for having recommended marijuana to a patient for medical purposes.

(d) Section 11357, relating to the possession of marijuana, and Section 11358, relating to the cultivation of marijuana, shall not apply to a patient, or to a patient's primary caregiver, who possesses or cultivates marijuana for the personal medical purposes of the patient upon the written or oral recommendation or approval of a physician.

(e) For the purposes of this section, "primary caregiver" means the individual designated by the person exempted under this section who has consistently assumed responsibility for the housing, health, or safety of that person.

SECTION 2. If any provision of this measure or the application thereof to any person or circumstance is held invalid, that invalidity shall not affect other provisions or applications of the measure that can be given effect without the invalid provision or application, and to this end the provisions of this measure are severable.[6]

Courts have dealt with various provisions of this measure in some detail and will no doubt have to do so in the future. A couple of matters are worth noting early on, however. The first is that several specific ailments are mentioned by name, followed by "or any other illness for which marijuana provides relief," which is fairly open-ended. Dennis Peron, who founded the San Francisco Cannabis Buyers Club and was largely responsible for the final wording of the initiative, told me this was done mainly for educational purposes. Even if the initiative failed, he said, people would have looked at their ballot booklets and noticed specific ailments for which at least somebody (generally, in fact, a respectable minority of the medical community) thought marijuana was useful.

Note that subsection (A) says that "seriously ill Californians have the right to obtain and use marijuana." How are they to obtain it? That question has loomed large in the aftermath, as has the question of what constitutes being "seriously ill."

In subsection (B) and in other places, the word "recommendation" is used rather than "prescription," and "recommend" rather than "prescribe." This terminology was employed primarily to avoid potential conflicts with federal law. The system of limiting access to certain drugs by requiring that a licensed physician write a prescription first was set up formally in the 1930s under federal statute (although a less formal prescription system existed before then and some states had already set up more formal regulatory schemes). The laws that control access to certain drugs through prescription are federal laws. The privilege licensed physicians have to write prescriptions for various drugs is granted as part of a federal regulatory system. The writers of Proposition 215 chose the possibly less precise words "recommend" and "recommendation" to avoid conflict with this system.

Subsection (C) gives as one of the purposes "To encourage the federal and state governments to implement a plan to provide safe and affordable distribution of marijuana." "Encourage" doesn't mean the same as "require," so this is not the language of an absolute mandate; nonetheless, it sends a strong message to governments as to what the people want it to do. In California, county and city governments are viewed under the law as subdivisions of the state government (although there are different kinds of charters for both counties and cities that provide different degrees of independence and freedom of action to the local subdivisions). Do the words "safe and affordable" imply that money is expected to change hands in whatever distribution system is set up? Does the reference to "distribution" imply that existing laws prohibiting the selling or distribution of marijuana are to be changed or softened for medical patients? Courts have wrestled with and will probably continue to wrestle with these questions.

The final subsection, defining the term "primary caregiver," refers to "the individual designated by the person exempted under this section who has consistently assumed responsibility for the housing, health, or safety of that person." What does that mean in practice? Is the "primary caregiver" anybody the "person exempted" says he or she is, as could be inferred? Can anybody who assumes responsibility for the "housing, health, or safety" or any aspect of those needs for a patient be called a primary caregiver? Can there be more than one "primary caregiver"? In most medical situations several people, including sometimes more than one doctor, several nurses, anesthesiologists, lab workers, orderlies, and others divide various aspects of caregiving. Indeed, in some senses the

administrator of a hospital or a nursing-home janitor could be viewed as
a caregiver; an argument could even be made that his or her contributions are equally important or more important than that of a person who
administers an IV. Does one of them have to be designated the "primary"
caregiver for this provision to be applicable? If not, why was the term
"primary" used?

If a person had a team of medical specialists who agreed that marijuana was a useful therapy and one person specialized in procuring
high-quality medical-grade cannabis for therapeutic purposes, it is that
person who would have to be exempted from the laws against cannabis
cultivation and possession for this law to provide the protection from
prosecution it was obviously intended to provide. But would it be accurate to term that person, who might furnish only a small but essential
facet of the overall medical care process, as the "primary" caregiver? Can
one person—perhaps somebody who grows medical marijuana profes-
sionally or has experience in obtaining it—be designated as the "primary
caregiver" for more than one patient, perhaps even for hundreds?
Doctors often have hundreds of patients. Can a primary caregiver
whose method of caring is to furnish marijuana to sick people or to
their doctors have hundreds of clients? Would use of the term "client"
imply too commercial a relationship when the initiative doesn't explicitly authorize "sales," even though its purposes include "safe and
affordable distribution"?

Perhaps most important, in anticipation of legal challenges to various
methods of implementation, can a cannabis club—an organization set
up to provide cannabis to medical patients who have provided some
form of proof that they have a recommendation from a bona fide
licensed physician—be viewed as a "primary caregiver" under the new
law as written?

Note that the proposition, after the "purposes" section, which
speaks of the "right to obtain and use" for patients and primary caregivers, specifically says that Sections 11357, relating to possession,
and 11358, relating to cultivation, "shall not apply to a patient, or to

a patient's primary caregiver, who possesses or cultivates marijuana." But California's code contains numerous other sections relating to marijuana, forbidding sales (written to include transactions where no money changes hands), transportation, possession for sale, cultivation for sale, possession with intent to sell, conspiracy to sell, giving away, transportation and possession in a motor vehicle, and on and on. The intent was to make illegal as many aspects related to marijuana as the authorities could imagine or that experience dictated were important. Does the specific exemption to Sections 11357 and 11358 mean that the full force of all the other provisions should still apply to medical marijuana patients and their caregivers? Or does the "purpose" section direct prosecutors and courts to apply these provisions to bona fide patients with a little leniency—not to act as if they've been repealed exactly but to wink a bit as long as they're convinced that a person is a bona fide patient with a bona fide physician's recommendation rather than a recreational smoker pulling a scam?

It is also significant that Proposition 215, Section 11362.5, says nothing about the amounts of marijuana a patient and/or caregiver can possess without being subject to arrest or prosecution—or "sanction." In the 1970s California made simple possession of an ounce or less of marijuana an infraction, to be punished by a fine (very much like a traffic ticket) instead of by prosecution that could lead to jail time. Possession of more than an ounce can lead to criminal prosecution, and possession of large amounts (variable from local jurisdiction to local jurisdiction) can be taken as evidence of possession with intent to sell or distribute. But how much is reasonable for a medical patient? Is that simply a matter to be determined between patient and doctor, with the authorities having no say in the matter, as the proposition's silence on the issue could reasonably be taken to infer? Or do the authorities, with other laws against possession, trafficking, and the like still on the books for non-medical users, have a legitimate interest in setting limits on how much a medical patient or caregiver can possess or grow? How does California's constitution, which provides that an initiative put in place by a vote of the people cannot be changed except by a vote of the people, play into the issue? Would it permit authorities to set limits without getting approval through another vote of the people?

With a good will—a sincere desire to carry out the wish of the people in a reasonable manner—most of these potential problems could be worked out, and in some localities they have been. But to a shrewd prosecuting attorney determined to prove that that initiative was poorly written (and put in place only by duping the people to boot) and completely impractical in the real world, these questions can—and, as we shall see, did—provide opportunities to stymie or slow down efforts, even careful, good-faith efforts, at implementation.

CHAPTER TWO

How Medical Marijuana Prevailed

In retrospect it might have seemed inevitable. The state legislature had twice voted to make known its desire to authorize marijuana for medical use, aware that it might precipitate a legal tussle with the federal government and willing to take that risk, only to have the legislation vetoed each time by Republican Governor Pete Wilson. Few polls were done on the issue prior to Proposition 215 being circulated, but those polls showed at least majority support for allowing marijuana to be furnished to people through a doctor. San Francisco voters had approved an advisory initiative on medical marijuana with a majority of almost 80 percent, as had those in Santa Cruz. Several county boards of supervisors and city councils had weighed in on the subject. Numerous stories had run in the popular press about the growing use of marijuana by AIDS patients, who claimed it held off the debilitation and weight loss associated with "AIDS wasting syndrome." A number of newspapers had conducted phone-in polls—not "scientific" in that they are not limited to a sample chosen to mirror the population at large but often not bad at offering a rough approximation of what people are thinking—that showed substantial majorities in favor of medical marijuana.

While it might seem that the public in California had made up its mind and was just waiting to be asked, the passage of Proposition 215 was a long way from a sure thing. If events had not fallen out as they did, we might still be writing about when Californians would endorse the medical use of marijuana rather than why and how they did so. Numerous mistakes were made along the way that might have backfired more severely, and some proponents were concerned right up until election day that if the opponents figured out how to attack the initiative's wording the right way they could turn the tables quickly.

The process began in late 1995 around the kitchen table of Dennis Peron, a longtime marijuana law reform and gay rights activist who had gotten Proposition P, an advisory initiative endorsing the medical use of marijuana, on the San Francisco ballot in 1991, whereupon it passed with a 79.3 percent majority. He had since run the large-scale Cannabis Buyers Club in San Francisco. Discouraged that the second piece of medical marijuana legislation in two years had been vetoed, Peron and several friends and fellow activists decided that the best way to see their desire to have marijuana for medical uses approved was through California's initiative process, which is not subject to a veto by the governor. John Entwhistle, Scott Imler, and a few others who were members of the Cannabis Buyers Club; Dale Gieringer, longtime executive director of California NORML (National Organization for Reform of Marijuana Laws); Dr. Tod Mikuriya of Berkeley, perhaps the country's leading medical authority on the medical uses of marijuana; and attorney William Panzer also participated. They wanted something similar to the law just passed by the state legislature, which provided a defense in court for people who had a doctor's recommendation for a small list of diseases against marijuana possession charges, along with a preamble to explain the purposes and intention of the new law and a bit wider latitude for patients than the legislature had approved.

"Some people think we just sat around the table one night and came up with it," Dennis Peron later told me, referring to Proposition 215. "It was considerably more complicated than that. We went through at least 20 drafts, and each of those was criticized and revised by people in the legislative counsel's office in Sacramento, who worked with us through then–San Francisco state Senator Milton Marks's good offices. We wrangled, revised, adjourned for a while to think about it, got suggestions from Sacramento, then went back to it many, many times before it was finally completed."[7]

Scott Imler, who then lived in Santa Cruz and now heads the cannabis distribution center in West Hollywood, has similar memories, and an interesting insight.

> When we used the term "primary caregiver," as best I can remember we had in mind a family member or a close friend, perhaps a wife, husband, lover, in-law, son, or daughter. Of course, we hoped that eventually marijuana would be made available through ordinary drug stores, but we didn't expect that to happen right away because of federal jurisdiction over the prescription system. So we figured that some patients would grow it, some would have friends grow it, and there would be an interim distribution system like the San Francisco Cannabis Buyers Club for some patients.
>
> The initiative was not drafted in isolation—far from it. We had done polls on the measure in the legislature and smaller-scale polls on different ways to word it. As I remember, the final version pulled a 68 percent favorable vote in polls. We worked very hard to write not only something that would protect patients' rights but something that would have a chance to win. Nonetheless—and I know there has been criticism of the way it was written—I'm glad it was written mostly by patients and patients' advocates rather than the professional politicians. There was a lot of experience with patients in that room.[8]

"I remember the day we filed it in Sacramento," John Entwhistle told me later.

It was a strikingly beautiful day, the same day Pete Wilson announced he was going to run for president, which stole away a good bit of the publicity we had hoped to get. But we still relished the irony. I remember Dennis, me, Anna Boyce [a nurse from Southern California whose husband's last illness had been eased by marijuana she thought should have been legally available], and Amy Casey [a veteran San Francisco AIDS nurse]. We were all dressed conservatively, in our Sunday best.

As we got to the Capitol building grounds, Dennis said to me, "John, we should light up a joint." So we did—a very good one—and smoked it as we walked up the long sidewalk to the building. We stubbed it out just before we got to the doors. But, you know, marijuana has an aroma that lingers, and it was still with us. As we walked through the doors, you could see people looking at us with expressions of slight puzzlement. You could tell they smelled the aroma, but since we were all dressed in suits and nice, conservative clothes and there wasn't anybody around with beads or tie-dyed shirts they weren't sure just where the aroma was coming from. It was beautiful. The dynamics turned out to be perfect, the energy was very good.[9]

In California the attorney general's office writes a title and description for every initiative as part of the process for certifying it for signature gathering. The authors of the initiative had named it the Compassionate Use Act. The office of Attorney General Dan Lungren, a law-and-order conservative and confirmed drug warrior (when in Congress in the 1980s he was instrumental in pushing legislation to expand the power of police to seize property in drug cases through the asset forfeiture laws), wanted to have the word "marijuana" in the title. Initiative proponents objected and exchanged several letters with the attorney general's office, but in the end the initiative was called the Medical Marijuana Act. It was certified and the period for gathering signatures began on December 1, 1995. Dennis Peron rushed into print an updated version of a little book on his long campaign for marijuana law reform featuring a cookbook from "Brownie Mary" Rathbun, the seventy-plus San Francisco fixture and media darling who for years had been baking marijuana-laced brownies for patients on the AIDS ward in San Francisco General Hospital, where she volunteered two days a week. Scott Imler and a group of patients were sent to open a campaign office in Santa Monica to handle the Southern California end of the petition drive.

It takes 562,000 signatures (from a total population around 30 million) to qualify an initiative for a ballot in California. Since the late 1970s professional signature-gathering firms have been in place that handle the details, including paying people (by the hour or by the signature) and training them to sit in front of markets, department stores, shopping centers, and other heavily traveled spots and collect signatures. Most people in the field say you should collect at least half again as many as the required number to account for the fact that some who sign will not be registered voters, some will sign more than once despite admonitions, and some signatures will be illegible or otherwise disqualified. The rule of thumb in California is that it takes about $1 million, in some combination of payments to professionals and the time of volunteers, to qualify a measure for a statewide ballot. Peron and company didn't have that kind of money. They couldn't afford to hire a signature-gathering company. They hoped to qualify strictly with volunteers, perhaps hiring professionals later if their fundraising efforts were more successful than they realistically expected them to be.

"We made every boneheaded mistake you can imagine and some you probably wouldn't imagine," Scott Imler told me.

> We had to throw away thousands of petitions we had printed with the wrong wording. We didn't really know Southern California. We were a bunch of patients, mostly from Santa Cruz and mostly gay. We would rub people the

wrong way, greet hostility with hostility, and get into arguments, which means during that time you're not getting any signatures. We did start providing for our medical marijuana needs as a group, pooling our resources and sharing what could be acquired, and that grew into the Los Angeles Cannabis Club.

By about seven or eight weeks into the petitioning process, however, it was painfully obvious that we weren't going to make it. I would guess we had maybe 70,000 or 80,000 signatures before the professionals from back East came in to save the day. We had asked them to help earlier and they hadn't, so there were mixed feelings. But it wouldn't have happened without them.[10]

It wasn't only the pros from back East. George Zimmer, president of the discount clothing company Men's Wearhouse (known for his "You're gonna like the way you look. I guarantee it" television commercials), headquartered in Oakland, was a multimillionaire who remained interested in what he viewed as progressive causes. Jeremy Tarcher, whose publishing company had been bought by Putnam some years before (and who was married to the late puppeteer and entertainer Shari Lewis) had long been interested in drug law reform issues. Steve Kubby, a medical marijuana patient who published an online winter and extreme sports magazine from his home in Lake Tahoe, knew Zimmer and urged him to help. Tarcher knew Bill Zimmerman, a longtime political consultant for Democratic candidates and liberal causes, who eventually became Proposition 215's campaign manager.

But the key commitment came from George Soros, the refugee Hungarian self-made billionaire speculator, who had formed the Open Society Institute in part to funnel $1 billion of his money to governments, entrepreneurs, and civic organizations in Eastern Europe and the former Soviet Union to try to help build a civil society after the collapse of communism. Soros was also sympathetic to drug law reform issues, having donated some $4 million—up to $6 million if you include money ear-marked for grants to others—to the Washington, D.C.–based Drug Policy Foundation, founded by American University law professor Arnold Trebach, and having formed the Lindesmith Center under the aegis of the Open Society Institute to pursue drug reform issues centered around the concept of harm reduction as an alternative to prohibition. The Soros policy initiatives were and are supervised by Ethan Nadelmann, formerly a political scientist at Princeton University, who had called for an end to the international drug war in a memorable arti-cle in *Foreign Affairs* almost 10 years earlier.

Along with Soros and Zimmer, Peter Lewis of Cleveland, head of Progressive Insurance Co., had an interest in the issue and money to spend on what he viewed as good causes. Later Richard Dennis, a Chicago commodities broker with a longstanding interest in drug policy, and Laurence Rockefeller contributed fairly substantial amounts of money to the Proposition 215 campaign. But it was really the triumvirate of George Soros, George Zimmer, and Peter Lewis who put in the crucial money to get Proposition 215 on the ballot.

"I know it was an intricate process to get the money together, but it happened before I came on so I don't know the details," Dave Fratello told me. A California native, he had worked in press relations for the Drug Policy Foundation in Washington, D.C., for several years and was later hired to work with Bill Zimmerman on what soon became Californians for Medical Rights. "I do know the money came in only because the polling showed it could win with a professional campaign."[11]

Before that, however, the goal had to be to get enough signatures to qualify the initiative for the ballot. Zimmerman was put in charge and hired professional signature gatherers. Some of the original activists were a bit chagrined to see the "suits from back East" taking over their baby. "Of course it hurt a bit," John Entwhistle says now, "but we let them do it. We could see that it [the initiative] had a chance to win with a respectable amount of money behind it and no chance without it. And most of all we wanted to win."[12] That desire didn't mean there wasn't friction between the old-line activists and the new pros; there was, and some squabbling and culture clashes continued throughout the campaign. But the bottom line, as Scott Imler, put it to me, was that "the pros came in and gathered 700,000 or 800,00 signatures in about five or six weeks. It was awesome."[13]

Californians for Medical Rights, headquartered in Santa Monica, began to take charge of the election campaign as soon as enough signatures had been gathered. Anna Boyce, a registered nurse who looked like anything but a creature of the counterculture, was to be a main spokesperson, and several doctors were recruited. A concerted effort was made to get the California Medical Association (CMA), an American Medical Association (AMA) affiliate, to endorse the initiative. The CMA did not endorse, but the California Association of Family Practitioners did, along with several nurses' associations and other organizations of health-care workers. Brochures featuring an elderly doctor in a white coat talking to an elderly patient were printed. Speakers and debaters were admonished to wear conservative suits and ties.

In late May 1996, according to Dave Fratello, the campaign conducted what is known as a benchmark poll. It included using a long questionnaire that kept respondents on the phone for 25 to 30 minutes, getting their opinions and attitudes on a wide range of related subjects from the condition of the health-care system in general to the proper role of the federal government vis-à-vis state government to various elements within the initiative. The purpose was to try to determine which arguments on both sides would be most persuasive, especially to undecided voters, and which "soft" voters on both sides would be susceptible to which arguments. The poll and focus groups showed that the weakest aspect of the initiative, potentially, was the authorization of cultivation by patients and caregivers. Poll respondents and focus group participants could imagine that aspect getting out of hand, with teenagers sneaking over a fence to steal marijuana from a cancer patient's backyard or hillsides full of cannabis.

For Fratello, the wording of the initiative contained several potential pitfalls from a strictly political perspective. "I had already decided I was coming and moved across the country before I had read the actual initiative," he told me several years later. "I had assumed that it was identical to the legislation sponsored by Senator [John] Vasconcellos in the legislature in 1995, but the actual initiative included some fairly radical moves in the direction of more open access and more widespread use than Vasco's bill, including an open-ended list of diseases. I could see a number of provisions that would be vulnerable to an intelligent or pointed attack from the opposition."[14] To cope with that possibility, the campaign took the initiative in stressing that Proposition 215 would not change the laws against recreational use or stop the war on drugs. It would simply provide a positive defense, either at the time of arrest or later in court, for people arrested on marijuana charges who had a recommendation from a doctor for a bona fide illness.

Opposition to the initiative was not long in coming, but it came mostly from law enforcement officials. Attorney General Dan Lungren and Orange County Sheriff Brad Gates became cochairmen of the campaign against Proposition 215. The major thrust of their campaign was that medical marijuana was simply a ruse to make marijuana fully legal and that marijuana is not a proper medicine. Sheriff Gates, for example, accused proponents of "using sick and dying people in their game to legalize marijuana. It wouldn't just legalize marijuana for medical use—it would legalize marijuana, period, with absolutely no controls on quality or dosage or who can get it." Juan Carlos Cobo, president of the Orange County Medical Association, which opposed 215, attacked the use of the word "recommendation": "We must keep the same controls on it that we do with all other medications: Doctors write prescriptions, patients pick them up at the pharmacy. So we can control the quality and quantity of the drug."[15] He didn't offer to lead a campaign at the federal level to reschedule marijuana so it could be handled that way.

Federal drug czar General Barry McCaffrey campaigned actively against Proposition 215 with television and other media appearances during several trips to California. Former presidents Jimmy Carter and Gerald Ford made a well-publicized appearance in California to urge voters to reject this "stealth initiative." Former drug czar William Bennett denounced it from the remote fastnesses of Washington, D.C. Aside from public officials, however, little citizen-oriented grass-roots opposition developed, and opponents, while they certainly used tax money in their campaign in ways that have never been accounted for, raised very little money from private sources.

Opponents found a statement made some years before by Richard Cowan, former national executive director of NORML: "The key is medical access, because once you have hundreds of thousands of people using marijuana under medical supervision, the whole scam is going to be brought up . . . then we will get medical, then we will get full legalization."[16] This statement was reprinted in almost all the opposition literature as evidence that medical marijuana authorization was simply a ruse, a clever ploy designed to get full legalization of marijuana for recreational use as well.

In fact, a number of people who favored full legalization of marijuana had serious doubts about the efforts to permit marijuana to be used medically, either through action at the state level or by pushing to have it rescheduled at the federal level so it could be prescribed by physicians under tight controls, as cocaine and morphine can be. In his book *Marihuana: The Forbidden Medicine,* Dr. Lester Grinspoon of Harvard University argued that the federal regulatory system is geared toward dealing only with single-chemical synthesized drugs patented by pharmaceutical companies. Even with rescheduling, the federal system would take so long and tie itself in so many regulatory knots trying to deal with a natural plant containing hundreds of chemicals—and further, one that many patients preferred to administer by smoking it—that marijuana would be effectively unavailable for many years anyway. "The only way out," he wrote, "is to cut the knot by giving cannabis the same status as alcohol—legalizing it for all uses and removing it entirely from the medical and criminal control systems."[17] Dr. Grinspoon and others also wondered, if cannabis were legalized for medical use and many of the "attractive victims" of current policy—AIDS patients, elderly cancer patients, people with glaucoma, and chronic pain sufferers—could get marijuana without much hassle, whether some of the emotional wind for full legalization would go out of the reformers' sails.

There's plausibility in both arguments—that medicalization will reduce the capacity to demonize marijuana and pave the way for full legalization and that medicalization could reduce the impetus for full legalization. Since California and other states that have passed medical marijuana statutes are still well short of full implementation and since nothing has changed at the level of federal law yet, it's too early to tell which way medicalization cuts in the larger debate over drug law reform.

As Dave Fratello and others have noted, leaders of the Proposition 215 campaign knew from about June on that they would have enough money to run a few television ads for about a week shortly before the election in November and that the opposition would probably not have enough money to buy television ads. They hoped that effort would be enough to carry the day because they didn't anticipate being able to raise a great deal more money to counter a full-scale media campaign.

In some ways the Proposition 215 campaign caught the drug war establishment napping. The war on drugs had not been seriously challenged in a political environment since the 1970s, when a number of states either reduced marijuana possession to an infraction with a fine rather than jail time and/or endorsed the medical use of marijuana, and many reformers thought full legalization was imminent. The drug warriors recovered nicely during the second half of the Carter administration, then benefited from the "Just Say No" campaign and increased spending during the administrations of Ronald Reagan and George Bush. But the institutions of the drug war had become something of a complacent autocracy. Its members had not had to defend their activities for many years or present their defenses in a political environment and had lost some of the knack.

In addition, the fact that the drug war had been almost entirely a government operation for the last decade and a half meant there was little significant private money or support either for expanding the drug war or for opposing efforts to modulate it. Even many of the "grass-roots" parents' organizations that sprang up during the 1980s were heavily subsidized by government agencies and so were unaccustomed to scrambling to raise money through voluntary means. The larger and more effective and savvy national pro-prohibition organizations, like Joseph Califano's Center on Addiction and Substance Abuse at Columbia University and the Partnership for a Drug-Free America (PDFA), which sponsored and got free air time for antidrug television commercials, were ostensibly nonpolitical nonprofit organizations that could not get involved directly in a political campaign. In that sense, then, Proposition 215 could be viewed as a "stealth" campaign in that it exposed the weakness of the standard pro-prohibition arguments in the public mind. My sense, however, is that few of the proponents anticipated just how vulnerable the drug war establishment would prove to be, at least on the issue of medicalization of marijuana.

Cultural differences between the two groups pushing for Proposition 215 continued to require almost daily attention. As Dave Fratello told me,

> Early on we conducted a focus group in, I believe, San Jose. A newspaper story about Dennis Peron's Cannabis Buyers Club had appeared that was different in tone from several of the friendly stories. It focused on what seemed to be a party atmosphere at the club, suggesting it was a bit out of hand and didn't very much resemble a medical clinic. We wanted to see how this way of viewing the cannabis clubs would affect public perceptions, so we let the members of the focus group read the article and asked them to discuss it. Many were laughing, others were saying the cannabis club seemed to them to be a joke, an excuse to get together and

smoke pot rather than anything medical. We let Dennis and John Entwhistle sit in on the other side of the two-way mirror so they could observe. They didn't seem to be very concerned about how people were reacting, but most of the rest of us were horrified. We thought there was a good chance that if this was the perception of what medical use of cannabis was like we could lose support rapidly.[18]

People like Scott Imler had other concerns. "I'm something of a diehard separatist when it comes to medical marijuana and other drug policy reforms," he told me in 2000. "I think the argument for medical marijuana is stronger by itself, when these other controversial issues can be separated from it. Even though I understood that we would lose without it, I had some concern about taking money from Soros and others who are known to have a broader drug policy reform agenda. The opposition did use that in the campaign, but it turned out not to have as much of an impact as I had expected."[19]

The issue of the San Francisco cannabis clubs came to the fore in August when a state task force, at the behest of Attorney General Dan Lungren, cochairman of the No on 215 campaign, closed down the Cannabis Buyers Club in San Francisco. State authorities said that undercover agents had penetrated the club and had evidence that marijuana was being handed out willy-nilly to all comers, including minors, with no real safeguards as to its being for medical use. Lungren said the closure had nothing at all to do with the fact that the club was a nerve center for the Proposition 215 campaign, but the closure did make campaign materials, lists, computers, and the like unavailable to Dennis Peron and other activists for several days. At the time very few people were aware of the extent to which the real campaign was being run from Santa Monica, by Californians for Medical Rights, which considered the San Francisco cannabis clubs a sideshow with the potential to blow up in the campaign's face. To many, the raid looked like an attempt to use law enforcement to cripple a political campaign of which it disapproved. The campaign materials were returned to Peron and his supporters within a few days, but in the final analysis the event seemed to work against Proposition 215's opponents in the minds of most voters.

In September, the newly formed Los Angeles Cannabis Club in West Hollywood, which had grown from the informal organization of Proposition 215 campaign workers around Scott Imler, was raided by Los Angeles County sheriffs. Imler had moved his campaign operation to West Hollywood, a small municipality within Los Angeles that, because of the composition of its population has some of the strongest anti–gay discrimination laws in the country and has had a gay majority on the city council for years. The small city finds it more feasible to contract with the Los Angeles County Sheriffs Department for police services than to maintain its own independent police force. Imler persuaded a local Methodist church to permit the club to continue operating under some form of religious sanctuary, and the police left it alone until the end of the campaign. Nonetheless, campaign operations were somewhat curtailed by the events.

In October, Peron was arrested by state law enforcement officials— not in San Francisco, where local law enforcement had consistently refused to cooperate with state efforts to close down the cannabis club, but across the bay in Alameda County. The judge considered a ruling barring Peron from speaking with the media from the time of his arraignment until his trial, scheduled for December, after the election, but decided against it.

At the end of September the nationally syndicated cartoon strip "Doonesbury," by Garry Trudeau, weighed in with a series of cartoons over a full week lampooning the police raid on the Cannabis Buyers Club and supporting Proposition 215. Dan Lungren, who was mentioned by name in the cartoon strips, was upset and asked Universal Press Syndicate (UPS) to pull the strip for the week or to run it with a disclaimer saying the cartoon was inaccurate. UPS declined to do either. Lungren expressed his concern in a letter to the *San Francisco Chronicle*: "This week's Doonesbury strips clearly advance the wink-and-nod attitude toward drug use that is most responsible for the addition of thousands of American kids to the drugged and at risk roster."[20] Trudeau didn't respond directly to the controversy, but he had made known his opinion on the general topic in the September 16 issue of *Time* magazine:

> Before we can get any traction on controlling pot, the generation that popularized the stuff has got to finally come clean about what made it so alluring in the first place—and then square that with current marijuana policy. A good start might be for every middle-aged public official in America to take the following oath: "I concede that I once did not view marijuana as dangerous. . . . It was after my appetite for recreational drugs had abated, and I produced children whom I did not believe capable of 'handling' marijuana as responsibly as I had, that I came to oppose decriminalization. I acknowledge that it was this fear, and not new medical evidence, that caused me to subsequently support mandatory sentencing for other people's children caught emulating the actions of my generation."[21]

It's easy to say in the aftermath that the "Doonesbury" incident, along with Lungren's overreaction, cut in favor of Proposition 215 with the California electorate. But proponents weren't sure if some Californians would view it as an outsider trying to sway an election one way or another. Others were concerned that some of the opposition arguments might begin to have enough of an impact to sway some of the "soft" pro-215 voters. "I didn't really think we had it in the bag until about eight o'clock election night," Dave Fratello told me.[22] "I was watching the tracking polls and they got as low as they ever did in the final weeks of the campaign," Scott Imler said. "It really seemed to me that the opposition had begun to muster its forces and its arguments in a way that was having an impact on the electorate. It's not just because a political campaign is an all-consuming ordeal that I was glad it ended when it did."[23]

In any event, Proposition 215 passed by a 56–44 margin on election night. But there was concern even before the election was over about whether the legislation would or could be implemented smoothly. In a wrap-up piece run the Sunday before the election in the *Orange County Register*, I wrote:

> When asked what they would do if Prop. 215 passes, law-enforcement officials seem shocked at having to think about such a possibility. At a recent forum at UC Irvine, they implied they would go on enforcing the marijuana laws as if Prop. 215 didn't exist—raising serious questions about whether they're devoted to enforcing the law as the people make it or making it up as they go along. At other times, they have implied that any and all enforcement of marijuana prohibition laws would cease, that they would be helpless to make the necessary distinction between people with a doctor-certified medical need for the herb and those who are using it to get high.
>
> Meanwhile, federal "drug czar" Gen. Barry McCaffrey says that if 215 passes, he'll order federal agents to arrest doctors in California who recommend marijuana.[24]

I had no desire to be so accurate a prophet on these matters.

"I really had mixed feelings on election night," Scott Imler told me. "On the one hand, I was exhilarated, obviously, at the result. On the other hand, listening to the vehement and unrepentant attacks on 215 and on the electorate that was so foolish as to have passed it, I had this strange feeling: 'Wait a minute,' I said to myself. 'We've all made our arguments and the people decided. We won. Why continue the attacks? It's over.'"[25] While Imler was entertaining these thoughts in Southern California, in San Francisco Dennis Peron fired up a joint in front of the television cameras.

In many ways the fight was just beginning.

CHAPTER THREE

Were the Voters Duped?

On election night 1996 California's Republican attorney general, Dan Lungren, who was positioning himself to run for governor and had been one of the most vocal leaders of the anti–Proposition 215 campaign, was virtually apoplectic. "This thing is a disaster," he told the *Los Angeles Times.* "What's going to happen? We're going to have an unprecedented mess."[26] Even though some polls had shown Proposition 215 would be approved, most of those in authority were taken by surprise. How could the voters reject the authority of drug czar Barry McCaffrey, President Bill Clinton, three former presidents, virtually every elected official, and the major party challengers for elective offices? And by a 56 percent margin, larger than the margin of any statewide candidate?

Former drug czar William Bennett had a ready explanation: the people had been cruelly duped. "That this initiative passed is a scandal," he said. "It's also understandable given the promotion and advertising that were used." Former Secretary of Health, Education, and Welfare (back during the Lyndon Johnson years and again in the Carter administration) Joseph Califano—who became a staunch antitobacco crusader, then launched his own antidrug organization, CASA (Center on Addiction and Substance Abuse) at Columbia University, pursuing a strong prohibitionist line—saw something almost sinister: "A moneyed, out-of-state elite mounted a cynical and deceptive campaign to push its hidden

agenda to legalize drugs," he declared. *New York Times* columnist Abe
Rosenthal started naming names, beginning with that of George Soros.
The Hungarian refugee (he fled both the Nazis and Communists) had
donated about $1 billion of his fortune, through his Open Society
Institute, to aid the new democracies and some hopeful entrepreneurs in
Russia and eastern European countries after the fall of the Berlin Wall.
He had also given, over the years, considerable sums to the Drug Policy
Foundation, which was skeptical of current prohibitionist policies, and
he had donated money to the Proposition 215 campaign, providing a
good deal of the financing for Californians for Medical Rights. That
made him, according to Rosenthal, "the Daddy Warbucks of drug legalization," whose "gobs of money" could be likened to "the fortunes
manipulated by drug criminals."[27]

Related to the question of whether those who voted to authorize the
medical use of marijuana genuinely understood the issues is the question
whether medicalizing marijuana—or even talking about doing so—will
"send the wrong message" to people, especially to vulnerable young people who might be inclined to discount information about the negative
aspects of marijuana and therefore be more inclined to use it and other,
more dangerous drugs as well. Robert Maginnis, in a paper for the
Family Research Council, founded by Christian right luminary and former presidential candidate Gary Bauer, worried that "Labeling
marijuana as a 'medicine' communicates that it is a safe substance. That
message will further erode the perceived risk in drug use by teen-agers.
According to PDFA [sponsor of "This is your brain on drugs" and other
commercials] the number of teens who agree with the statement 'taking
drugs scares me' declined from 47 percent to 36 percent in 1995."[28]

In his statement to the Senate Judiciary Committee on December 2,
1996, shortly after the passage of the California and Arizona initiatives,
Barry McCaffrey predicted that the passage of the two measures would
lead to an increase in drug use: "By our judgment," he said, "increased
drug abuse in every category will be the inevitable result of the referenda."[29] In the Institute of Medicine report commissioned by McCaffrey

within months of the passage of Proposition 215 and delivered in March 1999, the authors introduced their discussion of the topic thus: "Almost everyone who spoke or wrote to the IOM study team about the potential harms posed by the medical use of marijuana felt that it would send the wrong message to children and teenagers. They stated that information about the harms caused by marijuana is undermined by claims that marijuana might have medical value."[30] In short, youngsters and teenagers, listening to debate surrounding a ballot initiative or absorbing the information that marijuana has been authorized for medical use might figure "How bad can it be if they say it has medical uses?" and start puffing away, which would probably lead to heroin addiction before you knew it.

Not only does this contention give teenagers little credit for being able to make relatively simple choices if informed reasonably well, it ignores the crucial fact that almost all medications, especially prescription medications, have side effects, some of them quite severe. Doctors and patients together must balance the potential risks and benefits of certain medications constantly, sometimes by trial and error. As the IOM report continued: "Yet many of our powerful medicines are also dangerous medicines. These two facets of medicine—effectiveness and risk—are inextricably linked."[31]

The IOM report introduced and summarized the issues and studies that might have some relevance, if only by analogy, rather succinctly:

> The question here is not whether marijuana can be both harmful and helpful but whether the perception of its benefits will increase its abuse. For now, any answer to the question remains conjecture. Because marijuana is not an approved medicine, there is little information about the consequences of its medical use in modern society. Reasonable inferences might be drawn from some examples. Opiates, such as morphine and codeine, are an example of a class of drugs that is both abused to great harm and used to great

medical benefit, and it would be useful to examine the relationship between their medical use and their abuse. In a
"natural experiment" during 1973–1978 some states
decriminalized marijuana and others did not. Finally, one can
examine the short-term consequences of the publicity surrounding the 1996 medical marijuana campaign in
California and ask whether it had any measurable impact on
marijuana consumption among youth in California.[32]

The IOM authors note that two influential papers published in the
1920s and the 1950s aroused considerable concern among doctors and
licensing boards that liberal prescribing of opiates would increase the
number of addicts. There was historical reason to worry: most historians
believe that liberal use of morphine and other opiates during the Civil
War (when knowledge of the drugs and their effects was in its infancy
among doctors) left some veterans addicted and was associated with a
subsequent fashion for opiates in the late 19th century. Subsequent studies and decades of experience, however, showed otherwise. "Such fears
have proven unfounded;" the IOM report concludes, "it is now recognized that fear of producing addicts through medical treatment resulted
in needless suffering among patients with pain as physicians needlessly
limited appropriate doses of medications. Few people begin their drug
addiction problems with misuse of drugs that have been prescribed for
medical use." Diversion of opiates and cocaine from medical channels
into the black market "is not generally considered to be a major problem," according to the IOM report.[33]

The report then moves on to what is sometimes referred to as the
decriminalization movement in the 1970s, when a number of states
reduced the penalty for simple possession of small quantities of marijuana to an infraction, similar in seriousness to a traffic ticket, carrying a
relatively modest fine (in California it is $100 for possession of less than
one ounce, with criminal penalties that could carry jail time or a charge
for possession for sale taking effect at more than one ounce). Whether

this reform really amounts to decriminalization or not, it is a significant penalty reduction, one that has saved the states that undertook it significant amounts of money in policing and other enforcement costs. A study by Monitoring the Future, a widely recognized annual survey of values and lifestyles of high school seniors done under the auspices of the University of Michigan, "revealed," according to the IOM report, "that high school seniors in decriminalized states reported using no more marijuana than did their counterparts in states where marijuana was not decriminalized."[34]

Another report had somewhat different results, according to the IOM report.

> That study used data from the Drug Awareness Warning Network (DAWN), which has collected data on drug-related emergency room (ER) cases since 1975. [As Lynn Zimmer and John P. Morgan point out in *Marijuana Myths, Marijuana Facts,* reports of such cases do not necessarily mean that marijuana was the cause of the condition or accident, they simply mean that the patient had used marijuana recently enough to be detected. More detailed studies would be needed to determine whether marijuana (or other drugs) were the actual cause, or part of the cause, for the emergency that required treatment.] There was a greater increase from 1975 to 1978 in the proportion of ER patients who had used marijuana in states that had decriminalized marijuana in 1975–1976 than in states that had not decriminalized it. Despite the greater increase among decriminalized states, the proportion of marijuana users among ER patients by 1978 was about equal in states that had and states that had not decriminalized marijuana. That is because the non-decriminalized states had higher rates of marijuana use *before* decriminalization.[35]

There's another interesting wrinkle in the DAWN emergency room report: "In contrast with marijuana use, rates of other illicit drug use among ER patients were substantially higher in states that did not decriminalize marijuana use. Thus there are different possible reasons for the greater increase in marijuana use in the decriminalized states. On the one hand, decriminalization might have led to an increased use of marijuana (at least among people who sought health care in hospital ERs). On the other hand, the lack of decriminalization might have encouraged greater use of drugs that are even more dangerous than marijuana."[36]

All in all, concluded the IOM, "The differences between the results for high school seniors from the Monitoring the Future study and the DAWN data are unclear, although the author of the latter study suggests that the reasons might lie in limitations inherent in how the DAWN data are collected."[37] That leads us to several considerations that an intelligent observer should keep in mind when considering these and similar studies. The DAWN data track emergency room admissions and correlate them with recent use of a number of drugs (including alcohol, which was found to be present in more emergency room admissions than all other drugs combined). A case where somebody has recently used several different drugs will be reported as a positive for each one but will not tell the analyst which drug (if any) bears responsibility for the emergency. Add the fact that emergency room admissions are hardly the sum total of people's interactions with the health-care system (some people with very serious illnesses have never been to an emergency room) and that a certain (unknown) percentage of patients will not admit to use of an illicit drug unless they know they will get or have gotten a blood test that will reveal it anyway, and more of the DAWN system's limitations are revealed. The system can give a possibly revealing rough indication of the correlation between drug use and health problems in society, but it will be a necessarily incomplete picture. Because the data have been collected in roughly the same fashion since 1975 they can show some interesting trend lines that might be worth further study, but they hardly offer a complete or dispositive picture of the relationship between drug use and health problems. In theory, at least, a more complete picture that included people who sought treatment for health problems related to drugs in venues other than emergency rooms might show *more* health problems caused by marijuana and other illicit drugs than the DAWN studies suggest.

Similar questions surround Monitoring the Future and other studies of young people in various levels of schooling. No matter how anonymous the test or how strongly anonymity and confidentiality are guaranteed, some respondents will not tell the truth about illicit drug use. It is quite possible, therefore, that illicit drug use among various target populations has actually been higher than is reported in standard studies. Even this isn't for certain, however; some students might actually think it's "cool" to report drug use even though they haven't used drugs. Although studies that use the same methodology from year to year can suggest trends, they just might vary from year to year, depending on social or cultural factors that are difficult to isolate, by varying amounts. While studies can be helpful, therefore, no one study should be taken as fully authoritative. In general, if one has the time and the inclination, it's a good idea to read the complete versions of studies referred to in news accounts and in books (including this one). Often they will describe their own limitations and guide the reader to a more sophisticated understanding of what they demonstrate and don't demonstrate. Checking complete studies a few times can give you an idea of how reliably particular journalists and policy analysts use studies—whether they report them reasonably well, with an awareness of their shortcomings or incompleteness, or "cherry-pick" facts and statistics to make their own case, sometimes distorting the import of the study they cite.

What the different reports and surveys the IOM studied in relation to the effects of modest decriminalization in the 1970s on marijuana use do show is that the worst predictions of the drug warriors were not borne out. Maybe usage was roughly the same as in states that did not decriminalize. Maybe it was a little higher, but the difference was offset by a higher proportion of use of more dangerous drugs in states that did not decriminalize. Maybe the figures are unreliable. But there is no evidence at all of the kind of radical increase in marijuana use or in the use of other drugs following partial decriminalization that various opponents of medical marijuana predicted in the wake of the passage of the California initiative. It is worth bearing in mind that the situations are not precisely the same—we are inferring by analogy here. But the evidence that modest liberalization doesn't lead to radical increases in illicit drug use is strongly suggestive.

The IOM also discussed the Netherlands, which in 1976, without changing its laws formally, adopted a policy of police toleration for possession of up to 30 grams of marijuana, while still promising no official tolerance for hard drugs. In 1984 Amsterdam and other larger Dutch cities permitted "coffee shops" where people can buy and use marijuana and hashish openly. Numerous comments and claims about the success or failure of the Dutch policy have been bandied about in a war of dueling statistics and studies. Here is the IOM summary:

> In 1976 the Netherlands adopted a policy of toleration for possession of up to 30 g of marijuana. There was little change in marijuana use during the seven years after the policy change, which suggests that the change itself had little effect; however, in 1984, when Dutch "coffee shops" that sold marijuana commercially spread throughout Amsterdam, marijuana use began to increase. During the 1990s, marijuana use has continued to increase in the Netherlands at the same rate as in the United States and Norway—two countries that strictly forbid marijuana sale and possession. Furthermore, during this period, approximately equal percentages of American and Dutch 18-year-olds used marijuana.[38]

The upshot, according to the IOM? "The authors of this study conclude that there is little evidence that the Dutch marijuana depenalization policy led to increased marijuana use, although they note that commercialization of marijuana might have contributed to its increased use. Thus, there is little evidence that decriminalization of marijuana use necessarily leads to a substantial increase in marijuana use."[39]

What about the discussion of medical marijuana itself? Has it had the impact predicted—persuading a substantial number of teenagers that if marijuana has medical value it must be completely harmless and therefore there's no downside to smoking it? Obviously, not enough time has passed to make a definitive statement, but the Institute of Medicine team found a suggestive study:

> The most recent National Household Survey on Drug Abuse [compiled by the Substance Abuse and Mental Health Services Administration Office of Applied Studies] showed that among people 12–17 years old the perceived risk associated with smoking marijuana once or twice a week had decreased significantly between 1996 and 1997. (Perceived risk is measured as the percentage of survey respondents who report that they "perceive great risk of harm" in using a drug at a specified frequency.) At first glance that might seem to validate the fear that the medical marijuana debate of 1996—before passage of the California medical marijuana referendum in November 1997 [sic]—had sent a message that marijuana use is safe.[40]

The IOM report notes an unusual aspect to this household survey: "But a closer analysis of the data shows that California youth were an exception to the national trend. In contrast to the national trend, the perceived risk of marijuana use did not change among California youth between 1996 and 1997. In summary, there is no evidence that the medical marijuana debate has altered adolescents' perceptions of the risks associated with marijuana use."[41] It is tempting to say that, if anything, this report suggests that if you want to keep the perception of risk from declining among teenagers, the best way is to have an initiative and a lively debate in every state every year on medical marijuana. But that would be wrong.

Other concerns about approving the medical use of marijuana often arise when critics say the people just didn't know what they were doing or were duped when they voted for medical marijuana. One is the issue of drug dependence. The Institute of Medicine report's conclusions on this subject were in line with almost every government report since the Indian Hemp Commission report in 1898—which is that dependence is rare and relatively mild compared to drugs like nicotine and alcohol. In 1996, 68.6 million Americans—some 32 percent of the U.S. population over 12—had tried marijuana at one time or another, but only 5 percent were current users, and only a small portion of these could accurately be described as dependent. The IOM report notes:

> Most people with a diagnosis of drug dependence disorder also have a diagnosis of another psychiatric disorder (76% of men and 65% of women). Psychiatric disorders seem to be closely associated with drug use of all kinds; daily tobacco cigarette smoking among adolescent boys is more strongly associated with psychiatric disorders than is any use of illicit substances, but this doesn't mean that tobacco *causes* psychiatric disorders or that it is more likely to cause psychiatric disorders than any illicit drugs. It probably suggests that people with psychiatric problems are more likely to engage in risky behavior, or behavior perceived as risky or beyond normal social boundaries, such as smoking tobacco or using illicit drugs, but even that modest conclusion should be approached with caution.[42]

How common is marijuana dependence compared with dependence on other substances (recognizing that "dependence" itself is a slippery concept and isn't always defined the same way in different studies)? The

IOM noted that data from a National Comorbity Study of more than 8,000 people 15–54 "indicate that 4.2% of the general population were dependent on marijuana at some time. Similar results for frequency of substance abuse among the general population were obtained from the Epidemiological Catchment Area Program, a survey of over 19,000 people. According to the data collected in the early 1980s for that study, 4.4% of adults have, at one time, met the criteria for marijuana dependence. In comparison, 13.8% of adults met the criteria for alcohol dependence and 36.0% for tobacco dependence."[43]

The IOM team concludes:

> In summary, although few marijuana users develop dependence, some do. But they appear to be less likely to do so than users of other drugs (including alcohol and nicotine), and marijuana dependence appears to be less severe than dependence on other drugs. Drug dependence is more prevalent in some sectors of the population than others, but no group has been identified as particularly vulnerable to the drug-specific effects of marijuana. Adolescents, especially troubled ones, and people with psychiatric disorders (including substance abuse) appear to be more likely than the general population to become dependent on marijuana.
>
> If marijuana or cannabinoid drugs were approved for therapeutic uses, it would be important to consider the possibility of dependence, particularly for patients at high risk for substance dependence. Some controlled substances that are approved medications produce dependence after long-term use; this, however, is a normal part of patient management and does not generally present undue risk to the patient.[44]

The other concern expressed by many is that marijuana is a "gateway" drug—that is, use of marijuana not only precedes the use of other, more harmful drugs but might in some way cause or make more likely the use of other drugs. Studies showing that marijuana stimulates some of the same "pleasure centers" in the brain as do cocaine and heroin have purported to demonstrate this gateway effect, as have studies showing that high percentages of people who become heavy users of cocaine, crack, methamphetamines, or heroin began their use of illicit drugs with heroin. The Institute of Medicine report (chapter 3, "First Do No Harm") is especially perceptive on this topic, and it is worth quoting at some length:

> The fear that marijuana might cause, as opposed to merely precede, the use of drugs that are more harmful is of great concern. To judge from comments submitted to the IOM study team, it appears to be of greater concern than the harms directly related to marijuana itself. The discussion that marijuana is a "gateway" drug implicitly recognizes that other illicit drugs might inflict greater damage to health or social relations than marijuana. Although the scientific literature generally discusses drug use progression between a variety of drug classes, including alcohol and tobacco, the public discussion has focused on marijuana as a "gateway" drug that leads to abuse of more harmful illicit drugs, such as cocaine and heroin.
>
> There are strikingly regular patterns in the progression of drug use from adolescence to adulthood. Because it is the most widely used illicit drug, marijuana is predictably the first illicit drug most people encounter. Not surprisingly, most users of other illicit drugs used marijuana first. In fact, most drug users do not begin their drug use with marijuana—they begin with alcohol and nicotine, usually when they are too young to do so legally.[45]

Some people view refined sugar as a drug, and under certain legal definitions it fits the criteria. (Defining what a drug is turns out to be a lot trickier proposition than it might appear at first blush.) Since most heavy heroin users probably ate sugar at an early age, is this substance a "gateway" to ultimate heroin addiction? Obviously, a study that simply asks an addict what substances he or she used before trying heroin cannot answer this question. The IOM report helps to clarify some issues that are left murky in many discussions:

> The gateway analogy evokes two ideas that are often confused. The first, more often referred to as the "stepping stone" hypothesis, is the idea that progression from marijuana to other drugs arises from pharmacological properties of marijuana itself. The second is that marijuana serves as a gateway to the world of illegal drugs in which youths have greater opportunity and are under greater social pressure to try other illegal drugs. The latter interpretation is most often used in the scientific literature, and it is supported, although not proven, by the available data.
>
> The stepping stone hypothesis applies to marijuana only in the broadest sense. People who enjoy the effects of marijuana are, logically, more likely to be willing to try other mood-altering drugs than are people who are not willing to try marijuana or who dislike its effects. In other words, many of the factors associated with a willingness to use marijuana are, presumably, the same as those associated with a willingness to use other illicit drugs. Those factors include physiological reactions to the drug effect, which are consistent with the stepping stone hypothesis, but also psychosocial factors, which are independent of drug-specific effects. There is no evidence that marijuana serves as a stepping stone on the basis of its particular physiological effect. One might argue that marijuana is generally used before other illicit mood-altering drugs, in part, because its effects are milder; in this case, marijuana is a stepping stone

only in the same sense as taking a small dose of a particular drug and then increasing that dose over time is a
stepping stone to increased drug use.[46]

One wonders whether that last analogy is useful. The physiological
effects of marijuana are different from those of cocaine or heroin (not the
same effects only less pronounced), as the IOM report itself emphasized
a few sentences earlier. Presumably the IOM team wanted to give the
stepping stone idea as much respectful attention as possible as it
debunked it. Here is the key paragraph:

"Whereas the stepping stone hypothesis presumes a predominantly
physiological component of drug progression, the gateway theory is a
social theory. The latter does not suggest that the pharmacological qualities of marijuana make it a risk factor for progression to other drug use.
Instead, the legal status of marijuana makes it a gateway drug."[47]

Note how that last sentence is slipped in, with no prior or subsequent
comment on its significance, like a time bomb ticking or a gem hidden in
a cave. First, the report notes that "the latter interpretation"—the gateway version—"is most often used in the scientific literature." That leaves
the version that "progression from marijuana to other drugs arises from
pharmacological properties of marijuana itself" in the realm of discarded
hypothesis or folklore, something scientists consider so unlikely on the
basis of what is known already about those pharmacological properties
that it's not worth studying anymore.

Then, sure enough, a few sentences later comes the flat statement
"There is no evidence that marijuana serves as a stepping stone on the
basis of its particular physiological effect." No evidence. What about
studies (usually done on tissues in a lab rather than on human beings)
that suggest marijuana's impact on the brain is so similar to that of
cocaine or heroin as to give a marijuana user an irresistible urge to try
the harder drugs? They show certain aspects about how certain chemicals interact in certain laboratory conditions, some of which might turn

out to be important, but they're not evidence about how actual human beings behave.

Then the surprising conclusion: "Instead, the legal status of marijuana makes it a gateway drug."

What? So you mean that the only aspect of marijuana possibly leading to other drugs that scientists view as having any validity at all has to do with the fact that the government chose to make it illegal? That the most significant reason scientists can document that marijuana use is even associated with the use of heroin, cocaine, and other drugs is that a person who chooses to use marijuana must enter, to some extent, a criminal subculture in which other illicit drugs are available (and probably more profitable to the dealer) and in which pressures to "try something a little more interesting, a little more daring" abound not just from peers but from dealers with a personal interest in making that person a steady customer of more expensive exotica? That if marijuana were not illegal, no scientist would be likely to deem the notion of marijuana leading to or causing the use of other drugs worthy of further study because the likelihood was low and the studies to date showed no causative correlation?

In a word, yes. And a bit more is implied, though it is obviously not spelled out in the IOM report, which took pains to distance itself from the larger social and political debates that revolve ultimately around values rather than science and to make policy recommendations only within the narrow confines of its mandate: what known science suggests about marijuana as a medicine.

Most of those who want to keep marijuana illegal, and especially those who resist even the modest reform of allowing it to be used for medical purposes, insist that their position arises in part from their great concern for the welfare of "the children." Opening even this small chink in the wall of prohibition, they say, will put children at great risk of becoming addicted to drugs and facing lives of misery and frustration. Those who question their policy preferences are often accused of being callous and insensitive to the suffering of innocent children that would accompany any modest reform.

But the only aspect of marijuana that scientists accept as being a remotely respectable connection between it and more dangerous illicit drugs is the fact that marijuana is illegal. This implies that keeping it illegal means that a larger percentage of innocent children will go on to use more dangerous and addictive drugs sometime in their lives, quite possibly doing great damage to their psyches and to their potential to develop to their fullest as human beings. This, in turn, means that those who insist on keeping marijuana illegal should bear—morally if not necessarily legally—a huge portion of the responsibility for that suffering and heartache. Should state attorneys general and contingency trial lawyers start suing prohibitionists to recover damages inflicted on drug addicts (and the tax dollars spent on them) by the policies they have insisted on keeping in place, even as they have sued manufacturers of tobacco and firearms? Except for the fact that most of them would have to sue themselves, the rationale is at least as strong.

The IOM report didn't choose to tease out all those implications, but they are certainly there.

Now it is unlikely that California voters knew all of this, or even very much of it, during the campaign for Proposition 215 in 1996. What they did seem to understand—based on polling data and the impressions I got from working for a large daily newspaper, interviewing principals on various sides of the issues, writing about them regularly, and fielding telephone calls and reading letters in response to what I had written—is that marijuana had some troubling side effects, but other prescription drugs did also, and weighing the risks and possible benefits should be a matter for patients and doctors to decide. Most voters who supported Proposition 215 seemed to hope that a small "white market" for medical marijuana could be created or allowed to emerge, preferably with some modicum of the kinds of safeguards built into the prescription drug system. Then they wouldn't have to be confronted with images of people who appeared to be getting some benefit from marijuana in dealing with fairly serious ailments being hassled by the police or run through the court system. Few California voters seemed to want to legalize marijuana for recreational purposes—I'm not aware of any poll in 1996 that showed more than 29 percent support for full legalization—but they figured if sick people could get cocaine or morphine under a doctor's supervision, why shouldn't they have access to marijuana? It is unlikely that more than a few voters gave much thought to the problems that might be involved in implementing such a system, figuring that the authorities, the law's proponents, and other interested parties could get together and figure out a system that would work reasonably well.

If that was the hope, it was to prove an unrealistic one, at least in parts of the state.

CHAPTER FOUR

Implementation: The Lungren Interlude

California is a large and diverse state, with more different kinds of geography, topography, and climate zones, not to mention people, than most large countries. The political topography is complex as well, with numerous hills, valleys, and unexpected promontories. This diversity makes it difficult, even with the best will in the world and the best of intentions, to devise a single policy that can satisfy both patients and law enforcement personnel in Humboldt County in the northern forests and Imperial County in the southern desert, let alone all points between. Over the years there have been several semiserious efforts (at least put forward by reasonably serious people, most recently a high-ranking Republican state senator, Stan Statham, in the middle 1980s) to divide California into two, three, or more states. Even as a third-generation native with roots and relatives north and south who has traveled up and down the state numerous times by most of the available conveyances, I don't begin to claim to understand the state in its totality.

The California tourist board used to print brochures touting "the Seven Californias" to stress diversity and lure people to visit and spend their money in as many parts of the state as possible. The visitor's guide on the tourist commission's Web site now divides the state into 12 different regions. While these regions do not coincide precisely with political tendencies, they offer a framework that at least conveys a sense of how variegated California is.

With more than 32 million people, 158,869 square miles, a coastline stretching 840 miles on the Pacific Ocean, and 58 different counties,[48] California's size and diversity present potential implementation problems for any state policy. One with a strong emotional subtext is bound to present more problems.

The 12 Regions

The tourist board begins with the Shasta Cascade region in the far northeastern corner of the state. An area of mountains, including majestic Mount Shasta, forests, lakes, and rivers, it has excellent recreational attractions and a relatively sparse population. Politicos used to refer to this part of California and some farther south, in Gold Country and parts of the Central Valley, as the "cow counties." With mostly rural areas and small towns, it is generally politically conservative. Some parts of the region have been used for marijuana growing—and in general the marijuana issue, especially medical marijuana, tends to cut across political and ideological divides.

The North Coast stretches from the dense redwood forests near the Oregon border down along a rugged and sometimes strikingly beautiful coastline to the wine-growing counties of Napa, Sonoma, and Mendocino. The city of Mendocino, established by New England whalers, looks like a Cape Cod village—it served as Cabot Cove, Maine, for the *Murder, She Wrote* television series. Parts of Mendocino, Humboldt, and Trinity Counties, from about Willits north to Eureka and Arcata on the coast, have become known as the "Emerald Triangle" among illicit marijuana growers and users. Sometimes large patches are nestled into remote portions of national forests, which are used in part because it can be difficult to trace responsibility when authorities find "grows," and as government property they can't be seized or forfeited. Marijuana has for years been the leading cash crop in this region, and often those involved in the trade are not transplanted hippies but otherwise quite conservative country dwellers and Vietnam War veterans. Over the years the region has received extensive surveillance and attention both from federal authorities and California's aggressive CAMP (Campaign Against Marijuana Planting) programs. While some citizens have welcomed the helicopters and fatigue-clad troops trying to control illicit marijuana growing (innocent hikers and neighbors have been known to encounter armed guards and endure some tense situations), most have grown weary of them. Proposition 215 passed in the region by a healthy margin.

The San Francisco Bay Area includes Marin County to the north of the bay; Oakland, Berkeley and other cities in the East Bay area; San Francisco itself; and the San Francisco peninsula to San Jose, which includes Silicon Valley and Stanford University. Although the area is quite diverse, politically it has a reputation for being relatively liberal, but often in unusual ways. San Francisco, the only California city some east-erners would recognize as a "real city," votes Democratic but also includes extremely conservative enclaves. Stanford University houses the Hoover Institution, which is generally viewed as a conservative "think tank" (though more ideologically diverse than is generally recognized) but which has welcomed drug war critics from Nobel economist Milton Friedman to former Secretary of State George Shultz to former San Jose and Kansas City police chief Joseph McNamara. In 1998 Oakland elected as mayor former "Governor Moonbeam" Jerry Brown, who ran more as a nuts-and-bolts civic improver than as a New Age visionary. San Francisco had been home to serious and aggressive campaigners for medical marijuana and several medical cannabis clubs for several years prior to passage of Proposition 215, and most of its elected officials sup-ported it strongly.

California's Gold Country includes Sacramento, the state capital, and the 300-mile-long area stretching along state Highway 49 in the Sierra foothills Mother Lode region. Aside from Sacramento it is generally rural and more or less conservative. Steve Kubby, a supporter of Proposition 215 and later a Libertarian Party gubernatorial candidate, claims that when he and his wife were arrested for growing medical marijuana in their home near Lake Tahoe, he heard sheriff's deputies murmuring com-ments like "You might be able to get away with this in San Francisco, but this is Placer County and we voted against 215" loud enough for him to hear. I can't say firsthand if it's true, but it wouldn't be surprising.

The Central Valley from Yolo County north of Sacramento down to Bakersfield (which has been and still is a major oil-producing region) is one of the richest agricultural regions in the world, where fruit trees and massive vegetable fields grow along with grains and rice. Parts of it remind one of the Midwest, visually and culturally, and parts bring to mind Oklahoma or the prairie states. The area is generally conservative.

The High Sierra region, from Mono Lake and the Mammoth Lakes area in the southeastern Sierras to Sequoia/Kings Canyon and Yosemite National Parks through the Lake Tahoe area, is used for recreation by people in other parts of the state, especially for winter sports. It is rugged and fairly sparsely populated, generally conservative in attitude. (Hollywood used to love to set tales of small-town evil or bigotry in this general region.)

The Central Coast, stretching roughly from Monterey Bay to Ventura and Oxnard, is largely an agricultural region dotted with relatively small towns and some spectacularly beautiful scenery. Novelist John Steinbeck grew up in the agricultural/ranching area of Salinas and set several novels there and in nearby Monterey. The drive along the coast highway yields endless natural beauty, from Big Sur through San Simeon to Morro Bay. The mythical character Zorro fought evil in the Santa Ynez Valley area. Coastal Santa Barbara is a wealthy and relatively liberal enclave amid a generally conservative region.

Los Angeles County is a world unto itself, including Hollywood, Beverly Hills, the liberal westside, generally Hispanic East Los Angeles, predominantly African-American South Los Angeles, relatively conservative South Bay, working-class San Pedro, and numerous suburban cities to the east, including Monterey Park, which has become heavily Asian-American. Politically, the county generally divides its votes closely between Democrats and Republicans in statewide and national races, though it has leaned slightly more Democratic in recent years.

Orange County was long viewed as a suburban bedroom community for people who worked in Los Angeles, but it has become quite distinct, with thriving biomedical and high-tech industries and a superb performing arts center. It also has the largest number of Vietnamese in the world outside Saigon, in the thriving Little Saigon community in Westminster and Garden Grove, and a considerable Korean-American community. It was never quite the bastion of right-wing zealotry portrayed in myths of old, but it does produce reliable majorities for statewide and national Republican candidates, though it has elected a few Democrats of late.

The Inland Empire, including San Bernardino, Riverside, Victorville, the recreational and winter sports meccas of Lake Arrowhead and Big Bear in the San Bernardino Mountains, and the valley down to Temecula (home to recently developed wineries), combines established rural towns with fast-growing new suburban developments such as Moreno Valley and is generally conservative in politics.

The Deserts, stretching from Death Valley through Palm Springs to the Mexican border, east of old Highway 395, are sparsely populated and fought over by recreationalists and environmentalists who live somewhere else. There are a few resort cities, lots of sand, few people, and landscapes ranging from depressingly bare to austerely beautiful. Voters are generally conservative, with strongly individualist sentiments.

San Diego County, home to one of the larger naval bases in the country and almost perfect weather, includes the lovely coastal towns of La Jolla, Carlsbad, and Oceanside and the Marine Corps base at Camp Pendleton. Inland are Escondido and some mountains and growing towns such as Poway and Rancho Bernardo and areas surrounding La Mesa. The region generally votes Republican—former Governor Pete Wilson got started in politics as mayor of San Diego—but has become less distinctly conservative in recent years.

Sacramento's Political Culture

One other factor, although probably not unique to California, that is certainly important in assessing the state's political ways is the relative isolation of the state capital in Sacramento and a general lack of interest among large portions of the populace in what goes on there, which may be related phenomena. In the era of the automobile, one could make a case that no location is truly isolated anymore, but if it is possible, Sacramento is. The major population areas of the state are in the Los

Angeles basin and around the San Francisco Bay. Sacramento is about 80 miles east and north of San Francisco, in the Central Valley, in an area that used to be primarily agricultural. It has no dominant industry besides government and agriculture. In a state with numerous areas with very attractive climates, Sacramento's is one of the less desirable. Although the larger newspapers all have Sacramento bureaus, state capital news is not a top priority for any of them. None of the Los Angeles television stations has a news bureau in Sacramento. There is a strong tendency, then, for the political culture of the city to be relatively insular. It takes a powerful surge of interest for any political group or movement to mobilize a sizeable crowd for a demonstration or bout of concerted lobbying in Sacramento. People in the legislature and executive branches, therefore, tend to see mostly those who are in the capital permanently—those with a persistent and ongoing interest in how the resources commanded by state government are sliced up and served. That means permanent, large-scale special interest lobbies tend to dominate not just the political landscape but the social life of the town. Perhaps the situation is not any better or worse than in other state capitals, but in California few people pay much attention to Sacramento except sporadically, so the politics of governing is carried on with little oversight or feedback from the rest of the state.

It is said all politics is local, and even with significant input and a good deal of posturing and influence from state and federal officials, much of the response, especially regarding the practical situation of patients, to Proposition 215 becoming Section 11362.5 of the California Health and Safety Code was influenced more by local officials and attitudes than statewide or national proclamations. With the kind of diversity just described, it should not be surprising that local responses were quite varied.

Early Reactions to the New Law

After the election-night celebrations, many patients who had been using or were thinking about using marijuana for therapeutic or medical purposes found they still had more questions than answers when it came to actually exercising the rights the electorate had granted them. The new law definitely gave them the right to possess, use, and cultivate marijuana so long as they had even an oral recommendation from a licensed physician. But would physicians, few of whom outside a tight circle of doctors with an intense interest knew much about either the benefits or risks of marijuana, be willing to write recommendations? Would local police respect their new right? Would they leave anybody alone who had so much as a slip of paper with a doctor's name scrawled on it (or even a tale of sickness and a doctor's phone number), or would they be inclined to arrest people with recommendations and let the courts sort it out? Would a copy of a doctor's recommendation be sufficient to protect patients from arrest, or would the government (state or local) set up a system of government-issued identification cards? If identification cards were issued, would they be mandatory or voluntary, and what expectation would patients have that their privacy would be protected?

Even with the new law, where would patients get marijuana, especially if they didn't live in one of the few cities with an established cannabis club? The new law gave them the right to grow it, but it takes six months for a marijuana plant to reach maturity and many patients don't have facilities to grow plants or an especially green thumb. Some were disabled people living in small apartments or group homes. And while the new law encouraged government to set up distribution systems, it did not explicitly exempt patients and caregivers from existing laws against sales, transportation, and distribution. Would a distribution mechanism be able to charge enough to cover basic costs and a profit, would it have to operate as a nonprofit outfit, or would it be able to charge money openly at all? Was there any chance that ordinary pharmacists would eventually start to carry marijuana and other cannabis-based products with roughly the same control mechanisms—triplicate forms and the like—used for cocaine and other controlled substances available through prescription?

All these questions—which for many patients boiled down to the question of whether they would be able to get the medicine the law said they were entitled to use through an aboveboard "white market" or would have to continue to rely on the black market—were overshadowed by the larger question of whether federal laws against any use or possession of marijuana would trump the new state law and make the reforms contemplated by Proposition 215 essentially null and void.

The federal government responded, but not right away.

On November 6 Californians for Medical Rights, Bill Zimmerman's organization, renamed itself Americans for Medical Rights (AMR) and announced plans to put medical marijuana initiatives on the ballot in five or more states (although it kept its old stationery and sometimes called itself CMR when commenting on Proposition 215 implementation issues). On November 7 the Wo/Men's Alliance in Santa Cruz was granted nonprofit status by the California secretary of state, stating its intention not only to "research, prepare, and disseminate reports . . . based on information gathered directly from patients using marijuana" but also to "ensure that seriously ill patients have access at no charge to a safe supply of marijuana as prescribed by a physician."[49]

Americans for Medical Rights tried to launch a preemptive strike against national drug warriors when it filed, on November 20, a complaint with the state's Fair Political Practices Commission against the White House Office of National Drug Control Policy (ONDCP) for its failure to disclose how much in taxpayers' funds it had spent for ONDCP director Barry McCaffrey to campaign against Proposition 215. Dave Fratello said the group didn't question the propriety of McCaffrey—or of California Attorney General Dan Lungren or Joseph Califano of the Center on Addiction and Substance Abuse, also named— taking a position on 215. But "State election laws require a full accounting of in-kind contributions to campaigns,"[50] and McCaffrey's press events, AMR claimed, amounted to in-kind contributions, meaning his expenses and those of all his staff should be reported. The complaint was never investigated.

On November 21, Jeff Jones of the Oakland Cannabis Buyers Club announced that membership stood at "775 meticulously screened patients, and we are growing carefully." Jones also thanked the city council for resolving that "arrest of individuals involved with the medical use of marijuana shall be a low priority for the city of Oakland." The protocols developed for the Oakland club—requiring, among other things, a new member to produce a written medical diagnosis signed by a doctor on stationery bearing a license number followed by a telephone call to the doctor to confirm—were shortly thereafter sent to other clubs in the state and to people known to be interested in starting a club.[51]

Orange County Sheriff Brad Gates flew to Washington, D.C., to confer with McCaffrey and with representatives of the American Medical Association and the U.S. Drug Enforcement Administration (DEA) on federal and local law enforcement response to Proposition 215. He continued to criticize the new law, claiming that "the advertising campaign was done very effectively and the information didn't allow the voters to see all the facts." The proposition was carefully worded to create confusion, he continued. "They left loopholes." The *Orange County Register* report on the counterattack included a comment from Dr. S. Clarke Smith of Anaheim, who argued that law enforcement officers were more concerned about the possibility of losing "billions of dollars . . . forfeited in the name of protecting our youth from pot."[52] Dr. Smith told me that shortly after publication of the article that quoted him, a strapping, healthy-looking young man in his thirties came in to his office complaining of back pain and asking him to prescribe marijuana. "I told him to hold his horses," said Dr. Smith, "that we would have to do complete tests and try several other alternatives before going that route. He looked terribly disappointed but said he would come back for a later appointment to start tests. He never did. I still believe he was a deputy sheriff."[53]

On December 1 MedEx Santa Cruz was established "to provide in-home delivery of safe and affordable cannabis."[54]

The federal counterattack against the new California and Arizona laws began in earnest on December 2 with a hearing of the Senate Judiciary Committee at which Committee Chairman Senator Orrin Hatch of Utah gave the administration until January 1, 1997, to provide a battle plan against the new state laws. "We can't let this go by without a response," he said. Senator Jon Kyl of Arizona declared that he was "extraordinarily embarrassed" that his home state had passed an initiative allowing marijuana and other drugs to be used medicinally and eliminating imprisonment for possession of drugs. The law, he predicted, "begins the road to destruction of people's lives." Nobody asked him to rate going to prison against using marijuana under a doctor's supervision on a life-destruction scale. John Walters, who had been deputy director of the drug policy office during the Bush administration, criticized the Clinton administration for not moving faster to counteract the California and Arizona initiatives. "The law is on the books," he said. "The question is whether the officials in this administration are going to enforce it or not."[55] Presumably, he meant the federal law, not the laws passed by the voters of two states.

Republicans like to paint themselves as opponents of overweening centralized power in the federal government. The leaders of the Republican majority that swept into power in Congress in 1994 on the strength of the "Contract with America" declared themselves devoted to "devolution" of power from the central government in Washington, D.C., to the states and to the most local levels of government. Republicans have supported "block grants" from the federal government, which state or local government leaders may spend as they choose, to replace grants that come with all kinds of intricate rules, regulations, and mandates. But toward the end of 1996 Republican leaders were invoking federal supremacy to slap down the voters of two states who had been insolent enough to disagree with federal mandates in an area Republicans of a previous era might have said was none of the government's business. In the case of the federal prohibition against prescribing marijuana for medical uses, as we shall see, the policy was in fact the result of an arbitrary decision by an unelected bureaucrat who made the decision against the strong recommendation to the contrary by his agency's chief administrative law judge after extensive hearings.

Walters, who had been a Republican appointee, demanded that the Clinton administration, at the very least, exert federal supremacy by revoking the federal licenses to prescribe controlled substances of any doctor who recommended marijuana. Republican members of the Judiciary Committee urged the Drug Enforcement Administration to deputize local police to confiscate illegal drugs under federal law to reduce the police departments' possible liability for defying new state laws and a legal challenge by the Justice Department to the new laws. They also called for increased federal prosecution of small-scale drug cases that had theretofore been considered too minor to demand federal attention.

There was a time, as late as the early 1990s, when most Republicans deplored increased federalization of local police. Presumably, when the issue is medical use of certain drugs, conservative principles fade into insignificance.

In California, Dan Lungren in early December 1996 told a meeting with 300 law enforcement representatives that the new law should be implemented conservatively, though he didn't rule out working with federal agents to help enforce federal laws against marijuana possession. "It would be our view that marijuana would not be available for acne, hangnails, stress, or arthritis," Lungren told the enforcement officials, an interesting slip of the tongue in that the initiative had specifically mentioned arthritis along with "any other illness for which marijuana provides relief." He noted that under the California Constitution the legislature does not have the power to overturn or amend an initiative passed by the people, but statutes, for example, that prohibit medical users from operating heavy equipment might be in order. He noted that marijuana sales remained illegal under state law. Dave Fratello of Californians for Medical Rights chose to see the bright side: "What was noticeably absent today was a battle cry, that Lungren is going to be part of defeating this even though voters passed it," he told reporters.[56]

On December 4 the district attorney in Amador County asked a judge to dismiss a pending marijuana case "as defendant has medical reasons to use marijuana,"[57] and the sheriff subsequently mailed the patient two grams of marijuana that had been confiscated. On December 17 in Sonoma County an attempt by attorney Bill Panzer to get a case—involving a nurse's aide with epilepsy and a friend designated as a caregiver who were arrested in August—dismissed on the basis of Section 11362.5 was rebuffed. The judge in that case also declined to have the patient's doctor named "in camera" (in chambers) to protect his identity, saying if he wanted to testify it would have to be in open court. Also on December 17 Dennis Peron's attorney, J. David Nick, moved to have the case stemming from the August raid on the Cannabis Buyers Club moved from Alameda County to San Francisco. Nick also argued that the grand jury should be reconvened to consider the "medical necessity" defense created by Section 11362.5 and the contention that the raid itself was an improper attempt to influence the election.

After several weeks of leaks and rumors, the federal government on December 30 announced its plan. "Federal law-enforcement provisions remain in effect," said Barry McCaffrey. "Nothing has changed." He announced the administration's intention to punish doctors who prescribe drugs deemed illicit under federal law by revoking their federal licenses to prescribe certain drugs and by prosecuting them if deemed appropriate. He also announced an advisory to the transportation industry that workers who test positive for certain drugs would not be permitted to use new state laws as an excuse. Attorney General Janet Reno and Department of Health and Human Services (HHS) Secretary Donna Shalala joined McCaffrey in continuing to call the initiatives a "hoax" passed as a result of a "stealth" campaign. "This is not medicine," said McCaffrey. "This is a 'Cheech and Chong' show." Presumably he was speaking of doctors who might recommend medical marijuana—in fact, he singled out Dr. Tod Mikuriya of Berkeley by name for personal ridicule—not the press conference. The officials noted that not only were letters being sent to state and local medical licensing groups warning "unequivocally" against prescribing illegal drugs, but doctors who didn't heed the warning might be banned from treating Medicare or Medicaid patients. They also announced that the Internal Revenue Service (IRS) would be ordered to scrutinize the tax returns of doctors who prescribed marijuana.[58]

Bill Zimmerman, who had managed the Proposition 215 campaign, was quick to respond: "McCaffrey has decided to proceed with his most deplorable and indefensible option—targeting physicians," he said. "This strategy is a measure of our government's hysteria over marijuana. Doctors must now fear federal agents simply for informing their patients that this particular drug might help them."[59] Zimmerman said that Californians for Medical Rights, which was staying in existence for the foreseeable future, was organizing a court challenge to the administration plan to attack doctors.

Interestingly, the officials did not announce a court challenge to either the California or the Arizona law to uphold the doctrine of federal supremacy. To date the federal government has not challenged any of the state medical marijuana laws in court for contradicting federal law, relying on bureaucratic and administrative procedures to try to thwart them.

1997

On January 8, 1997, Superior Court Judge David Garcia in San Francisco ruled that the passage of Proposition 215 entitled the San Francisco Cannabis Buyers Club, closed the previous August, to operate. Garcia told prosecutors from the state attorney general's office: "I don't think you or I are going to say that the people of California were totally ineffectual in trying to pass a medical marijuana law. The defendants are ordered to operate as a nonprofit organization and to maintain records showing that they have been designated as primary caregiver by members who have recommendations from physicians."[60] The attorney general's office vowed to appeal, contesting the ruling that a club can be a caregiver under Section 11362.5.

On January 9 cultivation charges in Plumas County against Cynthia Ann Powers, a multiple sclerosis patient, were dropped by District Attorney James Reichle. In Alameda County charges against Harold Sweet, who has glaucoma, were dropped.[61]

On January 14, 1997, four medical marijuana users, including a San Francisco assistant district attorney, Keith Vines, and Santa Cruz activist Valerie Corral, along with several doctors who treat AIDS and cancer patients, including Marcus Conant, Arnold Leff, Neil Flynn, Milton Estes, Stephen Follansbee, Stephen O'Brien, Robert Scott, Duby

Tripathy, and Donald Northfelt, filed suit to challenge the federal government's plans. On February 27 the White House, while filing papers seeking dismissal of the suit, sought to clarify the policy. Doctors could discuss marijuana as medicine with their patients so long as they didn't recommend it, either orally or in writing. The California Medical Association and the American Medical Association both urged Dr. Conant to drop the suit, and CMA attorney Alice Mead "recommends that physicians not sign or complete those forms [patient forms usually prepared by cannabis clubs] and that they should not prepare their own similar forms."[62] On March 17 the AMA and the CMA urged a settlement of the suit and issued guidelines for members. The guidelines still recommended that doctors not write recommendations or assist patients to obtain marijuana but said that doctors should be able to discuss the risks and benefits of medicinal marijuana use with their patients and to document the discussion in the medical record without interference from the federal government.

On April 11, 1997, U.S. District Court Judge Fern Smith, a Reagan appointee, issued a temporary restraining order against any federal government action—not just the threats to go after licenses but threats related to Medicare and other agencies such as the IRS—against California doctors who recommend marijuana to their patients.[63] On April 30, after hearing further arguments from the government, Judge Smith reaffirmed the restraining order. It remains in effect.

On January 13, perhaps in response to criticism that he talked about relying on science when in fact the dearth of recent research on marijuana was due to the federal government's refusing to allow its supply of marijuana to be used for research on human beings, Barry McCaffrey announced that his office would commission a $1 million study of the medical potential of marijuana by the Institute of Medicine. The Institute of Medicine is a branch of the National Academy of Sciences that does not maintain an ongoing bureaucracy but is convened by the NAS when a public policy matter requires objective answers to medicine-related issues, recruiting scientists to undertake specific projects.

On January 15 the San Francisco club, renamed the Cannabis Cultivators Club, reopened for business at 1444 Market Street.

On January 30, Dr. Jerome Kassirer, editor in chief of the *New England Journal of Medicine,* wrote an editorial in the journal titled "Federal Foolishness and Marijuana." It derided the federal government's policy as "misguided," "out of step with the public," and "inhumane." Dr. Kassirer called for reclassifying marijuana from Schedule I (drugs of abuse with no therapeutic value) to Schedule II (drugs subject to abuse with some therapeutic value). He denounced "the absolute power of bureaucrats whose decisions are based more on reflexive ideology and political correctness than on compassion."[64]

On February 6 state Senator John Vasconcellos of San Jose announced that he would be developing and introducing legislation to implement Proposition 215. Dennis Peron was wary, saying "Prop. 215 doesn't need any help."[65]

As federal authorities strove to thwart the new law and as state and local law enforcement officials sought to understand it, patients and activists began to try to implement it while keeping a cautious eye on the federal government and, in many cases, local law enforcement agencies. By early February six new clubs working to educate patients and doctors and to make cannabis available to bona fide patients had opened, bringing the total in the state to 17.

In Orange County, activist Marvin Chavez, who had found that marijuana helped ease the pain of his rare genetic back disorder, ankylosing spondylitis, organized the Patient, Doctor, Nurse Support Group and asked for an appointment with Sheriff Brad Gates to discuss the development of guidelines to allow the group to operate within the law and with the cooperation of the sheriffs department. Sheriff Gates, one of the two cochairmen of the No on 215 campaign, would not meet with Chavez. He still believed the voters hadn't known what they were doing when they passed the law, as he told a *Register* reporter on February 8. He also announced that he had retained a law firm to try to reverse the effects of 215 and said that it was his intention to report to the federal government the names of any doctors who recommended marijuana. (This was before the April court ruling.)

In Los Angeles, Metropolitan Transit Authority police arrested Willie Perkins for possession of marijuana even after he showed them a membership card in the Los Angeles Cannabis Club. Dan Lungren announced his intention to crack down on clubs that distribute marijuana and stated his opinion that even after the passage of 215, California law still provides that no money can be exchanged for marijuana, even if the transaction is called a donation.[66]

On February 24, 1997, Lungren issued an information bulletin to law enforcement agencies with guidelines on how to take account of Section 11362.5 when enforcing California's marijuana laws. These guidelines made it clear that it was not his intention to make it easy for patients to exercise the rights the people had given them by vote. The first clause set the tone: "It is not incumbent on a police officer to inquire whether the individual cultivating, possessing, or using marijuana is doing so for medicinal purposes. It is the responsibility of an individual to claim that he/she has an affirmative defense." In the second clause, the procedure for handling somebody claiming a Section 11362.5 defense was outlined: "The officer should detain the person for the purpose of making those inquiries necessary to determine whether there is a legitimate affirmative defense." Among the qualifications specified were these: "Patients must be seriously ill. Minor injuries, colds, common flu, most skin cancer, stress, etc. are not covered." The directive also said: "Patients cannot cultivate or possess amounts greater than necessary for their personal medical needs. This precludes commercial and most cooperative style operations. Questioning by an officer should help determine whether the amount is consistent with what was recommended by the doctor for what length of time and for what illness. . . . NOTE: One marijuana plant produces approximately one pound of bulk marijuana. One pound will make approximately 1,000 cigarettes. Therefore, one can argue that more than two plants would be cultivation of more than necessary for personal medical use."[67]

The guidelines also urged that the following specific questions be asked of each patient: "What is the nature of your serious illness? How long ago was it diagnosed and by whom? Do you use marijuana to provide relief from this illness? Have you tried other drugs? If so, what drugs? Have you tried Marinol? How many marijuana cigarettes do you smoke per day because of your condition? . . . Did the physician conduct an examination and make a determination that marijuana would be beneficial? How long have you been seeing the doctor? Has he/she done any follow-up examinations to monitor your condition? How often are you examined by your physician?"[68]

It is difficult to remember that the promulgator of these guidelines was the same Dan Lungren who had reminded all concerned that the California Constitution did not allow a law passed by the people to be amended by the legislature. The operative clause of Proposition 215 states that "Section 11357, relating to the possession of marijuana, and Section 11358, relating to the cultivation of marijuana, shall not apply to a patient, or to a patient's primary caregiver, who possesses or cultivates marijuana for the personal medical purposes of the patient upon the written or oral recommendation or approval of a physician." It doesn't say "shall not apply unless it's more than two plants," nor does it authorize the police to second-guess a doctor's recommendations or practices or even to inquire as to the nature of the disease. Any such provision—the guidelines also created a much narrower definition of the admittedly ambiguous term "primary caregiver" than was contained in the law passed by the people—is in fact an amendment to the initiative and an amendment explicitly designed to narrow and reduce the rights the initiative grants to patients and physicians. If the legislature doesn't have the right to amend an initiative passed by the people, on what authority does the attorney general do so through a set of guidelines that are not subject either to legislative or judicial review?

These guidelines have never been rescinded or superseded.

On March 1 police in Mountain View, Santa Clara County, returned six plants and some growing equipment seized from Edward Willis, a 43-year-old electrician with AIDS. Santa Clara County Assistant District

Attorney Karyn Sinunu commented, "We respect the voters' call. In certain circumstances, upon a doctor's recommendation, we will honor a patient's right to use marijuana for medical purposes."[69]

On March 6, a lawsuit was filed in the First District Court in Washington, D.C., by life-extension scientist Durk Pearson, his partner, Sandy Shaw, and several doctors against Barry McCaffrey, Donna Shalala, and Janet Reno, to enjoin the federal government from any interference in state medical regulation and control of medical marijuana. The suit contended that the Ninth and Tenth Amendments reserved the right to implement such regulation to the states and that since no interstate commerce was involved, the federal government had no power to interpose its will. As of this writing, several responses and counterresponses had been filed in the case, but it had not yet been heard. A decision in Pearson's favor could change everything. Durk Pearson, co-author with Sandy Shaw of the 1978 bestseller *Life Extension: A Scientific Approach,* had won a case in January against the Food and Drug Administration (FDA), arguing successfully that the FDA's refusal to allow scientific studies showing benefits to be quoted on packaging or in advertisements for vitamins and nutrient supplements violated the First Amendment. The attorney who won that case, constitutional lawyer Jonathan Emord of Washington, D.C., was handling the medical marijuana lawsuit.[70]

On March 11, San Jose City Attorney Joan Gallo announced a proposed ordinance to regulate the locations and operations of "medical marijuana dispensaries," authorizing them to be only in commercial areas and at least 1,000 feet from churches, schools, and day-care centers. Smoking would not be allowed on the premises. On March 25 the city council passed the proposed ordinance and San Jose became the first city in the United States to officially permit and regulate the distribution of marijuana to patients. Peter Baez and Jesse Garcia announced that they planned to open a dispensary soon on San Carlos Street.[71] Also on March 25 Mendocino County District Attorney Susan Massini (in the North Coast area) warned marijuana growers that having a contract with a medical cannabis club would provide them with no legal protection. "They will not be immune from felony prosecution even though they've reached a contract with an organization that may be perceived in San Francisco as being legal," she said.[72]

Meanwhile, in Los Angeles on March 18, prosecutors decided to drop their case against Willie Perkins.

On April 5 the Ukiah Cannabis Buyers Club began registering patients at a local theater. On April 9 Jeff Webb of Oroville, after being stopped for a license plate violation near the Yuba-Sutter County line, informed California Highway Patrol officers that he and his wife were caregivers delivering medical marijuana to patients. Three small bags with San Francisco Cannabis Cultivators Club seals containing less than two ounces were found. The two were arrested and charged with transportation and possession for sale. And on April 10 a warrant was issued for the arrest of Jean Baker, 39, director of the Humboldt Cannabis Action Network, after she failed to appear in court on cultivation charges. She claimed she was being harassed for negotiating contracts with local growers. The district attorney's office said she was observed at a site where marijuana was later found growing. Sheriff Dennis Lewis said that his understanding is that under Proposition 215, "Patients and caregivers can grow for personal use, but there's no mention of proxies growing large fields for clinics or clubs." Dennis Peron of the San Francisco club had long claimed that the caregiver status members assign to clubs like his can be reassigned to growers to protect them from cultivation charges.[73]

In Sacramento in early April, AIDS patient Ryan Landers announced that he would ask the city council to help his group open a Capitol City Cannabis Buyers Club. "We want this to work and we want everybody to feel comfortable with what we are doing," he told the *Sacramento Bee*. "Patients are working with law enforcement." Dale Kitching, head of the Sacramento County district attorney's narcotics unit, said he told Landers that he thought what Landers proposed went beyond what Proposition 215 allowed, but he hadn't threatened to arrest him and would take a wait-and-see attitude.[74] By late April the club had changed its name to the somewhat less controversial Sacramento Patients Access Clinic and had directed a series of very pointed questions to the California Medical Association in response to the guidelines issued in March.[75] Although he continued to negotiate with city officials, Landers was never able to establish a facility in Sacramento, and for the next several years police and the district attorney's office carried out a policy that amounted to arresting patients and letting the courts sort out whether their medical claims were valid.

On April 21, federal Drug Enforcement Administration agents raided a cannabis club called Flower Therapy in San Francisco, confiscating 331 marijuana plants and growing equipment. John Hudson, who had been a member of the Cannabis Buyers Club, had formed the club the previous September, after the first club had been closed in August. The April raid occurred when nobody was at the club; the DEA did not confiscate records or other property, including sealed bags of dried marijuana marked for medical use. No charges were filed and the club reopened the following day, but the raid stirred up considerable opposition. San Francisco District Attorney Terence Hallinan, the only prosecutor in the state who had endorsed Proposition 215 during the campaign, complained that he had not been notified of the raid and would have opposed it if he had been, even offering to testify "to the fact that this group was trying to comply with the laws of the state of California." Dave Fratello of Americans for Medical Rights noted that "only ten days since having a federal judge's restraining order block the government's 'war on doctors,' federal officials are now launching a war on patients." He argued that this raid showed "that the DEA is not interested in preventing abuse of Proposition 215; the agency is interested in preventing any access to medical marijuana." Dale Gieringer of California NORML said that "By shutting down Flower Therapy's cultivation operation, the federal government is forcing patients to be dependent on the black market's high prices and less scrupulous foreign smugglers. The administration's policy is morally and constitutionally bankrupt, and is a direct affront to the people of California who voted for Prop. 215."[76]

Attorney General Dan Lungren's office kept close tabs on legal developments surrounding Section 11362.5. For example, Lungren's Update #4, issued on May 12, presented discussions of 14 different cases in California, including a brief summary of the legal issues involved and the dates of the next scheduled actions. It also took notice of the *Pearson v. McCaffrey* suit filed in Washington, D.C., and of the Proposition 215 implementation legislation introduced by state Senator John Vasconcellos.

An example of the advice doctors were getting from within the profession can be gleaned from a memo issued on May 19, 1997, by the Permanente Medical Group in Oakland, a regional administrative headquarters for Kaiser Permanente HMOs (health maintenance organizations) throughout Northern California. It noted Judge Fern Smith's ruling to prohibit the federal government from punishing doctors but went on to advise:

> This ruling does not permit doctors to assist their patients to purchase or otherwise obtain marijuana, which is still a controlled substance under federal law. You are still advised not to sign forms from buyer's clubs, as this may expose you to some type of federal enforcement action. Regional attorneys continue to advise that only the attached letter should be used by physicians whose patients bring in a buyer's club form or request a letter of diagnosis. If you sign the attached letter, a copy should be placed in the patient's medical record.
>
> This ruling is currently in effect—however, the federal government may appeal the ruling, and it may be overturned by a higher court. If that happens, we will let you know. In the meantime, you may discuss the pros and cons of marijuana use with your patients without fear of federal sanctions, you may orally recommend marijuana, and you may sign the attached diagnosis letter for your patients if you so choose.[77]

The approved diagnosis letter was as follows:

> To Whom it May Concern:
>
> [Mr./Ms./Miss/Mrs. [Patient's Name] is under my care at Kaiser Permanente Medical Center for [Diagnosis: for example, AIDS, AIDS chemotherapy, Cancer (specific type)/Cancer Chemotherapy, Lupus, Crohn's disease, Multiple Sclerosis] with [describe symptoms: for example, pain, nausea, anorexia, spasms, Wasting Syndrome, etc.]. If [Patient's Name] chooses to use marijuana therapeutically, I will continue to monitor and to provide appropriate medical care for his/her medical condition. I am a physician licensed to practice medicine in the state of California. You are welcome to call [provide appropriate phone number] to verify this information.
>
> > Sincerely.
> > [Physicians' Name], MD
> > [Physician's Department Name]
> > California Physician's License Number:
> > [Physician's License Number]
>
> I request that my physician provide the foregoing information.
>
> > [Patient Signature]
> > [Patient Name]

The original of this letter may be given to the patient; a copy shall be placed in the patient's medical record.[78]

Over the next few months the cases of Sue Ellen Elm in Santa Cruz; Mike King, 52, a former deputy sheriff in Tulare County with back injuries arising from the pursuit of a suspect; and Alan Ager, a podiatrist in Marin County with 134 marijuana plants in his yard, which he said constituted an effort to lay in a year's supply to deal with chronic back pain, crept through the preliminary phases of the court system.[79] The most highly visible case involving radically different understandings of what California's new medical marijuana law authorized began on July 29: Los Angeles County sheriffs' drug investigators arrested cancer patient Todd McCormick in an old, gutted mansion in the fashionable and expensive Bel Air district of Los Angeles that contained 4,000 plants in varying stages of development. Federal charges were filed that would carry a mandatory minimum sentence of 10 years in prison.[80] Actor Woody Harrelson, who had been a public advocate of drug law reform and especially of the reintroduction of hemp for food and fiber for several years, posted the $500,000 bail after McCormick had spent two weeks in jail.

I spoke with McCormick, a cancer patient since the age of two who had used marijuana for various kinds of discomfort arising both from the cancers and from his treatment since the age of nine, over lunch in Santa Ana a few weeks after his release on bail. A slight, frail young man with an air of earnestness, he told me he was growing so many plants as a scientific experiment, to test the different effects of different strains of cannabis on different symptoms. "Most of those plants were seedlings," he told me. "I would have gotten rid of the males once they could be sexed and some would have died. I probably would have ended up with 2,000 fairly mature plants of more than two dozen different strains. Then my plan was to test them on myself to see if different strains had different effects on different symptoms." He had preliminary plans to make the marijuana available to other certified patients as well and to keep meticulous records so as to form a database suitable for scientific study, but those plans had not been completely worked out when the arrest occurred.[81]

McCormick didn't say so at the time, but publisher Peter McWilliams, author of more than 30 books (mostly on getting comfortable with computers), five of which spent time on the *New York Times* bestseller list, later revealed that he had financed McCormick's project. McWilliams suffered from cancer and AIDS and was using marijuana medically himself. He said he had given McCormick a sizeable advance so he could set up his growing project, then write a book on the results of his research, which McWilliams's company, Prelude Press, planned to publish.

On August 15 the first appeals court decision relating to Proposition 215 was handed down by the First District Court of Appeals in the case of *People v. Trippett*. Pebbles Trippett, a medical marijuana patient and activist, had appealed her conviction in a 1995 Contra Costa County case in which she had been found to have marijuana in her car while driving and had been convicted of transportation under Health and Safety Code Section 11360, which was not specifically mentioned in Proposition 215. The appeals court ruled that Proposition 215 could be applied retroactively in some but not all cases and that it created an "implied defense" for transportation for personal use. "The voters could not have intended that a dying cancer patient's primary caregiver could be subject to criminal sanctions for carrying otherwise legally cultivated and possessed marijuana down a hallway to the patient's room," the court said, but a literal reading of Section 11360 could make that action an offense. It urged lower courts to apply Section 11360 to those who qualified as patients under Section 11362.5 with common sense and a little leeway. The court also ruled that Proposition 215 did not necessarily permit a patient to possess unlimited quantities of marijuana but only what was reasonably consistent with the patient's personal medical use: "The statute does not mean, for example, that a person who claims an occasional problem with arthritis pain may stockpile 100 pounds of marijuana just in case it suddenly gets cold. The rule should be that the quantity possessed by the patient, and the form and manner in which it is possessed, should be reasonably related to the patient's current medical needs." The court declined to translate that into a specific number of plants or a specific quantity of dried marijuana, noting that such decisions would of necessity have to be determined on a case-by-case basis, primarily between patient and doctor, with the authorities intervening only when quantities seemed unreasonable. The appeals court did not rule on Pebbles Trippett's guilt or innocence, remanding the case to a lower court for retrial with these principles in mind.[82]

After preliminary legal maneuvering the civil trial of Dennis Peron, Beth Moore, and others arising from the August 1996 closure of the San Francisco Cannabis Buyers Club was delayed again on August 20, 1997. The case had been narrowed to a civil matter involving the maintenance of a public nuisance under state law. Senior Assistant Attorney General John Gordnier, who coordinated antidrug enforcement in the attorney general's office, handled the case personally, and moved successfully to prevent a jury trial and to block Attorney General Lungren's appearance as a witness.[83] On August 22 the case of Alan Ager, the Marin County podiatrist with 134 plants, ended in a hung jury, 10–2. The Marin district attorney announced he would refile charges and seek a new trial.[84]

On August 26, 1996, "Conservative Attorney General Lungren and liberal lawmaker John Vasconcellos stood shoulder-to-shoulder Tuesday to announce they had agreed on a three-year state study of marijuana," as the *San Francisco Examiner* put it. Senate Bill (S.B.) 535, the bill they endorsed, had been scaled back considerably from what Vasconcellos originally had in mind, in part to obtain Lungren's endorsement and to improve the bill's chances of passage through the legislature with a margin high enough to make a veto by Governor Pete Wilson less likely. Vasconcellos had originally included guidelines for quantities and a state distribution program that would have involved voluntary registration and issuance of state identification cards for patients, but these steps were considered unlikely to win majority legislative support. In its final form the bill consisted of a three-year medical marijuana research program, to be conducted by the University of California (UC) at $1 million per year, and received endorsements from the California Medical Association and the American Cancer Society. It was an "urgency measure" to go into effect immediately rather than on January 1 of the following year as most new laws in California do, so it required a two-thirds vote. By the end of the legislative session in September, Vasconcellos, a veteran of numerous legislative struggles, determined that it would not receive the necessary two-thirds majority and decided to hold it over until 1998. (Legislative sessions in California are two years in length, with legislation not acted upon by the end of the first year still up for consideration at the beginning of the second year.)[85]

By October 1997, California NORML, in its monthly newsletter, wrote that "Dozens of cases have come to the attention of California NORML in which patients or caregivers have been apprehended for possession or cultivation of marijuana. While many authorities have been respectful of Proposition 215 in allowing patients with proper medical documentation to keep their medicine, innumerable patients have complained of police harassment, raids on gardens, and improper treatment by authorities." The newsletter went on to note that "Among the most contested issues is how much marijuana patients may possess or cultivate for 'personal medical use' under Prop. 215. Because of variations in medical consumption, storage needs, plant yields, etc., the garden size needed to satisfy personal use varies greatly. Drug agents have raided outdoor gardens with as few as a half dozen plants on the grounds that they were too large for personal use. (The government supplies 5 to 10 pounds per year of cannabis to the eight patients in the medical marijuana program, an amount that typically requires growing dozens or scores of plants.)" By October the NORML newsletter listed 18 cannabis clubs or distribution organizations around the state, although they ranged from flourishing and active outfits with thousands of members or patients to one or two people with the idea of beginning a program backed by little more than good intentions.

On October 8 UC San Francisco professor Dr. Donald Abrams, after more than three years of delays and refusals, got a go-ahead from the National Institutes of Health (along with a $1 million grant and the promise of research-grade marijuana from the government's plantation in Mississippi) to proceed with a research project on medical marijuana. Dr. Abrams's original intention had been to study whether cannabis really leads to weight gain and appetite stimulation in AIDS patients, but the project had been changed to emphasize safety aspects—impact on the immune system, viral load and hormone levels, and whether THC affects the metabolism of protease inhibitor AIDS drugs. The plan was to study three groups of 21 patients each, with one group smoking marijuana, one taking Marinol tablets, and one taking placebo tablets.

In October a Sacramento court ruled that a doctor's recommendation obtained after a defendant's arrest for possession and cultivation did not create a valid Proposition 215 defense. San Mateo County Supervisor Mike Nevin suggested that the county establish medical marijuana outlets at local clinics and distribute marijuana seized by law enforcement. This idea has surfaced periodically in the ongoing debate over implementation of Proposition 215 but has never been implemented.

During the first nine months of 1997 I spent a good deal of time on the telephone trying to track implementation, not only with legislators and their aides in Sacramento but with people who were running cannabis clubs, people who were thinking about running cannabis clubs, and their lawyers. What struck me was that beyond a few essentials, there was wide disagreement among them over how a "safe and affordable" supply of marijuana could be furnished through a small, legitimate "white market" to legitimate patients.

Some believed almost nothing could be done until implementing legislation was passed at the state level to assure uniformity and respect for certain protocols, while others believed the key was to set up distribution systems at the local level so they would be responsive to localized needs rather than subject to a uniform and possibly constricting state policy. Some thought it was essential for distribution organizations to have comprehensive medical information on members or clients, while others thought that any information beyond a bare-bones recommendation from a doctor, without even a diagnosis as long as the doctor was properly board certified, could create potential privacy-invasion problems for patients and should not be compiled. Some believed that it would be too risky to begin operating until they had ironclad local political support from a city council, county board of supervisors, or local police chief or sheriff, while others thought the best plan would be to set up a distribution system first, then notify local officials. Some believed the best approach would be to have a local government entity designate a piece of government property as a site for growing cannabis for medical needs and perhaps even have government officials operate it, while others insisted that the actual cultivation be done privately and resisted even the idea of government regulation or oversight. Some thought cultivation or distribution facilities should have a policy of being available at any time for a "pop inspection" by local police, while others feared such a policy could compromise patient privacy or invite harassment and was not required under Proposition 215. Some thought patients should be strictly limited as to the amounts they could cultivate, while others rejected the idea of any limits.

Almost everybody I talked with was sure that his or her approach was the one best approach and that other approaches were likely to end in failure or disaster. Perhaps that was inevitable given the wide variety of local conditions and political attitudes in California and the individualistic character of most of those likely to be interested in so esoteric an enterprise as distribution of medical marijuana, not to mention the varying levels of practical experience among them. And perhaps it reflected a healthy period of trial and error that was necessary at the beginning of any new set of social institutions. But it made for a good deal of confusion, even among those who were sincerely trying to do the right thing, and a certain amount of mutual hostility among people whose goals should have been similar. Medical cannabis distributors regularly sniped at one another, directly or indirectly, and occasionally one would call the police on another, justifying the act by saying that if the other's practices were allowed to continue, the whole movement would be discredited.

On October 17 proprietors of 15 cannabis clubs met in Santa Cruz at a meeting organized mainly by Scott Imler, whose Los Angeles club in West Hollywood enjoyed cooperative relations with local officials and had not been raided since the September before the election. In December 1996 his core group had begun meeting with West Hollywood city officials including the mayor and city manager, as well as the sheriffs who provided police services for the area, going through several drafts of guidelines and protocols before settling on a version all parties could live

with. The group filed applications for recognition of nonprofit or chari-
table status with the Internal Revenue Service, the state Franchise Tax
Board, and the state Board of Equalization, and worked with local planning and zoning authorities. "If there's a piece of paper required by some
government agency we file it scrupulously and completely," Imler told
me recently. "I can't say that I like doing it much, but we have 780 members who stand to lose access to a secure supply of their medicine if we
screw up."[86]

At the meeting in Santa Cruz Imler outlined what he believed were the
15 keys to success, the first being early and open communication with
law enforcement. "I think the West Hollywood sheriffs, since they were
in on the planning from the beginning, now feel as if they have almost an
ownership interest or at least a stake in our club," he told me some years
later. "They'll tell us if we're starting to mess up and help us to fix it
before it becomes a big problem."[87]

The Los Angeles club requires a prospective member to fax the doctor's recommendation letter before making an appointment with the
club. The club verifies that the doctor actually wrote the letter and checks
that the doctor is in good standing with the state medical board before
the first meeting. The Los Angeles club requires not only that a patient's
diagnosis fit the Section 11362.5 criteria but that it also meets the legal
doctrine of medical necessity under federal law, as applied most recently
to medical marijuana by the Ninth Circuit Court of Appeal. This is a
stricter standard than is required by Proposition 215 itself. The club also
requires that for illnesses other than cancer, AIDS, glaucoma, multiple
sclerosis, and epilepsy, the doctor separately certify that "imminent
harm" is likely if the patient does not receive medicinal marijuana.
Again, this is a stricter requirement than Section 11362.5 sets up. The
rationale is that those five diseases were specifically mentioned in the
lawsuit by physicians against McCaffrey et al. and in the restraining
order that enjoins federal officials from harassing doctors, so Imler concluded that providing medicine for those diseases can be done with
virtually complete protection from federal attention but that an extra
level of protection for other diseases would be prudent.

Most of the first meeting was taken up with an explanation of the Los Angeles club's rules and regulations, which the club representative explained are more complex and stricter than is specifically required under California law, and why it has chosen to operate this way. A form is required to certify informed consent to all the rules and regulations, and a new member must sign a stack of papers in duplicate. Only then does the admissions director issue a photo identification card. Different grades of cannabis are then available on a sliding-scale suggested donation basis. Imler told me the suggested donation is very close to current black market prices, although it really is voluntary and the suggested donation for people on Social Security insurance or disability is 20 percent of the normal donation. As of spring 2000, the club grows about a third of what is distributed, and a third is provided by members, who receive some form of reimbursement or compensation. That means a third still comes from the black market. The police wink at that because they would rather the amount be diverted to patients than sold to teenagers and because the club has moved steadily toward its goal of growing all the cannabis its members require in-house.[88]

In October two Marin County supervisors proposed an ordinance under which the county would give out cards to patients who have verified illnesses that a licensed clinician deems suitable for treatment with marijuana. The cards would be valid for one year and cost $25. And in Monterey County, about 100 miles south of San Francisco, the sheriffs department raided the Monterey County Medical Marijuana Care Centers, seizing seven pounds of marijuana and the records of more than 100 members. The center was subsequently closed. In November the Drug Enforcement Administration announced that state, local, and federal agents had seized more than 553,000 marijuana plants in California during the 1997 growing season, compared to 351,000 plants in 1996.[89] An FBI (Federal Bureau of Investigation) report noted that during 1996 there were 641,642 arrests nationwide for marijuana offenses, of which 85.2 percent were for possession. That was more than double the 300,000 or so arrested in 1991 and in 1992, the last years of the Bush administration, and brought to 2.1 million the number of people arrested for marijuana offenses during the first four years of the Clinton administration.[90]

In October an Alameda County superior court judge sent the criminal case against Dennis Peron and associates back to San Francisco to avoid "the appearance of improper forum-shopping" by the attorney general. On December 12 the First Appellate District ruled that Judge David Garcia's ruling the previous January was incorrect, that under the terms of Section 11362.5 cannabis clubs could not be considered "primary caregivers" and were therefore not immune from laws banning sales even if they operated on a nonprofit basis. Peron claimed that "the court has nullified the will of the voters as expressed in the success of Prop. 215."[91] Attorney General Lungren immediately sent out a bulletin to district attorneys and other local law enforcement officials stating, in part: "When the issue of whether the so-called 'buyers' clubs' could be primary caregivers under Proposition 215 arose, this office sought to resolve the issue through the judicial process. It was our opinion that California's citizens had approved a narrow measure that clearly did not contemplate sales of marijuana through 'clubs.' Many of you have clubs operating in your jurisdiction. This letter is to advise you of the ruling in *People v. Peron* so that you can prepare to take appropriate action. If you have any questions or need assistance with this issue, please contact either George Williamson or John Gordnier."[92]

Lungren may not have been aware of it, but by that time most of the other clubs in California, with the exception of Orange County's group, were organized as cooperatives of patients rather than as caregivers, and those that hadn't been quickly took steps to change their organizational structure and document the change. As cooperatives of patients—groups of patients joined together to pool their resources and to grow and/or acquire as much medicinal marijuana as possible, then divide it up among the members—they therefore had the same legal status as patients. As patients, they were clearly protected from prosecution for cultivation, possession, or use and under the Trippett decision were to be given a certain amount of leeway on transportation. After the *People v.*

Peron decision, then, no club organized as a patients' cooperative was shut down by law enforcement for several years on the grounds that it was illegitimately assuming the role of a caregiver, though some were shut down or closed for other reasons.[93]

The *People v. Peron* decision also clarified somewhat certain fuzzy areas of the law. It noted that the attorney general's "contention—that a primary caregiver cannot serve more than one patient—has no support in the statutory language." So while the San Francisco club was adjudged not to be a primary caregiver, Lungren's attempt to impose an almost impossibly narrow interpretation on the patient-caregiver relationship was turned back. And while the court noted that sale and distribution were still illegal, "bona fide primary caregivers for Section 11362.5 patients should not be precluded from receiving bona fide reimbursement for their actual expense of cultivating and furnishing marijuana for the patient's approved medical treatment." After some discussion the court became even more specific: "A primary caregiver who *consistently* grows and supplies physician-approved or—prescribed medicinal marijuana for a Section 11362.5 patient is serving a health need of the patient and may seek reimbursement for such services."[94] Trial courts in subsequent cases have interpreted these guidelines rather differently.

On the official medical front, the American Medical Association's policymaking committee on December 9 called for free discussion between doctors and patients regarding marijuana as a treatment option and for clinical trials to test marijuana's possible benefits to be held as quickly as possible. On December 14 and 15, researchers from the Institute of Medicine, commissioned by drug czar McCaffrey in January, held a Basic and Clinical Science Workshop at UC Irvine in Orange County. The IOM panel, headed by Stanley J. Watson, a research psychiatrist from the University of Michigan, and John A. Benson, a professor emeritus at the Oregon Health Sciences University, heard from patients and caregivers, including William Britt, Peter McWilliams, Todd McCormick, nurse Anna Boyce, Dr. Del Dalton of Laguna Niguel, Marvin Chavez, and Etienne Fontan of the Cannabis Alliance of Veterans. Andrew Kinnon;

Kenneth Smuland; Vic Hernandez; Bonnie Metcalf of the Yuba County co-op; Joanna McKee of Green Cross in Seattle; Jeff Jones, a patient and head of the Oakland club; California NORML coordinator Dale Gieringer; and Chris Conrad, author of a book called *Hemp for Health,* also participated. In addition, the panel heard from research scientists from Wake Forest University, Brown University, Michigan State University, Medical College of Virginia, University of Arizona, UC San Francisco, University of Vermont, and elsewhere on topics including the neuropharmacology of cannabinoids and their receptors, cannabinoid withdrawal, tolerance to cannabinoids, immune system modulation, marijuana and glaucoma, how cannabinoids act to kill or mask pain, and others.[95]

On December 26, Dennis Peron announced that he would run for governor as a Republican, facing Attorney General Dan Lungren, the clear favorite, in the June 1998 primary.

1998

After a year with Proposition 215 on the books, the data for marijuana arrests in California counties showed some interesting anomalies. Alpine County, in the eastern Sierras just south of Lake Tahoe, had the sharpest decline in marijuana arrest rates, down 93.06 percent, while Plumas County, in the eastern Sierras just south of Lake Tahoe, showed the sharpest increase in arrest rates, up 92.39 percent. But Alpine still had almost twice as many arrests per 100,000 population (327.06) as did Plumas (175.72). Marijuana arrests declined in 35 California counties but increased in 23 counties, including the highly populated southern counties of Los Angeles (7.00 percent), Riverside (13.17 percent), San Bernardino (16.88 percent), and Ventura (4.56 percent). Interestingly, the arrest rate declined slightly more in Orange County (–5.07 percent), where the only local cannabis club had almost no cooperation from local officials, than in San Francisco County (–4.14 percent), where several cannabis clubs worked closely with local officials. The arrest rate declined more in San Diego County (–8.62 percent) than in Santa Cruz County (–5.32 percent). The arrest rate in Alameda County, home to the

Oakland Cannabis Club, generally considered the most effective and responsible of the clubs in California, went up 6.25 percent.[96]

What all this means, beyond the fact that California is a diverse state full of the surprising and the unexpected, is not immediately clear.

On January 1, 1998, CHAMP (Cannabis Helping Alleviate Medical Problems), a buyers club on Church and Market Streets in San Francisco, closed, in part due to Attorney General Lungren's threat in December to close cannabis clubs and in part because of labor-management tension. This closure would prove fortuitous because on January 9 the U.S. Department of Justice filed suit against almost all existing cannabis clubs in Northern California—the Cannabis Cultivators Club and Dennis Peron; Flower Therapy and John Hudson, Mary Palmer, Barbara Sweeney, and Gerald Buhrz (their landlord); the Oakland Cannabis Buyers Cooperative (formerly Club) and Jeff Jones; the Marin Alliance for Medical Marijuana and Lynette Shaw; the Ukiah Cannabis Buyers Club and Cherrie Lovett and Marvin and Mildred Lehrman; and the Santa Cruz club. The suit was a civil action rather than a criminal case (meaning no jury trial would be forthcoming) under the rarely used civil provisions of the 1970 Controlled Substances Act and sought to enjoin all the clubs from dispensing marijuana.[97] Dennis Peron commented that the federal government was "defying the people of California. First they threatened the doctors, now they're threatening the patients." Dave Fratello of Americans for Medical Rights said, "Today's announcement continues a vicious and politically inept attempt by the Clinton administration to kill this issue. When will they learn it is not going away?"[98]

On January 12 state Senator John Vasconcellos announced plans to convene a statewide Medical Marijuana Summit to which he planned to invite Governor Pete Wilson, California Attorney General Dan Lungren, and U.S. Attorney General Janet Reno to meet with patients, caregivers, attorneys, and others. "I'm appalled, dismayed, that our state and federal governments have acted so arrogantly in the face of California voters' decisive support of Proposition 215," he said. Vasconcellos, a Democrat, continued: "I'm particularly angry that a president who won this state by a smaller margin than voters approved Proposition 215 has the temerity to send his federal law enforcement into our state to undo the decision of our citizens. If there was a mistake made by the voters in 1996, it wasn't to pass 215; it was to elect a president with so little regard for the wishes of the voters." Vasconcellos said he would push harder for S.B. 535, his bill to subsidize medical marijuana research, and would be developing a bill to facilitate distribution. "No one can argue with an ounce of credibility that voters passed Proposition 215 believing that sick people and their caregivers could only get marijuana from street pushers. We who are policymakers and purport to be leaders have an obligation to swiftly, smartly effectuate the will of the voters," he said.[99]

On January 14 Marvin Chavez, who had been operating the Orange County Patient, Doctor, Nurse Support Group out of his home since passage of Section 11362.5, was arrested and charged with transportation and sales of marijuana. Undercover police had forged a doctor's recommendation letter and begged Chavez to supply marijuana before the process of checking on the validity of the doctor's recommendation had been completed, complaining of severe back pain, one of the conditions for which Chavez himself used marijuana. When he relented, he was arrested. Chavez was held in jail for several days, then released on his own recognizance after promising to cease distribution of medical marijuana pending the resolution of the case, although he was allowed to continue to use marijuana medicinally himself.[100]

On January 21, the Arcata City Council unanimously passed Ordinance 1276, which "recognizes that the assistance of medical marijuana associations . . . may in some situations help promote the safe and lawful access to and consistent and affordable distribution" that Proposition 215 had called for and provided protocols and guidelines for such associations. It also "recognizes that lawful remuneration consistent with state law may occur between qualified patients and primary caregivers."[101] Arcata is just north of Eureka, in the far northwestern corner of the state. The ordinance was the result of months of work and consultation among Jason Browne of the Humboldt Cannabis Center,

Arcata Police Chief Mel Browne (no relation), patients advocate Robert Harris, and others. Harris had been calling me for months with updates on the sometimes agonizing process of achieving consensus among the disparate interests.

The ordinance authorized the Humboldt Cannabis Center, a co-op of 32 patients and caregivers who pay a $20 monthly fee that entitles them to a share of a crop grown by center members at two different locations. Additional cannabis was sometimes to be available for an additional contribution. Photo identification cards are issued by the police department, which is also given the authority to conduct inspections of the facilities and the financial and other records of the club, mainly to ensure that doctors' recommendations are valid and maintained properly but without having access to diagnoses and other information that might compromise patient privacy. The co-op is still operating, without more than normal day-to-day problems and complications and without interference from either the state or the federal governments. Police Chief Browne and the co-op were later the subjects of a flattering piece in *Time* magazine.

The following day, January 22, a San Diego municipal court judge ordered that possession charges be dismissed against Michael Ganey, who used marijuana with a doctor's recommendation for pain relief for a degenerative disorder in his wrists and ankles. The judge also granted a motion for the return of his confiscated property, less than an ounce of marijuana, but attorney James Silva had to threaten contempt proceedings before the Harbor Patrol, which had seized the marijuana and arrested Ganey, honored the court order.[102]

On February 1, CHAMP reopened under new management. The fact that it was closed when the federal civil lawsuit was filed meant that it was not affected by the injunction to close. Over the next few months CHAMP's membership grew dramatically as patients and caregivers from other clubs sought alternatives. On February 3 the Thousand Oaks City Council moved to close a cannabis club in Ventura County, giving the district attorney authority to obtain a court order to shut it down based on a fairly broad interpretation of the appellate court decision in *People v. Peron* to the effect that a club could not be a caregiver. The order did not prevent the club's cofounders, Andrea Nagy and Robert Carson, from continuing to grow marijuana for their own personal use, since they had doctors' recommendations, and they were allowed to take the plants under cultivation at the club to their home.

On March 9 Mendocino County Superior Court Judge Henry K. Nelson upheld a previous ruling that marijuana seized from Christopher Brown should be returned. The possession and cultivation case had already been dismissed under Section 11362.5, and the judge found that the amount of marijuana Brown possessed, around 11 ounces, was reasonably related to his needs. On March 15 Dennis Peron rented a 20-acre plot of property with a house, a pond, and a few outbuildings in Lake County and announced that he planned to move there and grow medicinal marijuana in a different way than had been possible in the city (see chapter 12). On March 16 San Francisco District Attorney Terence Hallinan filed an amicus curiae (friend of the court) brief in the federal civil case, stating that if the clubs are closed down patients will be put at risk and "what is now a reasonably well-controlled distribution system will devolve into a completely unregulated and unregulatable system."[103]

On March 23, one day after a cooperative police chief was replaced by another with a different attitude, the San Jose cannabis club, the Santa Clara County Cannabis Center, was raided and police seized patient records. Cofounder Peter Baez was arrested and charged with selling marijuana to someone who did not have a valid doctor's permission slip. The police also accused Baez, an AIDS patient, and cofounder Jesse Garcia of making a profit on the club's operation and of habitually selling to people without a doctor's recommendation, charges that might have had some validity. Whether they did or not, on May 8 the San Jose club officially went out of business. "We've been killed by the police and the district attorney," said Baez. "My credit is out. I can't get any more marijuana."[104]

Meanwhile, the political season in California was getting into full swing in this election year. On the Democratic side Lieutenant Governor

Gray Davis—who had been chief of staff to Jerry Brown when he was governor but had spent the intervening years as an assemblyman and secretary of state, quietly building a reputation as a moderate Democrat who was especially tough on crime—was battling it out with two millionaires. Representative Jane Harman, heir to the Harman-Kardon audio equipment fortune, and Al Checchi, who had made his millions in the airline industry, had both been opposed to Proposition 215, though they said they supported more federal research into medical marijuana. Harman and Checchi had more money to spend, but Gray Davis had a respectable war chest as well. On the Republican side Attorney General Dan Lungren, who had likewise built strong party ties as a congressman from Long Beach through most of the 1980s and into the 1990s, faced no serious opposition. Two minor-party candidates, Libertarian Party candidate Steve Kubby, who had played a role in getting 215 passed, and Green Party candidate Dan Hamburg, formerly a Democratic congressman, supported medical marijuana and more extensive drug law reform.

In the crucial—at least for the future of medical marijuana implementation—race for attorney general, state Senate Majority Leader Bill Lockyer of Santa Clara, a veteran legislator who had first been elected to the state assembly in 1972 but was facing California's recent term limit law, faced state Senator Charles Calderon of the Whittier area and former Congresswoman Lynn Schenk, neither of whom had supported Proposition 215. Lockyer had supported medical marijuana, needle exchange, and other drug reform issues in the legislature and promised to begin implementation of Proposition 215, as he said Republican Lungren had failed to do. On the Republican side Dave Stirling, previously an assemblyman from the Whittier area east of Los Angeles and for the last four years top deputy to Dan Lungren in the attorney general's office, faced token opposition. He also said he would move more positively to implement Section 11362.5, even as he defended Lungren's record in that area. The primary was to be held in June.

On April 2 nine federal marshals burst into Todd McCormick's home to arrest him for bail violations. He wasn't there. Having heard of the incident, he turned himself in the next morning. A drug test had found traces of THC in his urine. (A condition of his bail was that he not smoke marijuana.) He said it was from Marinol, which had been prescribed legally for him. Nonetheless he was taken into custody. He remained in jail until April 14, when federal Judge George King ordered his release because there was no legal basis for his arrest; in fact, a drug test taken on March 31, some days after the test that had shown traces of THC, had been negative, but the results of that test were not released before he was placed in custody. Judge King asked the prosecutor whether there was some obscure bit of case law that authorized such an arrest and the prosecutor said he didn't know of any. Peter McWilliams, McCormick's friend and publisher, was livid. "This was prohibited by the Bail Reform Act of 1984. This is not new law," he said. "The government had to know it was illegal. Apparently people can be locked up just because the government asks for it. That's how dangerous to all of our liberties the federal war on California medical marijuana patients has become."[105]

On April 8, in San Diego, the cases against Steve McWilliams and Dion Markgraaff, who had organized the San Diego Caregivers Club, were consolidated so they would be tried together. McWilliams, a colorful former cowboy who used cannabis for chronic pain resulting from several auto accidents and migraines, was stopped at a border checkpoint many miles from the border while taking 11 marijuana plants to a paraplegic club member. Investigators then searched his home, on a ranch owned by a cancer patient who used marijuana medicinally, and found a cooperative marijuana garden with about 400 plants inside a barn. The names of the patients to whom the plants belonged were on the walls. McWilliams was charged with cultivation, maintenance of a location for distribution, and conspiracy to cultivate for distribution, but based on the principle established in the Trippett case, transportation charges were dropped. Markgraaff was charged with conspiracy to distribute, sales to an undercover agent, and cultivation at the club's Ocean Beach location. According to the San Diego Union-Tribune, the club served several hundred members from two locations, one in the Hillcrest section near downtown San Diego and one in Ocean Beach. Both locations were closed down after the two were arrested.[106]

On April 11, Marvin Chavez of the Orange County Patient, Doctor, Nurse Support Group was arrested again, this time along with codirector Jack Schachter, and charged again with selling to undercover officers who posed as patients and caregivers. At the direction of Deputy District Attorney Carl Armbrust, police from several city police forces mounted a "sting" operation involving a phony doctor's recommendation (although one that was verified because the phone number given was answered by a police officer who posed as a doctor) and an undercover officer who met with Chavez several times to gain his confidence and tell about the suffering his "uncle" was undergoing. Finally, although he had agreed after his previous arrest not to participate in the distribution of marijuana, Chavez gave a quarter-ounce packet to the "nephew" and was arrested.

Meanwhile, David Herrick, a former San Bernardino County sheriff's deputy who had retired with a disability after a car rolled over him and who used marijuana to cope with the chronic pain resulting from his injuries, remained in jail. He had volunteered in 1997 to help Chavez and had been caught in a motel room with seven plastic bags each containing a quarter-ounce of marijuana, marked "for medical use only" and with the club's name and address emblazoned on them. Herrick acknowledged that he had planned to distribute the bags to certified patients but was arrested anyway. He spent almost a year in jail before his trial, at which the judge refused to allow him to mention Proposition 215 in his defense. He was found guilty of two counts of selling marijuana and acquitted on two counts, and the judge gave him a four-year sentence. His conviction was eventually overturned on appeal for prosecutorial misconduct by Deputy District Attorney Armbrust, but by that time Herrick was almost ready to be released.

On April 20 lawyers for B. E. Smith filed motions in federal court in California's Eastern District to dismiss charges on grounds that Smith had been unfairly targeted by the federal government for openly growing medical marijuana plants. A 50-year-old Vietnam veteran who used marijuana for pain relief and posttraumatic stress, had announced his intention to grow marijuana for medicinal purposes to the Trinity

County Board of Supervisors in rural northern California. The sheriff threatened to use federal law to deal with Smith. Smith publicly planted 20 plants along the side of a relatively major road, receiving national television attention, and local law enforcement left him alone. He increased the planting to 87 plants and posted a sign explaining the maladies of the patients for whom he was growing the plants—one paralyzed from the waist down, one an amputee. In September federal agents tore up the plants and charged Smith and his landlord with multiple violations of the federal Controlled Substances Act. Smith's attorneys claimed the federal government had acted in part to deny him a Section 11362.5 defense under state law. They pointed out that a 1994 memo by the U.S. Attorney advised agents not to bother with federal attention to plots with fewer than 200 plants on federal land or 500 plants on private land and the fact that no federal indictment had ever been brought in the district for fewer than 100 plants. They wanted the case dismissed for selective and discriminatory prosecution, but the judge declined and preparation continued to get the trial underway.[107]

On May 13, federal Judge Charles Breyer issued a preliminary injunction against five cannabis clubs in Northern California (the Santa Cruz club having folded) in the civil action that had been filed in January. He made it clear that the only issue before the court was whether the clubs violated federal law by distributing marijuana to patients. The constitutionality of Proposition 215 was not in question. He enjoined the clubs from "manufacturing" or distributing marijuana but left open several possible defenses if they continued to operate and were cited for contempt. If they were cited, their case would be tried before a California jury, and they might be able to use a medical necessity argument, a "joint possession" argument, or a substantive due process right to be free of unnecessary pain argument.[108] Several clubs closed for a while, but most reopened, although some did so as registration and information centers that did not distribute marijuana.

The Oakland club announced on May 21 that it would remain open but that every transaction would include a statement that marijuana was purchased or cultivated jointly by members for medical use, which attorneys had said might fit within the guidelines Judge Breyer had outlined. As the press conference began, a staff member told club president Jeff Jones that a DEA agent, posing as a patient, was in the club trying to purchase marijuana. Jones excused himself for a moment, talked briefly with the DEA agent, and asked if he would come into the next room for final processing of the paperwork; he then introduced him to the assembled media as a DEA agent trying to set up a "sting." With a "deer-in-the-headlights" look, the agent scrambled down the hallway to the elevator (the Oakland club is on one floor of an unremarkable downtown office building). When he emerged on the ground floor, the television cameras had already gotten there ahead of him and took pictures as he tried to cover his face.[109]

The federal government filed a motion on July 7 to hold those clubs that had reopened in contempt so the U.S. Marshal could close them forcibly. The hearing on that motion was scheduled for August 14.

Senator Vasconcellos's Medical Marijuana Summit on May 26 was a hearing of the Public Safety Committee, which he chairs, on S.B. 1887, which he had written to facilitate local government action to implement Section 11362.5. Nobody from the federal government attended. But Dan Abrahamson of the Lindesmith Center in San Francisco and Gerald Uelman, former dean of Santa Clara University's law school (and former O. J. Simpson lawyer), discussed Title 21, Section 885(d) of the U.S. Code, which grants immunity from prosecution to officers "lawfully engaged in the enforcement of any law or municipal ordinance relating to controlled substances." It was written to cover undercover narcotics officers, but it might cover people deputized to handle a municipal ordinance on medical marijuana like Arcata's. San Mateo County Supervisor Mike Nevin described how his county was supplying marijuana to patients under the auspices of a research program run by the county health department. San Francisco District Attorney Hallinan urged the state to give local health departments explicit authority to check doctors' recommendations and distribute marijuana. John Gordnier of the attorney general's office and representatives from the Sacramento police and sheriffs department stressed that federal law had supremacy and it would be unwise to take steps toward implementation until the federal government rescheduled marijuana. Randy Mendosa from the Arcata Police Department described the city's program and said it was working well.[110] As a result of the hearing Senator Vasconcellos rewrote S.B. 1887. It was passed by the state senate quickly but on June 30 failed to pass in the Assembly Health Committee.

On July 7 the Oakland City Council unanimously approved a policy statement on medical marijuana allowing a patient (or a primary caregiver for each patient) to possess up to 144 plants and up to six pounds of cannabis. The numbers and quantities were based on the amount of cannabis the federal government provides to the eight patients still receiving marijuana legally through the Investigative New Drug program, about seven pounds a year. Working groups consisting of patients, doctors, attorneys, growers, police officers, and representatives from the city attorney's and city manager's offices agreed that the number of plants needed to provide that quantity of processed cannabis was 48 flowering plants and 96 nonflowering plants in an indoor garden, or 30 flowering plants and 60 nonflowering plants in an outdoor garden, where plants presumably can be expected to grow more robustly. The police department's policy thereafter would be not to cite, arrest, or seize either plants or cannabis within the stated limits if a person established patient status. If a patient or caregiver could not immediately establish status, the police would not uproot or confiscate plants but take clippings and photographs. The owner would then have two business days to establish caregiver or patient status. Dried marijuana could be seized in such circumstances but would have to be stored for two days to give the person an opportunity to establish patient status, whereupon it would be returned.[111]

In the June primary, the first "open primary" in which voters could cross party lines to vote for any candidate they preferred, Gray Davis outdistanced his millionaire Democratic opponents, Jane Harman and Al Checchi, whose spending and mutual sniping canceled each other out, to win the Democratic nomination for governor. Dan Lungren won the Republican nomination for governor, although the 65,275 votes Dennis Peron received might have been enough to keep Lungren from polling more votes overall than Davis did, a closely watched indicator. (Davis received 35 percent to Lungren's 34 percent.) In the attorney general race Bill Lockyer won the Democratic nomination handily and Dave Stirling took the Republican nod.

During the general election campaign Davis started out ahead and kept increasing his margin in the polls. One indicator was in October, when the California Correctional Peace Officers Association (CCPOA), the prison guards' union, announced its support for Davis. The CCPOA, through shrewd lobbying and campaign contributions, had since 1980 made itself one of the most powerful political forces in the state, outstripping the doctors, lawyers, insurance industry, and teachers' unions in size of campaign contributions by the late 1990s. It had given the seed money to put California's three-strikes law on the ballot in 1994. It had supported Lungren generously in his runs for attorney general and had supported Republican Pete Wilson in his two races for governor. Political analysts are still debating whether CCPOA's support tipped the scales for Davis or whether it was an indication that Davis already had won the race and the prison guards wanted to be on the winning side. In any event, however, Davis trounced Lungren, leading a Democratic sweep that saw Republicans hold onto only two statewide posts, the relatively minor posts of secretary of state and insurance commissioner, while Democrats increased their majorities in the state legislature and in the state's congressional delegation. Bill Lockyer beat Dave Stirling to become the new attorney general.

On the level of individual patients encountering law enforcement personnel the record continued to be mixed. In Ventura County, on June 19, the district attorney decided not to file charges against 62-year-old Dean Jones after a doctor confirmed that he had recommended marijuana for high blood pressure, migraines, and back problems, and police were ordered to return 13 plants seized from his backyard in a May 27 raid. In San Bernardino County police seized

18 plants from wheelchair-bound Gene Weeks, a 48-year-old Vietnam veteran, and kept him in custody three days without allowing him access to the marijuana he used medicinally or to his conventional diabetes medication.

On July 24 Peter McWilliams, who acknowledged he had financed Todd McCormick's growing project in Bel Air, was indicted as a "drug kingpin," arrested, and denied access to his conventional AIDS medications while in custody. In July an Orange County judge allowed prosecutors access to medical files seized from Marvin Chavez's Patient, Doctor, Nurse Support Group, and in August Chavez turned down a plea-bargain deal that would have meant no prison time but would have prohibited him from being involved in marijuana distribution programs, setting up a trial in November. In August heavily armed DEA agents raided Dennis Peron's farm in Lake County, destroying 130 plants nearing maturity, but filed no charges.

In September police in Berkeley responding to a call about children trespassing in backyards found 12 plants at the home of singer-songwriter Buzzy Linhart, who wrote Bette Midler's hit "Friends." He produced a bona fide doctor's recommendation for glaucoma and the police helped him move the plants indoors and left. The next day a police officer who disagreed with that decision got a warrant (failing to mention the medical recommendation or the incident of the previous day) and arrested Linhart and confiscated the plants.[112] On September 23 Placer County sheriffs raided the home of Michael Baldwin, a respected dentist, and despite being shown recommendations for medical marijuana arrested him and his wife and confiscated enough plants and marijuana to fit into two shopping bags. "Proposition 215 does not apply in Placer County," one deputy murmured as the two were handcuffed.[113] In Los Angeles Sister Somayah, a sickle cell anemia sufferer who had informed the city council that she was growing plants for herself and other certified patients, was arrested in early October by four narcotics officers who claimed she had too many plants—30 small and 2 large. One of the arresting police was an officer against whom she had recently lodged a complaint.

In late August Judge Charles Breyer rejected the city of Oakland's decision to deputize Jeff Jones's Oakland Cannabis Buyers Cooperative as drug enforcement officers and thus immune from federal prosecution as "creative but not persuasive." He also turned down the Justice Department's request that the club be closed down immediately, leaving open the possibility of a jury trial centering around the issue of medical necessity. On October 13, however, Judge Breyer rejected the use of a "medical necessity" argument and authorized U.S. marshals to shut down the Oakland club. Breyer also rejected the defense's claim that the federal government did not have a "rational basis" to prohibit marijuana, saying he lacked the authority to judge it.[114] The Oakland club obeyed the court order, shutting down at the close of business on October 19, and appealing the decision to the Ninth Circuit federal appeals court. Attorney Gerald Uelman said he was convinced that Judge Breyer's decision would be reversed. Two weeks later Judge Breyer allowed the club to reopen as an educational resource and purveyor of hemp products such as caps and clothing items.

In Washington, D.C., the House of Representatives, with no hearings and virtually no debate, passed House Joint Resolution 117, by a 310–93 margin, declaring it to be the sense of Congress that marijuana is a dangerously addictive drug and that Congress is unalterably opposed to state propositions intended to legitimize the medical use of marijuana. The *Orange County Register* editorialized, "it told thousands of patients and their doctors—who believe that marijuana can alleviate their conditions, often with less serious and dangerous side-effects than 'standard' prescription medications—that Congress is pleased to see them continue to suffer or to obtain relief only at the price of becoming criminals."[115]

The Marvin Chavez Case

On November 10, after many delays, including those involved in getting new attorneys after Marvin Chavez lost confidence in those who advised him to take a plea bargain, the trial of Chavez, founder of the Orange County Patient, Doctor, Nurse Support Group, finally began in Orange County's West Court in Westminster, with Superior Court Judge

Thomas Borris presiding. I covered the trial for the *Orange County Register*'s editorial page, writing daily dispatches in the form of editorials and columns to supplement the news coverage with analysis that attempted to put each day's events in context. Before the trial I visited Chavez's modest home in Santa Ana, from which he ran the group, watching how meetings were conducted and getting to know other members of the group.

Marvin Chavez, born in 1954, might not have been the perfect squeaky-clean proponent of medical marijuana an advocate might prefer, as he was always frank to admit. He grew up in the working-class town of Huntington Park, near East Los Angeles. He dropped out of high school at 17 and got his mother's permission to join the Marine Corps Reserve before his 18th birthday. He served for the next six years, while working on construction jobs, sometimes getting a job as an extra in a film, and doing odd jobs. Eventually he started his own small contracting and remodeling company. He married and fathered two children. Like many others in the 1980s he developed a cocaine habit. He had several minor run-ins with the law, one in the 1970s involving having a gun (properly registered) in a car he was driving and several convictions for driving under the influence. In 1991, after some confusion over a diversion program he had begun attending after being caught in possession of cocaine, he was sentenced to two years in Tehachapi state prison. He volunteered for a work furlough program, and one day, while he was being transported in a van to a work site, he suffered a back injury when the van hit a parked car. Prison officials didn't take the injury seriously, figuring he was a typical malingering convict.

Transferred to a Chino prison, he worked in the dining room. One day in 1992 he slipped while mopping the floor, injuring his back once again. This time he was unable to walk or stand straight and prison officials provided a back brace and prescription painkillers until his release in 1993. Upon release, Chavez found himself still in constant pain. The medication also had massively depressive side effects. "I became a hermit," he told me. "I didn't want to be around people. I literally spent two

years in my bedroom, leaving only to go to the doctor, who couldn't figure out what was wrong with me. The injuries shouldn't have been that
debilitating."[116] Eventually he went to a different doctor who ran blood
tests and discovered that he was suffering from a rare genetic disorder,
ankylosing spondylitis, whose onset and progressive degeneration can
often be triggered by trauma to the back. Eventually, victims of ankylosing spondylitis will have almost all their bones fuse until they are
completely paralyzed. The process is extraordinarily painful.

From reading in the library Chavez learned that cannabis can sometimes be effective for chronic pain, especially back pain. Scott Imler had
just begun a cannabis club in Santa Monica about that time, in the early
stages of the Proposition 215 campaign. Chavez discussed the medical
use of cannabis with his doctor and his doctor finally gave him permission to try it. "I started using cannabis and came out of my bedroom,"
he later wrote. "My depression and the side effects from all those prescription medications disappeared."[117] Later, when he was making
presentations for the cannabis co-op he founded after Proposition 215
passed, he used to carry a gallon-size plastic bag filled with prescription
medication bottles. Cannabis had replaced all of his several dozen prescription medications, he claimed, and it relieved pain more effectively
without the kind of side effects that had made him a virtual hermit. Why
wouldn't he prefer it and want to make it available to other people suffering various ailments for which it might be effective?

Whatever it was that got him out of his bedroom, once he left he
began a burst of activity. He campaigned for Proposition 215, and after
it passed, since nobody else in Orange County seemed prepared to do so,
he started the Orange County Patient, Doctor, Nurse Support Group. He
got a business license from the city of Garden Grove, and when the city
council decided to rescind the license because it had figured out the group
had something to do with marijuana, he appeared before a city council
meeting to plead his case and explain his vision. The local media covered
these activities quite extensively. He wrote several letters to Orange
County Sheriff Brad Gates (cochairman of the No on 215 campaign),

explaining his intentions and expressing the hope that his organization would be able to cooperate with local law enforcement because while his desire was to stay on the right side of the law, he recognized that he might need some guidance. He made several attempts to get an appointment with Sheriff Gates but was rebuffed.

He developed a relationship with a local doctor who was a pain management specialist and knew something about marijuana and was willing to offer seminars and explain the pros and cons of marijuana for various ailments—and to write recommendations when warranted. Chavez worked on various forms for the group—sample recommendation slips for doctors to sign, application forms, agreement forms, designation of caregiver status forms—and publicized its work whenever possible. The group agreed that marijuana would be made available in quarter-ounce bags with a label that read "Not for Sale—For Medical Use Only" and would suggest a donation of $20, although a donation would not be required and donations over and above to cover overhead and other expenses would be gladly accepted. Chavez recruited a local nurse to be in charge of verification of physicians' recommendations. He printed posters and held regular educational meetings at the cooperating doctor's office and in other locations. At first dependent on the black market for cannabis, he began growing plants at his house and urged other members who had the capacity to grow as well, so eventually the group would furnish all the marijuana it needed through its own resources.

All this would have been a strange way to begin a large-scale criminal drug operation, which is what authorities alleged he was doing when they arrested him.

As noted earlier, Chavez was first arrested in January 1998 through an undercover "sting" operation, then arrested again in April when another undercover officer spun a tale of excruciating pain and persuaded him to act against his better judgment and furnish a small bag of marijuana. All these activities were coordinated by Deputy District Attorney Carl Armbrust, a vigilant drug warrior on the verge of retirement, who had prosecuted David Herrick, the former San Bernardino

County sheriff's deputy who was helping Chavez. I described Armbrust this way in a column in November: "Tall, balding, gaunt (one might almost say cadaverous), this former career Air Force officer projects a stern demeanor at first. But he is also approachable, pleasant and reasonable to talk with even when he disagrees with you, and has a wry sense of humor. He's fond of exaggerated pronunciation (may-ree-wanna). I think he's doing a terrible thing in pursuing this case rather than dropping it, but heaven help me, I like him."[118]

He pursued what he viewed as a legally proper if somewhat narrow interpretation of Proposition 215. He acknowledged that patients were allowed to possess, use, and cultivate marijuana and perhaps even transport it in light of the Trippett decision. But sales were still illegal, and the law defined any transfer, even if no money changed hands, as a sale. Calling a payment a "donation" was an obvious ruse. He also told me and other journalists, in conversations in the hall during pauses in the court proceedings, that what he really believed was that beneath the innocent exterior, Chavez was an extremely sophisticated marijuana dealer who was using the sympathy surrounding the medical marijuana issue to run a very lucrative large-scale drug-dealing operation that netted tens of thousands a month, and if this case ever got to trial he would bring in witnesses and experts to prove it. He never did. There was absolutely no evidence for this theory and Armbrust surely had to know it when he was peddling it.

In July Judge Robert Fitzgerald ruled that during Chavez's trial no mention of Proposition 215 or marijuana as medicine would be permitted, not even Chavez's disease or his own personal therapeutic use of marijuana. Faced with the possibility that conviction was a virtual certainty under such terms, Chavez rejected a plea-bargain offer that would have involved no jail time but would have prevented him from any involvement in marijuana distribution during a several-year probation period. Convinced that while he had made mistakes he had done nothing wrong, he preferred to take his chances rather than to admit wrongdoing. This attitude exasperated his attorneys and he soon replaced them with James Silva, an earnest young New Yorker with offices in Venice, California, who has also represented medical marijuana defendants Andrea Nagy in Ventura and Steve McWilliams in San Diego, along with J. David Nick, a San Francisco defense lawyer who cross-examines relentlessly and has handled marijuana cases since 1992, representing "Brownie Mary" Rathbun, Dennis Peron, and the Oakland cannabis club.

Judge Thomas Borris, 45, who finally got the case in the Westminster court, had been presiding judge in the Orange County's West Court since 1993, when Republican Governor Pete Wilson appointed him. A graduate of a Buena Park high school, where he played football, he earned a bachelor's degree at Claremont College and his law degree from Loyola Marymount University. He was deputy district attorney from 1980 to 1990, when he went into private law practice until 1993. A charming man with a sense of humor who loves sports analogies, he seemed like the most patient and thorough judge to have had the case. He explored pretrial issues completely, giving both sides plenty of time to make their cases. He announced early on that Chavez's attorneys would be able to talk about Proposition 215 and Chavez's belief that he was helping to implement it. Chavez's partisans had the best feeling about Borris that they had about any judge, but they reminded themselves from time to time that he was named Judge of the Year in 1995 and District Attorney of the Year in 1984 by the Orange County Narcotics Officers Association. You don't earn those honors by making a habit of giving accused drug dealers much leeway.

At least 20 members of the Patient, Doctor, Nurse Support Group, several with canes, some in wheelchairs, some with limbs missing, supported Chavez by attending each day of the trial. Steve McWilliams, Andrea Nagy, and Gene Weeks (from Victorville) also came whenever possible. Judge Borris had decided not to allow Dr. Tod Mikuriya, physician for a patient in Chico to whom Chavez had mailed some marijuana, to testify. Perhaps the most shocking testimony in the case came from an undercover narcotics officer who had posed as a man with severe back problems to persuade Chavez to trade him some marijuana for a donation. He testified that while he had vaguely heard of Proposition 215, he wasn't familiar with its provisions, had never read it all the way through, and had never had any training in how it would affect his day-to-day activities. If true, this was a shocking lapse not only on his part but on the part of his department. If false, then he perjured himself.

Although Judge Borris permitted Proposition 215 to be discussed during testimony, when he gave his instructions to the jury, they were that the jurors were not to consider Proposition 215 or medical marijuana at all, that their job was to determine whether sales had occurred and whether in some cases entrapment by police should be grounds for returning a not guilty verdict. On November 19, the jury returned not guilty verdicts on two of the four counts involving undercover police but guilty verdicts on the two other counts, as well as five misdemeanor counts of furnishing to patients. On the charge of mailing more than an ounce of marijuana to a woman in Chico, it found him guilty of transportation. Sentencing was scheduled for January 8, 1999.

The End of the Lungren Interlude

On November 22 the Marijuana Policy Project released its analysis of the annual FBI Uniform Crime Report (which is not especially uniform from year to year but still useful). It noted that the number of marijuana arrests during 1997 was the highest in American history at 695,201. Some 38.3 percent of the arrests were for simple possession. On any given day about 37,000 Americans are in federal or state prisons and local jails for nonviolent marijuana offenses.

On December 10 a Lake County jury found Charles Lepp of Hidden Valley not guilty after he was arrested with 131 plants in his yard. Lepp was a 46-year-old Vietnam veteran who had had bypass surgery and had chronic back pain and whose wife had thyroid cancer. He said he was growing also for a friend suffering pain from an on-the-job injury. The jury acquitted Lepp even though the doctor's recommendation was verbal and the doctor denied having made it. Afterward, Lepp told reporters:

The jury believed me. The reason they couldn't convict me was that they looked at me and saw themselves, their mother, their brother, their sister. I told them, "I've done nothing wrong. I'm like you." But if I were black or gay they might've tried to backdoor me. But I'm a white middle class goddamn war hero, military intelligence. I have letters of support from the V.A. with combat duty in Vietnam in 1972. Ninety percent of what's wrong with me can be traced to my service years. I need marijuana. When I take pain pills—I've had to take hundreds a month—it tears me up. I get bad when I drink alcohol. On weed I've never met anyone who doesn't like me.[119]

On December 18 a Sacramento police detective testified in the case of Bob Ames, a patient-activist who was growing marijuana in the yard at his home, that his understanding of department policy was that regardless of any paperwork demonstrating medical status, all people caught with cannabis were to have it confiscated, all plants were to be killed, and anyone in possession was to be arrested. The courts could sort it out thereafter.[120]

On December 28 incoming Attorney General Bill Lockyer announced a list of priorities that included making Proposition 215 work for all concerned. He called his predecessor "overly zealous in continuing to oppose [215] even after the people had adopted it."[121]

CHAPTER FIVE

Implementation: The Lockyer Years

Bill Lockyer might well be in the state senate still if not for California's term limit law. He began his legislative career as an assemblyman, elected in 1972, then moved to the state senate in 1982. He was senate Democratic leader from 1992 to 1998; he represented the San Jose area as a modestly liberal Democrat, affected and influenced by his younger years in the 1960s but taking care, in an area on the edges of Silicon Valley, not to seem hostile to business, especially high-tech business. He traveled up and down the state in his position as senate majority leader, speaking to newspaper editorial boards and civic groups, a pattern most cynical newspaper people associate with planning to run for governor or U.S. senator someday. Charming and articulate, he was said to be an effective party legislative leader—sometimes tough but always looking to form a consensus that wouldn't leave too many resentments, knowing there would be times when people who weren't with you today would vote with you if you didn't alienate them too badly this week. At age 57 he wouldn't surprise people if he still had aspirations to be governor sometime. But in 1998 it was Lieutenant Governor Gray Davis's turn, provided he could get by two relatively flamboyant millionaires spending huge sums of their own money. Davis had been Governor Jerry Brown's chief of staff in the late 1970s and had worked his way through various elected positions—assemblyman, state controller, lieutenant governor—

showing an ability to raise considerable sums of money and not to alienate, if not necessarily to excite, any significant faction of the Democratic
Party. Bill Lockyer, who had practiced briefly as an attorney and didn't
have as many chits to call in statewide as Davis, declared for attorney
general. Several Californians from both parties have used the position to
become governor or to launch serious bids, including Jerry Brown's
father, the legendary Democratic Governor Edmund G. "Pat" Brown,
and Evelle Younger, George Deukmejian, and Dan Lungren on the
Republican side.

The Republican nominee was Dave Stirling, who had been an assemblyman from the Whittier area in Southern California and then a top
assistant in the attorney general's office under Lungren. When he met
with the *Register* editorial board he said he would work to implement
Proposition 215 but emphasized that there were a number of legitimate
interests to balance and the existence of federal law to consider. Lockyer,
on the other hand, had been an open supporter of Proposition 215 in
1996, telling voters that when his mother was dying of cancer he decided
then that it was ridiculous for her not to have legal access to a medicine
that seemed to help others coping with the nausea and vomiting associated with cancer chemotherapy. Without going so far as to commit to an
active challenge to federal policies—although he emphasized that in the
long run an important key to acceptance and implementation would
have to be rescheduling at the federal level—he said that he would work
actively with all the interests involved to see that the promise to patients
embodied in Proposition 215 was finally fulfilled.

With John Vasconcellos chairing the Public Safety Committee in the
state senate and Lockyer in office as attorney general, medical marijuana
activists looked forward to serious steps toward implementation of
Proposition 215 at last. To be sure, Governor Davis, who had positioned
himself as a moderate's moderate during the campaign, had run as a
no-nonsense crime fighter and as a supporter of the death penalty and
of California's controversial three-strikes law. By May 23, 2000, he
had established a record that led Evelyn Nieves to write in the *New
York Times,* "Halfway into his second year in office, the governor is

establishing himself as more of a conservative on criminal justice issues than his Republican predecessors, or any other elected official in California—if not the nation." But nobody knew in 1998 if he had a position on how, when, or if systematic access to medical marijuana for certified patients should be implemented. (If he had visited the *Register*'s editorial board he would have been asked the question, but he didn't.)

In interviews prior to assuming office in January 1999, Lockyer almost always mentioned implementation of Proposition 215 as one of his goals. He told the *San Francisco Chronicle,* for example, for a January 4 story, that his predecessor, Dan Lungren, seemed to have a "zealous determination to not even allow this medical experiment" and that he planned to approach the issue differently. He reminded people that he had supported and voted for Proposition 215 in part because he had seen his mother die at age 50 and his younger sister at age 39, both of leukemia. After seeing how they had suffered, he said, "I concluded that if we can give them morphine, why can't we give them marijuana?" He acknowledged that working out a way to make medicine available without bringing reprisals from the federal government would be difficult and said he thought there should be tighter regulation of the cannabis clubs. "We need to operate clinics, not cults," he said.[122]

Lockyer had other items on his agenda as well. Within a few days of assuming office he had rescinded or withdrawn rulings or opinions Lungren had issued on topics such as abortion counseling in school clinics (Lungren was against, Lockyer for). He moved to establish himself as an environmental activist by defending a pending ban on Jet Skis and similar water craft in Lake Tahoe and increasing the budget for prosecution of violators of environmental, civil rights, and consumer protection laws by $2 million. He also had to decide whether California would stay signed on to the massive antitrust lawsuit against Microsoft brought by state attorneys general as the U.S. Justice Department was deciding whether to bring a federal antitrust case against Microsoft. Lungren had signed on, and several California high-tech companies, including Sun Microsystems, Netscape, and Intel, had been active in urging prosecution of Microsoft for antitrust violations. As Lockyer prepared to assume

office, people helping him with the transition hinted that he would probably appoint a task force on medical marijuana to draft legislation for the
state government to implement Proposition 215.

From their farm in Lake County, Proposition 215 author Dennis
Peron and John Entwhistle faxed news releases saying the initiative
didn't need to be "implemented" because it had become law on midnight
of the day it had passed, and state officials and law enforcement officers
needed to start obeying the law instead of trying to nullify it or imposing
legislative tweaks. They did have one suggestion for a simple change, in
light of the fact that some jurisdictions had chosen to interpret Section
11360, which forbids sales and transfers of marijuana so tightly as to
preclude even compensation for expenses: Why not simply add the
phrase "except for medical uses" to the laws forbidding sales and transportation of marijuana? That wouldn't constitute a change in
Proposition 215, as the previous year's legislation would have, it was in
the spirit of clarifying what the voters had tried to accomplish, and it was
fully within the power of the state legislature to do, since those sections
were originally put in by the legislature and not by popular initiative. It
would be simple and easy to understand and would make the law much
simpler for police, many of whom said they were confused, since Section
11362.5 seemed to make it legal for patients to possess, use, and cultivate cannabis but left it unclear whether they could transport, sell, or
even give it away. Perhaps the idea was too simple for a legislature com-
posed mostly of lawyers. Despite the fact that the state legislative counsel
had drafted a proposed bill with the proper legal language, not a single
member of the legislature could be found to sponsor this simple liberalizing clarification.[123]

The Kubby Arrest

The need for a consistent approach to the treatment of medical mar-
ijuana patients was put into high relief on January 19, 1999, when Steve
Kubby and his wife, Michele, were arrested at the home they rented in
Olympic Village near Lake Tahoe and taken to the Placer County Jail.
Steve, 52, had been the Libertarian Party candidate for governor in 1998,

in addition to having played a role in the passage of Proposition 215 in 1996. He campaigned not just openly but almost insistently, both as a medical marijuana advocate and as a patient. He had been diagnosed with adrenal cancer more than 20 years before, and he claimed that smoking medical marijuana as he had done for 20 years, making it the only medicine he used, helped to keep it in remission. He had a doctor's recommendation as did his wife, who had been diagnosed with an extremely painful gastrointestinal disorder called irritable bowel syndrome. The two were cultivating medical marijuana in a basement section of the house, away from the normal living area to which guests were invited. They had consulted with Jeff Jones of the Oakland club and with Dr. Mikuriya as to how many plants they would need to grow a six-month supply. They had shared the fact that they were growing with only a few of their very closest friends.

An anonymous letter sent to the El Dorado County sheriff from Santa Monica the previous September, during the election campaign, had alleged that the Kubbys were not only growing marijuana but actively selling it and using the election campaign to "launder" their pot-selling profits. Although the letter was anonymous and the accusations were, according to Don Atkinson of the El Dorado County Sheriff's Department, "weak and non-specific,"[124] Atkinson forwarded it to Placer County, where the Kubbys actually lived. Placer County had for several years been an active participant in the North Tahoe Task Force, a joint federal-state-local narcotics suppression effort financed mainly with federal funds and whose priorities might be inferred from the fact that its official stationery depicts a marijuana leaf inside a law enforcement badge. Within 24 hours Placer County had initiated a surveillance operation. Placer County Sheriff's Deputy Ed York began the police report by noting that Mr. Kubby had openly advocated medical marijuana use and enclosing copies of some of the hundreds of statements he had made while campaigning for governor.

A few days after the investigation was opened, Steve received a tip that he was a target of an investigation and was told to watch for a green Jeep with darkened windows. The Kubbys noticed a vehicle matching that description several times in their neighborhood and in town when they were shopping or picking up mail. Steve also told Peter King, the *Sacramento Bee*'s state political columnist, off the record during a campaign interview, that he thought he was under surveillance. After the Kubbys' arrest King wrote a column that described the encounter this way: "Now, with the interview winding down, the otherwise free-wheeling politician asked to go off the record. Kubby confided that he was concerned about a drug-police payback. He had received a tip: A stakeout of his Lake Tahoe residence was under way. Specifically, he had been warned to watch out for a green Jeep Cherokee with tinted windows."[125]

From the first time they spotted the green Jeep, the Kubbys stepped up documentation of their gardening activities. They posted copies of their medical recommendations at the door of their "grow room," along with copies of the Oakland guidelines and records showing how they were within the guidelines. As they became aware of more intensive surveillance through evidence that their garbage cans had been rifled, they began putting notes in the garbage marked "Attention: Law Enforcement," giving details about Steve's illness and stating that he would die without marijuana, that he was growing it for himself and his wife, and that at no time did he intend to possess more than a six-month supply of 3.5 pounds.

All this apparently did not deter the investigation. The police used high-power binoculars and telescopes to look inside the Kubbys' house, including their bedroom, from a distance. They crept close to the house at night with listening and recording devices. They obtained electric company records showing an unusually high use of electricity. In short, they proceeded as if they were convinced that the Kubbys were major marijuana dealers growing plants so they could sell and distribute marijuana under cover of a medical excuse.

When more than a dozen local police armed with automatic weapons arrived at the house late one Tuesday evening, the Kubbys thought they were prepared. They showed the police the grow room and the doctors' recommendations and explained why they believed what they were doing was well within the law. The police hesitated and called the district attorney's office. After the call, they proceeded with the arrests, confiscating all the plants and records, as well as the couple's computers, which they used to run a winter sports online magazine, and taking the two to jail. Fortunately, a neighbor was able to take their two-year-old daughter, Brooke, into her home. Bail was set at $100,000.

Steve was able to place a telephone call to his 23-year-old son from a previous marriage, Skye, who was living in Las Vegas, who began placing phone calls and sending e-mails to friends, supporters, and journalists, as well as to his attorney, Dale Wood of Truckee. I found an e-mail message from Skye Kubby when I got to the *Register* office the next morning, having, like Peter King, interviewed Steve Kubby during the campaign as part of the *Register* editorial page's political coverage.

I called Skye, who said that he had his father on the other line and could make it a three-way conversation. Steve explained briefly what had happened, swore he had a valid physician's recommendation (which he did), and explained some of his concerns about his physical condition. One of the indications that he needs medication, he said, was a release of adrenalin from the usually dormant adrenal cancer tumor. This caused his blood pressure, which was normally high to begin with, to "spike" to dangerous levels. For some reason, marijuana kept these episodes under control. Since being taken to jail, he said, he had had three such episodes, which had left him weak and vomiting. He had not been allowed to see Michele, but from what he could gather from the people at the jail her physical condition was shaky at best. Of course, his repeated requests to use marijuana medicinally while in jail had been laughed off. Prisoners often have a hard time getting an aspirin in jail, and Placer County wasn't about to provide marijuana to an accused drug dealer.

After calling the North Tahoe Task Force to confirm the arrest and talking to the Kubbys' attorney, Dale Wood; attorney Robert Raich, who was a member of the Oakland city medical marijuana working group; and Bill Lockyer's office, I wrote the *Register*'s editorial for the next day.

It explained what had happened, noted that Lockyer's office had said that the attorney general's policy would almost surely be not to intervene in a local decision to prosecute, and concluded that this was an unsatisfactory answer. "It should be the attorney general's job to make sure that law enforcement officials abide by the statewide law. California voters passed Prop. 215 more than two years ago. The proposition itself hasn't been challenged in court and has not been overturned. . . . It's time for law enforcement and the courts to respect that law." We quoted Robert Raich, who said: "I can't think of anybody to whom Prop. 215 more directly applies than Steve Kubby. He has a physician's authorization and he was growing only for his and his wife's personal use. It's troubling that he won't have access to his medicine while in jail, but it's even more troubling that he is in jail at all. Prop. 215 was written to keep patients out of jail."[126]

The following day, shortly after one of the deputies at the jail had asked Steve Kubby if he could get his friends to stop sending angry e-mails to the sheriff's department—the first indication aside from a few phone conversations Steve had that anybody on the outside knew of or cared about his plight—Dale Wood got the bail reduced and the Kubbys were released. Without their computers, however—which have not been returned to this day—they were unable to continue their online magazine business and were forced to declare bankruptcy. About the time they decided they might have to think about spending some time with Michele's parents in Orange County to cut their expenses while they regrouped and prepared for trial, their landlord informed them that he was thinking seriously about exercising his option to terminate their lease within a month, given all the notoriety and controversy surrounding them. They decided to make the move.[127]

On January 29, after a continuance from January 8, Judge Thomas Borris sentenced Marvin Chavez to six years in prison for marijuana sales. Judge Borris, who had instructed the jury not to consider Proposition 215 in its deliberations (and would later receive probation after wrapping his SUV around a tree while driving with a blood alcohol content two and a half times the legal limit), made it clear that the sentence was heavy in large part because Chavez had previously broken his promise to a court not to have anything to do with transferring marijuana to other people, even for reputedly medical purposes. Deputy District Attorney Carl Armbrust, who had retired after Chavez was convicted and came out of retirement to be present for the sentencing, commented, "Marijuana is still an illicit drug in the United States and California is still part of the United States." Defense attorney James Silva said, "The message sent out from Orange County today is 'hide.'"[128] Silva and co–defense attorney J. David Nick filed an appeal on the grounds that the jury had not been allowed to consider Proposition 215. The appeal is still pending, but Marvin Chavez was released on bail pending the appeal's outcome—by Judge Borris—in April 2000. While in prison Chavez repeatedly petitioned prison doctors and prison officials to let him use marijuana for his medical conditions and was repeatedly denied.

On February 18 the *Sacramento News and Review* ran an article by Michael Pulley noting that Placer County, where Steve and Michele Kubby lived, has been especially aggressive in prosecuting medical marijuana patients, including making 30 arrests in neighboring Sacramento County. Several of the cases had been dismissed or led to acquittals, but Placer County officials continued to arrest even patients who showed them a written recommendation from a physician and let the courts sort matters out. Pulley's article also noted that the California Medical Board, which licenses physicians, was investigating a "handful" of doctors, mostly on the basis of complaints filed by law enforcement agencies suggesting that they prescribed marijuana more than was warranted.

On February 25, 1999, Senator John Vasconcellos announced publicly the formation of Attorney General Lockyer's task force on medical marijuana—cochaired by Vasconcellos and Republican Santa Clara County District Attorney George Kennedy, who had opposed Proposition 215—in an angry op-ed article in the *Los Angeles Times*:

What kind of a government carries on a crusade against the will of its voters, favors pain and even death for some of its people?

From a president still distancing himself from youthful experimentation with marijuana, a drug czar who has effectively declared war on American citizens and a Congress that forbids the counting of votes on a Washington, D.C. ballot initiative on medical marijuana (sure to pass), our federal government continues to bungle the issue of medical marijuana.

There is an utter disregard of states' rights, an effort to try to silence the proponents of medical marijuana, to threaten the integrity and livelihood of California physicians and, ultimately, to engage in a campaign against the health and care of sick and dying Californians.

In November 1996, 56% of California voters passed Proposition 215, which allows the medicinal use of marijuana—a critical treatment and care option for sick and dying patients. The voters declared they want their relationship with their physician (rather than the government) [to] be the arbiter of their health and healing modalities.

In good faith, California local government and law enforcement leaders have spent the past two years working with patients, physicians and providers of medical marijuana to ensure responsible, compassionate implementation of Proposition 215.

Yet our federal government has assumed it knows best what's good for our people. It has engaged in activities that demonstrate an outrageous disregard for the will of our California voters (and since November, Arizona, Oregon, Washington and Alaska voters as well).

How ironic that Bill Clinton—who won our state by a smaller margin than voters approved Proposition 215—has the temerity to send federal law enforcement into our state to contravene the decision of our citizens.

Until the beginning of this year, our state and federal governments colluded to thwart the voters' mandate. Former California Atty. Gen. Dan Lungren publicly vowed to respect the voters' decision, yet then proceeded to take every action he could to ensure that Proposition 215 could not be safely implemented. To the extent he refrained from overtly violating our voters' mandate, he relied on the feds to do his dirty work.

Together, they closed most of the providers of medical marijuana in California, threw several legitimate caregivers in jail and currently are preventing a seriously sick defendant—author Peter McWilliams, now in failing health as a result—from access to medicinal marijuana.

Fortunately, California has begun, since the inauguration of a new attorney general and governor in January, to look more respectfully upon the will of our people.[129]

Brave words.

By the time of Steve and Michele Kubby's preliminary hearing in early March, the judge had received a letter from Dr. Vincent DeQuattro (M.D., F.A.C.C., F.A.C.P.)—professor of medicine at the University of Southern California Medical Center, director of hypertension studies, and chief of the hypertension diagnostic laboratory—"in behalf of my patient, Steve Kubby." Dr. DeQuattro noted that every patient with malignant pheochromocytoma that had, along with Kubby, been referred to a specialist in Michigan for experimental treatment had died long ago. Only Kubby had survived the disease. "I am convinced by Steve's blood pressure response during his recent incarceration when he was without marijuana therapy, that he still harbors a malignant pheochromocytoma. In some amazing fashion, this medication has not only controlled the symptoms of the pheochromocytoma, but in my view, has arrested growth."[130] Dr. DeQuattro would later conduct an extensive series of medical tests on Steve Kubby, documenting that he still had an adrenal cancer tumor kept in control by cannabis and that after 20 years of daily heavy cannabis use his health (apart from adrenal cancer and high blood pressure), including his lungs, and his mental capacities were on the high side of normal for a male his age.[131] The letter seemed to have no impact on the court. The trial, on 19 counts of cultivation for sale, sale, conspiracy, and more, was scheduled for March 19.

On March 2, Massachusetts Democratic Congressman Barney Frank introduced the Medical Use of Marijuana Act, which would set aside federal controls on marijuana so states could set their own policies. Specifically, it would take marijuana off Schedule I (reserved for uniquely dangerous drugs with no known therapeutic uses). It would also modify the Controlled Substances Act and Food, Drug, and Cosmetic Act so that none of their provisions would restrict (a) the prescription or recommendation of marijuana by a physician for medical use, (b) an individual from obtaining and using marijuana prescribed by a licensed physician, or (c) a pharmacy from obtaining and holding marijuana for dispensing under a prescription system in those states where it is legal for a physician to prescribe or recommend marijuana. The bill to date has received not so much as a preliminary committee hearing.

On March 17, 1999, the Institute of Medicine finally released its report, ordered by drug czar Barry McCaffrey and the White House Office of National Drug Control Policy, on the status of scientific knowledge of medicinal or therapeutic uses for marijuana. As discussed more extensively elsewhere (see chapter 6), the report concluded that "the combination of cannabinoid drug effects (anxiety reduction, appetite stimulation, nausea reduction and pain relief) suggests that cannabinoids would be moderately well-suited for certain conditions such as chemotherapy-induced nausea and vomiting and AIDS wasting" and that research into other possible therapeutic uses would be warranted. It also concluded that the risks associated with marijuana use are modest, that the morbidity threat is zero, that the risk of developing dependence is slight, and that there is no scientific evidence whatsoever for the notion that anything about the pharmacology of marijuana increases the risk that users will "progress" to harder drugs.[132]

As the *Orange County Register* editorialized the next day, McCaffrey had said at the time he commissioned the report two years previously that "he was doing so not to delay implementation [of medical marijuana initiatives] but so that decisions could be based on science rather than popular opinions. Now he has his report."[133]

McCaffrey might have taken a number of actions with the report. He might have noted, by confirming that there were some potential therapeutic uses for marijuana combined with a low abuse potential, that the report convinced him that marijuana should be moved to Schedule II so physicians could prescribe it and further research would be easier to carry out. While noting that he didn't control the process by which such decisions are made, he could have said that he felt sure his recommendation, along with this fine scientific report, would carry some influence. It wouldn't change the laws in any other way, he might have said, and it would take the issue of medical marijuana off the table. He could have declared that his office would redouble its efforts to enforce the laws against recreational smokers and the traffickers who supply them and that he recommended that penalties be increased against those who fraudulently claim a medical reason for smoking marijuana. He could have ensured us that Congress would go along.

But McCaffrey did not choose such a course. His first comment was "What marijuana legalizers won't tell you is that a substance found in marijuana can be delivered through various legal means," referring to Marinol, the THC pill. In subsequent comments he generally adhered to the line taken by White House spokesman Joe Lockhart: "What we found out is that there may be some chemical compounds in marijuana that are useful in pain relief or antinausea, but that smoking marijuana is a crude delivery system. So I think what this calls for is further research."[134] Government spokespersons never went on to say—and tried to avoid acknowledging on the rare occasions when they were challenged—that the report, in the next paragraph after it raised doubts that smoked marijuana had much of a future in medicine, said that since it would take years to develop alternatives, certain patients should be allowed immediate access to marijuana for smoking. None noted the report's suggestions for speeding up the Food and Drug Administration's approval process or the tentative arguments that in the case of marijuana, whose medical use preceded the existence of the FDA, the process could under existing law be bypassed altogether. None acknowledged that the report left no shred of scientific justification for keeping marijuana on Schedule I. And instead of using the report as it was putatively intended—to provide a base of scientific knowledge from which to craft or revise policies so as to be, at the least, not in direct contradiction to scientific knowledge—all government spokespersons who deigned to discuss the report after the two-day news cycle called for more research and keeping current policies while the research was conducted. If this report, which was based not only on hearings and direct research but on a survey of every single scientific study of marijuana available worldwide, was not to be the basis for revising laws and regulations to be in line with science, what future research project or report would offer enough authority?

In California the reaction from Attorney General Lockyer and his office was perhaps surprisingly cautious. His office issued a statement saying: "Current federal law prohibits doctors from prescribing medical marijuana and has made medical research difficult. We look forward to the federal government building on this report's findings so that we can wisely implement Prop. 215."[135] In other words—as he confirmed to me in an interview a couple of months later—Lockyer figured that effective implementation of 215, which would mean getting the police out of the picture for the most part (except in some cases where people used phony doctors' recommendations and the like) and treating marijuana as a medicine to be used under proper medical supervision, hinged on having marijuana rescheduled at the federal level, which would eliminate potential legal conflicts between the federal and state governments. But his office told me the day the IOM report came out, and he told me later, that he was not ready, for example, to file an amicus curiae brief on behalf of John Gettman's rescheduling petition, which was first filed in 1995, or even to endorse it publicly. Nor was he quite ready to join the *Pearson v. McCaffrey* lawsuit, which contended that so long as there was no nexus of interstate commerce, and especially in light of the Ninth and Tenth Amendments (which reserve to the states and people all rights and powers not specifically granted to the federal government), the federal government had no constitutional authority to impose its rules on medical use of marijuana on a state that had voted to authorize such use.

Not long after the IOM report was issued, Lockyer traveled to Washington to talk with McCaffrey and Attorney General Janet Reno about the possibility of developing some semblance of cooperation that would make it possible to honor the wishes of California voters who passed Proposition 215 without coming into conflict with federal law. He encountered General McCaffrey at his military-bearing intimidating best and a federal stone wall. As the *Sacramento Bee* reported, after the meeting Lockyer told reporters that "both were very clear that medical marijuana use violates federal law" and that McCaffrey said a massive additional research effort is required before there would be any chance of that status changing. When Lockyer mildly suggested that under California law he had, or soon would have, authority to have the state government sponsor or conduct certain kinds of marijuana-related research, McCaffrey told him in no uncertain terms that such research projects would also be a violation of federal law and that Lockyer himself might run the risk of being thrown in prison if he authorized such research.[136] The *Orange County Register* editorialized on April 2, 1999, "It is dismaying—an inversion of the democratic process—for an unaccountable, appointed federal official to threaten an elected California official with arrest for trying to implement a state law passed by the people of the state. Mr. McCaffrey's bullying attitude is intolerable."[137] But apparently it was effective.

Based on several personal meetings, I like Bill Lockyer and I think he is a thoroughly decent human being. He has an active mind and a wide range of knowledge. But some aspects of the very skills that have made him a successful politician make it difficult for him to be as forceful an advocate for medical marijuana patients and the full implementation of California law, especially vis-à-vis the federal government as an institution. As a legislative leader his strong suits were negotiation and compromise sufficient to reach, if not an actual consensus, at least a result all the interested parties could live with. That process emphasized gathering information and quietly sounding out potential adversaries as to what they would need to be able to sign on before a real legislative push was undertaken rather than confrontation or issuing a public ultimatum. Even though he was senate majority leader, that was a legislative position, akin to herding cats, rather than an executive or a command position. An effective political leader is more likely to be good at stroking egos and suggesting accommodations than at issuing orders or reminding subordinates that policy comes from the top and those who can't go along should start looking for another position. Lockyer was one of the best at that quintessentially political process. It is far from being a personal criticism to suggest that his experience and his inclinations in the political process were not the best possible experience for running the huge bureaucracy that the California attorney general's office is or for responding to a bully like Barry McCaffrey by saying something like, "Bring it on, sucker. I'll make sure the television cameras are rolling when you send your goons to arrest me."

Furthermore, for liberal Democrats of a certain age, there's a kind of respect bordering on reverence for the federal government as an institution. Since the time of Franklin Roosevelt, for most liberals it is the federal government on whom they pin their hopes for a more compassionate, just, and equal society. Within their memory it was the federal government that improved welfare programs or set standards when some states were intolerably stingy with their own programs. It was the federal government that broke the back of racial segregation in the South by

talking tough and occasionally sending in troops when Southern politicians counseled massive resistance and vowed to battle for "segregation
forever." It was the federal government that prevented certain states from
racially gerrymandering voting districts so as to ensure that black politicians could never be elected. It was the federal government that
developed and imposed uniform environmental and antipollution standards when many state governments were reluctant to address such
problems, hostile to the idea of doing so, or bought and paid for by big
corporate polluters. It has been the federal government that has pushed
for more generous health-care benefits, both through direct government
provision and through mandates. It was the federal government that
erected the rudiments of a "social safety net" and has tried to defend it
against attacks from corporate interests and right-wing ideologues.

For most liberals in the United States the federal government has been
and is an essential engine of social progress. It is difficult enough for them
to entertain the idea that the government might have gone a bit too far
in certain areas or pushed programs in such a way that they have become
counterproductive in relation to the original goals of a peaceful, compassionate society that respects and defends the legitimate rights of
citizens of every race, color, and ethnic background. It is a huge leap to
think about the possibility that the federal government has become, even
in part, an oppressive institution that should be resisted. To embrace the
concept of states' rights against the federal government is something people like Bull Connor or Orval Faubus or George Wallace did and decent
people deplored. For many people who were old enough to be politically
aware or who had their political beliefs deeply influenced during the civil
rights struggles of the 1960s, the very term "states' rights" carries with it
an inescapable association with an illegitimate and morally indefensible
propagation of racism and segregation.

Finally, the attorney general of California is the chief law enforcement officer of the state, and he is bound both by his office and by the
reality of his day-to-day duties to take the interests and concerns of
law enforcement officials to heart. It would be legally possible for an

attorney general to issue a new set of guidelines stating that medical marijuana patients would be the lowest possible priority, that patient and caregiver rights were to be protected scrupulously, that the benefit of the doubt should be given to patients, that law enforcement personnel were directed to cooperate with patients to develop guidelines and practices that used the phrase "To ensure that patients and their primary caregivers who obtain and use marijuana for medical purposes upon the recommendation of a physician are not subjected to criminal prosecution or sanction" as the Prime Directive because the voters had so decreed. After all, Article V, Section 13 of the California Constitution states:

> Subject to the powers and duties of the Governor, the Attorney General shall be the chief law officer of the State. It shall be the duty of the Attorney General to see that the laws of the State are uniformly and adequately enforced. The Attorney General shall have direct supervision over every district attorney and sheriff and over such law enforcement officers as may be designated by law, in all matters pertaining to the duties of their respective offices, and may require any of said officers to make reports concerning the investigation, detection, prosecution, and punishment of crime in their respective jurisdictions as to the Attorney General may seem advisable. Whenever in the opinion of the Attorney General any law of the State is not being adequately enforced in any county, it shall be the duty of the Attorney General to prosecute any violations of law of which the superior court shall have jurisdiction, and in such cases the Attorney General shall have all the powers of a district attorney.[138]

And many law enforcement officials, especially those on the streets rather than those in executive positions, would welcome a directive— almost any directive—from the attorney general on how Section 11362.5 is to be implemented, so long as it reduced ambiguities and uncertainties.

Some of the surveillance and arrests of medical marijuana patients have come about not so much because of malice or even resistance by police officers but because of the confusion and ambiguity (some real, some manufactured) that have surrounded the law from the outset. It is hardly surprising that police officers would view a "make an arrest and let the courts sort it out" attitude as erring on the side of caution and justifiably so.

Furthermore, the California Constitution, in Article III, Section 3.5, states:

> An administrative agency, including an administrative agency created by the Constitution or an initiative statute, has no power:
> (a) to declare a statute unenforceable, or refuse to enforce a statute, on the basis of it being unconstitutional unless an appellate court has made a determination that such a statute is unconstitutional;
> (b) To declare a statute unconstitutional;
> (c) To declare a statute unenforceable, or refuse to enforce a statute on the basis that federal law or federal regulations prohibit the enforcement of such statute unless an appellate court has made a determination that the enforcement of such statute is prohibited by federal law or federal regulations.

Neither the federal government nor anybody else has even brought a case contending that Section 11362.5 is invalid because of conflict with federal laws or regulations (or for any other reason), let alone having an appellate court issue a decision to that effect. Therefore, an argument could be made that every public official or law enforcement officer who has said that Proposition 215 can't be implemented properly because of potential conflict with federal law, from the governor down, stands in violation of the California Constitution. The California Constitution clearly calls for California laws to be enforced and implemented fully, even when reasonable doubt exists as to whether they conflict with federal laws, until such time as an appellate court has made a definitive determination that a conflict with federal law actually exists.

But almost everything in Bill Lockyer's approach to politics and in his personal experience—not to mention whatever further political ambitions he may harbor—militates against telling law enforcement officers that they're going to do it his way or he'll prosecute them. Like most politicians, he is likely to pay little if any political price by offending a relatively small number of legitimate medical marijuana patients by temporizing and delaying, while he could pay a substantial political price by offending law enforcement unions and professional associations, all of which are politically active and politically savvy, by being perceived as moving too quickly on the issue. Lockyer's experience, inclination, and style are not to issue orders and demand obedience. He is more likely, as he did as a legislative leader, to try to identify concerns, determine what the objections to a possible course of action might be, suggest compromises, and seek something resembling consensus from most of the interested parties—"stakeholders" as some would call them—before setting policy or taking drastic measures. One could easily argue that on balance and in general it's good for Californians that most attorneys general have been politicians who have sought consensus rather than use the potential power of their office to centralize all law enforcement policies in their hands. But the phenomenon makes the process of changing law enforcement attitudes rather sharply, as would be necessary for Section 11362.5 to work as intended, a slow, halting process subject to fits and starts.

It is hardly surprising, then, that Attorney General Bill Lockyer's task force on medical marijuana sometimes resembled a political convention more than a scientific body conducting an inquiry. Its 31 members included representatives from most of the interest groups that would eventually have to sign off if legislation based on the group's recommendations were to have a realistic chance of passing the legislature and being signed into law, including prosecutors, drug control police, advocates and practitioners of various distribution systems, doctors, addiction specialists, and attorneys who had tried marijuana and medical marijuana cases as defense lawyers. Interestingly, although several of the members used medical marijuana, nobody was appointed to represent the point of view of a patient who is simply a patient. Those who were medical marijuana users on the panel (some of whom acknowledged it and some of whom didn't) were there because they ran cannabis clubs or participated in activism or some other kind of advocacy. Dr. Tod Mikuriya, probably the country's most knowledgeable authority on medical marijuana, was not asked to be a member, although he attended all the sessions, which were open to the public. Dennis Peron, who had more to do with the final wording of Proposition 215 than any other single person, was not on the panel.

All sides soon discovered that if they let it be known a particular issue was so important to them that they might have to think seriously about publicly opposing the final report if the wording were not changed, they could get at least a little motion in their direction. The political calculation, at least in Lockyer's office and on the part of most old political hands, was that law enforcement was the interest group that was most essential to final approval; a bill might pass the legislature if some cannabis club operators opposed it as too restrictive, but if the California Peace Officers Association, then the California Police Chiefs Association, the California State Sheriff's Association, or even the California Narcotics Officers' Association publicly opposed it the chance of passage was rather low. Law enforcement soon recognized this, and although no group got everything it wanted from the task force report, the dynamic was to compromise in the direction of law enforcement concerns. A task force cochairman wrote an initial draft, for example, that formally called upon the federal government to reclassify marijuana, but that provision didn't make it into the final report.

The federal government, of course, loomed like a specter over the entire process, and especially since Bill Lockyer's close encounter with Barry McCaffrey and Janet Reno the result was to reduce some of the urgency of the deliberations. Special Assistant Attorney General David De Alba, who sat on the panel and was the attorney general's "point man" on the medical marijuana issue, told Alan Gathright of the *San Jose Mercury News* for an April 28 article (while the panel was still deliberating): "The attorney general has now realized that the best we can do is work toward having a system for distribution of medical marijuana in place if, and when, the federal government loosens its grip. The attorney general is not going to challenge federal authorities."[139]

The final report included a statewide registration system for patients and users. Participation in the registration system would be voluntary (an issue law enforcement representatives, who wanted it to be mandatory, didn't win) but would offer advantages. Each person who registered would receive a state identification card, not from the attorney general's office but from the state Department of Health and Safety (DHS), that would preclude him or her from being arrested unless extraordinary circumstances dictated otherwise. Jurisdiction over the entire program would be placed under the DHS rather than any law enforcement agency, and the DHS was directed to create more specific guidelines as to quantities or numbers of plants a patient could have at any one time. Specific information about diseases or conditions was to remain confidential; the police would have access only to a database with enough information for them to confirm whether a given patient identification was valid. Those who didn't register could still show a police officer a doctor's recommendation and have the protections of Section 11362.5 available in the case of prosecution and would not be subject to the quantity guidelines the DHS developed. But it would probably be more difficult and expensive for them to assert their rights and privileges under Section 11362.5 than for those who registered.

The task force report was converted into legislative language and inserted into S.B. 848, a "slot bill" Senator Vasconcellos had introduced before the March deadline for new nonemergency legislation with the understanding that it would eventually contain the Lockyer task force report. Senator Vasconcellos had also introduced S.B. 847, almost a duplicate of his S.B. 535 bill to fund a three-year study of medical marijuana by the University of California that had failed to pass the previous session. It passed in the Senate on June 2 with a bipartisan 27–7 vote and eventually passed in the assembly.

Lockyer and other advocates believed, according to an article in the July 13 *San Francisco Examiner* a couple of days after S.B. 848 passed in the Assembly Health Committee, "that the feds will steer clear if the state can get its marijuana-dispensing act together."[140] The next day Tom Umberg, the former Democratic California assemblyman who had become top aide to General McCaffrey, dashed that notion. He said that if California developed a registration system for medical marijuana patients, that would still not trump federal law, under which any use of marijuana is illegal. "This is not a commentary or critique on the bill," said Umberg. "The bill is mostly a work in progress and we're simply stating what federal policy is."[141] Umberg also claimed that the Vasconcellos bill ignored the recent IOM report (an interesting "pot-kettle" claim) that said marijuana smoke is carcinogenic. (Actually it said the smoke contains carcinogens, as do hundreds of other substances including broccoli, but acknowledged that no human case of marijuana-caused lung cancer had yet been found.)[142] Umberg neglected to mention, as usual, that the report acknowledged that there was no practical alternative at this time to smoked marijuana for some patients and that a pilot program to make marijuana available to individual patients should be begun immediately.

In the end a threat by Governor Gray Davis to veto the bill on the grounds that it was in contradiction to federal law torpedoed the bill. The fact that Dennis Peron and Steve Kubby opposed the bill seemed to be of little political moment in Sacramento, but Senator Vasconcellos was a legislative veteran who could count votes. He concluded he had enough votes to get S.B. 848 passed in both houses (although the rumor of a veto threat had peeled a few supporters away) but not the two-thirds majority necessary to override a gubernatorial veto. He withdrew the bill for the 1999 half of the two-year legislative session with the intention of putting it back on the agenda in 2000.

On September 13 a three-judge panel of the federal Ninth Circuit Court of Appeal ruled on an appeal from six Northern California cannabis distribution outlets and dealt a potentially severe blow to anti–medical marijuana hardliners. The outlets had challenged a ruling by federal Judge Charles Breyer ordering them to close because of the civil suit brought by the federal government. The circuit court ordered Judge Breyer to rehear the case of the Oakland Cannabis Buyers Cooperative with the doctrine of "medical necessity" in mind. That is a variation on the common-law doctrine that there may be circumstances in which necessity dictates that a law can be contravened or broken without the normal penalties ensuing, such as breaking trespass laws to rescue a drowning child. Specifically, the Ninth Circuit panel said: "In short, OCBC [Oakland Cannabis Buyers Cooperative] presented evidence that there is a class of people with serious medical conditions for whom the use of cannabis is necessary in order to treat or alleviate those conditions or their symptoms; who will suffer serious harm if they are denied cannabis; and for whom there is no legal alternative to cannabis for the effective treatment of their medical conditions because they have tried other alternatives and have found that they are ineffective, or that they have intolerable side effects."[143] The federal government had not even tried to contravene this evidence, the court said, relying almost solely on the argument that since Congress had decided to place cannabis in Schedule I, no court had the authority to contravene or amend this decision.

The civil suit was brought under federal law, not under California's new law, and the ruling of the Ninth Circuit covered federal law. It said, in effect, that even without a state law like California's Section 11362.5, there is the possibility of a medical exemption for cannabis use under federal law. The criteria would probably be tighter than under California's new state law. The decision suggested that it might be necessary for patients to have tried all the available alternatives for their condition before being able to claim a medical necessity defense rather than simply having a recommendation from a doctor as stipulated under Section

11362.5. But if not overturned (and the Ninth Circuit is overturned by the U.S. Supreme Court more often than any other circuit) the ruling could affect medical marijuana defenses under federal law throughout the country.

The U.S. Justice Department on October 27 asked the Ninth Circuit to convene an 11-judge panel to reconsider the decision of the 3-judge panel, arguing that "a court may not, under the rubric of 'medical necessity' set aside that judgment [by Congress, a questionable statement as we shall see in chapter 11], re-balance the factors already weighed by Congress, and conclude that the public interest exempts a class of persons from federal law."[144] In March 2000, the Ninth Circuit declined to rehear the decision. On May 10, 2000, the Ninth Circuit reaffirmed its opinion. Having refused the federal government's request for a rehearing, it formally remanded the case to U.S. District Judge Charles Breyer to consider arguments from patients associated with the Oakland cooperative that smoking marijuana to relieve medical conditions is a fundamental right that the government is powerless to prohibit under the U.S. Constitution. Judge Stephen Reinhardt noted, in a separate concurring opinion: "I would suggest . . . the district judge consider whether the constitutional claim should be resolved on summary judgment, rather than on a motion to dismiss, given the Supreme Court's emphasis on examining, in substantive due process cases, a claimed right's basis in 'our nation's history, legal traditions and practices.'" As of this writing no decision by the U.S. Justice Department as to whether to appeal that decision to the U.S. Supreme Court had been announced.

As decisions and events might have seemed to be moving in the direction of greater access for patients in higher courts, events at the local level continued to be consistently inconsistent. On March 18, Anna Boyce, the registered nurse who had helped to write Proposition 215 and was a key campaign spokeswoman, met with Orange County Assistant Sheriff George Jaramillo to discuss implementation of 215 and the sheriffs department's understanding that under the law somebody who tried to operate in Orange County as Marvin Chavez had would still be subject to possible prosecution. Boyce later told a reporter, "When we wrote this it never occurred to us that there would be distribution problems. We always assumed there would be centers where people could go for cannabis, because a few already existed."[145] It was a reminder that for the authors of the proposition and for many California voters, however subsequent court rulings might decide on specific language, Proposition 215 was a referendum on the buyers clubs' right to operate openly.

In San Diego in March, Steve McWilliams and Dion Markgraaff agreed to a plea bargain, pleading guilty to maintaining a place for distributing a controlled substance in exchange for dropping seven other felony charges. They received probation and community service after promising not to distribute marijuana. In Calaveras County Robert Galambos was found guilty on cultivation charges, but the jury deadlocked on possession for sale charges. Galambos had claimed he was growing for cannabis clubs in San Franciso and that his activities fit the definition of caretaker. In San Francisco in April two associates of Dennis Peron who had been running a cannabis delivery service called Compassion on Wheels, Jayne Weirick and Wayne Justman, met with an official in the city health department to discuss a possible city-sponsored clinical trial to test the efficacy of marijuana in conjunction with the drug disulfiram in the treatment of alcoholism. On April 10, 1999, Mary Rathbun—"Brownie Mary"—died in San Francisco at age 77.[146]

In Sacramento in April charges against Robert DeArkland, a 71-year-old retired building inspector and cancer patient with a doctor's recommendation, who had been arrested for having 13 marijuana plants, were dropped by the district attorney. DeArkland later filed a $10 million false arrest claim against Sacramento County. In Placer County in the case of Michael and Georgia Baldwin, a dentist and his wife, the judge suspended the trial for a week to allow attorneys for both sides to write new briefs and for the judge to decide whether the Baldwins should even need to mount a defense after the prosecution's performance. He later dismissed the cultivation charges but ruled the Baldwins must stand trial on sales charges. In Ventura, Andrea Nagy, who had run a cannabis buyers club and a growing garden, was raided by 20 police in full riot gear at 1:00 A.M. The police took 64 plants belonging to Nagy and her mother and told the Nagys that they would be notified by mail if charges were to be pressed. In Placer County the Kubby trial was postponed several times for technical reasons, then suspended until at least February because Michele Kubby was pregnant and her doctor recommended she not sit through a trial in that condition. The trial was postponed further after the Kubbys and their lawyers decided that the lawyers should testify during the trial, so different counsel was needed. After a closed hearing in which the judge was told some elements of the defense case, he decided to postpone again to give the new lawyers time to review the record in the case. The trial is scheduled to begin on August 15, 2000.

In May the Petaluma home of Ken Hayes, director of CHAMP (which became the largest cannabis co-op in California after Dennis Peron's club was closed), was raided and 800 plants (mostly seedlings) were confiscated. Hayes claimed he was growing for CHAMP patients. On May 21, B. E. Smith, having not been allowed to present any testimony relating to Proposition 215 or marijuana as a medication (even though actor Woody Harrelson accused the judge of "keeping the truth from the jury") was found guilty of possession and of "manufacturing" marijuana.[147]

In Orange County, with his trial date pending, Steve Kubby used the Internet over a period of a few weeks in late November to found the American Medical Marijuana Association (AMMA). AMMA's objective was to push for adoption of the Oakland guidelines statewide and to file lawsuits against top law enforcement and elected officials in cases where the AMMA sees a pattern of abuse or a policy of targeting medical marijuana users. The AMMA plans to file a complaint with California Secretary Bill Jones charging voter fraud when law enforcement officials led voters to believe that voting for Proposition 215 would amount to de facto legalization but have since acted as if the proposition never passed.

In September Richard Cowan, former executive director of NORML and now proprietor of a Web site called MarijuanaNews.com, wondered in virtual print whether Bill Lockyer was turning into "Lungren Lite" after Lockyer questioned whether the number of plants set in a proposed Mendocino County ordinance was too high. Mendocino District Attorney Norman Vroman noted that Lockyer's task force had been unable to agree on a number of plants so had no standing to complain about local decisions on the matter. "If the state wants to bring some definitive guidance, we will be happy to attempt to bring our policy into conformance," said Vroman. "Until then, we're going to continue the way we are."[148]

In March 2000 in Eureka, an arthritis patient with a doctor's recommendation was acquitted by a jury after up to 84 marijuana plants were found in his yard. Forty-eight-year-old Thomas Samuels had been arrested and had all but 10 plants seized in August 1998 because law enforcement officers thought 84 plants was simply too many for personal medical use, although Proposition 215 does not spell out a number because the authors wanted such questions to be decided between patient and doctor, not by law enforcement.

Richard Cowan's characterization of Bill Lockyer as "Lungren Lite" and Steve Kubby's contention that Lockyer has failed utterly to do his duty and in practice has been, if anything, worse than Dan Lungren might not be entirely fair. Lockyer did convene a task force on medical marijuana that did some good work and helped to educate the public and politicians about some of the issues surrounding Section 11362.5 implementation. He has said all the right things. But in practice his efforts have brought the state no closer to full statewide implementation of California's medical marijuana law than did Lungren's efforts to resist full implementation and shut down cannabis clubs. Patients might be forgiven the sentiment many have expressed to me that at least with Lungren you didn't get false promises and you knew where you stood with him.

Effective Local Efforts

Insofar as implementation has been successful, it has been because local officials and responsible patient advocates like Jeff Jones and Scott Imler have worked together, often in the absence of clear guidelines (or in the presence of outright hostility) from state and federal officials, to make some of the promises embodied in Section 11362.5 a reality. Many patients groups have worked quietly but tirelessly, shunning publicity or controversy, to get patients certified and medical marijuana provided to them without attracting attention from law enforcement. Courts in California have begun to order law enforcement agencies to return cannabis seized from patients if a Proposition 215 defense is established. And many individual patients are quietly growing their own medicine and providing for their medical needs, perhaps while glancing over their shoulders and wondering if some law enforcement agency will arrest them but with an increasing degree of confidence. John Entwhistle estimates, based on his extensive contacts with people who don't make a practice of speaking out publicly or to public officials, that as many as 250,000 patients in California are now regularly using marijuana as medicine with their doctors' cooperation and approval.[149]

Too many California doctors are still fearful of recommending medicinal marijuana or believe they don't know enough to recommend it intelligently or responsibly. No insurance plans yet offer reimbursement to patients who use marijuana medicinally, although a case could be made that it would be considerably less expensive than paying for many of the prescription medications for which they now offer routine reimbursement. Although Section 11362.5 could easily be interpreted to cover inmates in California's vast prison system who have medical conditions that could be alleviated by marijuana, most inmates find it difficult to get routine medical treatment, and it will probably be years before any prison doctor or administrator authorizes the distribution of marijuana to sick inmates. Finding it in the prisons would be no problem.

In March 2000 the city of Santa Cruz, where a cannabis distribution club had been forced to shut down for various reasons, passed an ordinance allowing people with illnesses such as AIDS to possess and grow marijuana. Shortly thereafter an old bed-and-breakfast inn in Santa Cruz was converted into the Compassion Flower Inn, which specialized in providing "a comfort zone for people with a medical need for marijuana," as Valerie Tischler, a former teacher who is a partner in the inn, put it to a *Los Angeles Times* reporter. "While it may be the nation's first, many more will follow."[150]

In Mendocino County, despite warnings from Bill Lockyer in September 1999, authorities continued to run a local identification card system under the auspices of the county health department that authorizes them to have up to two pounds of marijuana. "California voters have allowed for people with medical need to have pot," says Mendocino County District Attorney Norman Vroman. "That federal officials or state legislators think it's politically incorrect is beside the point in Mendocino County." And Mendocino County supervisors recently agreed to place on the county ballot a measure to legalize recreational use of marijuana—specifically by directing local police not to bother people with 25 or fewer "adult flowering female marijuana plants or the equivalent in dried marijuana."[151] All concerned agree that if passed, the measure would be advisory in character and not legally enforceable. But the medical marijuana movement began in California with advisory initiatives at the city and county levels.

In the May 22, 2000, issue of the *New Yorker* magazine, a 25,000-word article by renowned investigative reporter Seymour Hersh explored allegations that when he commanded an infantry division during the Persian Gulf War in 1991, General Barry McCaffrey authorized a four-hour attack, two days after top U.S. military leaders declared a cease-fire, on retreating Iraqi soldiers who should have been left alone to continue their retreat. The case is complex and not proven. (Several Army investigations shortly after the incidents exonerated McCaffrey.) But having any significant number of Americans consider the possibility that when he was in active service McCaffrey might have been a war criminal rather than a war hero cannot enhance his credibility as a drug warrior.

On July 17, 2000, U.S. District Court Judge Charles Breyer, responding to the Ninth Circuit Court's decision ordering him to reconsider the Oakland case with medical necessity in mind, issued a modification of his previous order stopping the distribution activities of Northern California cannabis clubs. Specifically, Judge Breyer ruled that under federal law the Oakland club could distribute cannabis to patients who meet four tests of medical necessity. The patients must (1) suffer from a serious medical condition, (2) face "imminent harm" if they do not have access to marijuana, (3) need marijuana for treatment of a medical condition or for treatment of symptoms associated with the condition, and (4) have no reasonable alternative to cannabis, having tried other available legal medications and having found that they are ineffective or that they produce intolerable side effects.[152] This "four-prong test," as lawyers refer to it, is obviously more stringent than what is required under California law. However, as Robert Raich, attorney for the Oakland cooperative, pointed out to me, Judge Breyer's modified injunction specifically authorizes distribution to patients with a medical necessity, whereas law and practice are unsettled where Proposition 215 and distribution are concerned. And the injunction does not require a physician's signature to establish a medical necessity. "Under the law if it's a necessity that settles it," Raich told me. "No authority figure is required."[153]

This development came on the heels of the establishment in San Francisco of a city-operated identification card system for medical marijuana users. And over the weekend of July 15, 2000, Dr. Donald Abrams of the UC San Francisco Medical School announced the results of his study of cannabis and AIDS patients at the international AIDS conference in Durban, South Africa. The government had pushed Dr. Abrams to modify his study from its original emphasis on the effect of cannabis on the appetite and ability to hold down medicines of AIDS patients to emphasize the possibility that cannabis might compromise the immune system. The research showed no damage to the immune system of AIDS patients, and although more research would be desirable to confirm the results, Dr. Abrams's study offers yet another example of a possible objection to the medical use of marijuana being discounted by rigorous scientific research.[154]

Perhaps because he is living the life of a farmer rather than that of an urban activist, John Entwhistle was unusually optimistic when I talked with him as I was completing this book, especially for somebody who has been an unrelenting critic of the way most state officials have approached medical marijuana implementation. "It's a big thing to turn around the habits and attitudes of 30 million people in a large and complex state," he said.

> We shouldn't be surprised if it is taking a while. And while I yield to few in my indignation over the way people like Steve Kubby and many others have been treated, and the utterly unnecessary suffering caused by official resistance to the will of the people, I think there are enough places now where the police are doing the right thing to say that real implementation has begun and will be successful. Ten years from now we may have forgotten that implementation problems were ever an issue. The solutions will come, as they always do, from the bottom up rather than from the top down and will occur so gradually and quietly that most people won't notice until the changes have been made. We won't have top officials to thank but the people who had the fortitude to take Proposition 215 seriously—and it was for the people, not the officials, that we wrote the initiative.[155]

CHAPTER SIX

Is Marijuana a Medicine?

The question of just what constitutes a medicine is not as easy or as cut-and-dried as it might seem at first glance. You could say that anything that makes you feel better, whether chocolate or sex or invigorating exercise or a relaxing evening (depending on one's condition or circumstances), is good for you and could be viewed as medicine. Indeed, most Americans use the term "good medicine" metaphorically and sometimes almost literally to describe some function or activity that promotes a sense of well-being.

Modern American medicine is a bit more specific than that most of the time. Developed in some measure since about the middle of the 19th century as a scientific discipline, a social and cultural mode of approaching health with a pronounced political aspect and a close relation with government, American medicine has numerous strengths and a few weaknesses. Notably more scientific and humane than the medieval European approach, which prescribed "bleeding" the patient well into the 19th century, the American approach emphasizes scientific diagnosis and specific cures for specific diseases. Licenses and state credentials for physicians, begun in the late 19th century and made mandatory in most of the country by the early 20th century, were designed to assure that each person with a doctor of medicine degree (along with other health-care workers) would meet certain criteria and have certain standardized levels of education and training. This emphasis on scientific training, strict standards, and peer review has given the United States what is probably the finest level of medical practice in the history of the world, but the system is also subject to criticism.

Some have complained that modern American doctors, especially specialists, are more like mechanics than like promoters of health: they're excellent if you receive an injury or have an identifiable disease but do little or nothing to promote overall health in a "holistic" fashion. Some have claimed that the doctor-patient relationship is, or has been, more like a master-subordinate relationship than that of a client attempting to improve one's health by seeking the help of a learned but caring counselor. Most doctors learn little about nutrition in medical school and few have advised their patients—at least until quite recently—on lifestyle issues that could affect their health. (Obviously, there are significant exceptions to these and other broad-brush criticisms.)

The fact that medicine is a state licensed profession has also caused many leaders of the medical profession to act more like the keepers of an economic cartel than promoters of a scientific and compassionate approach to human well-being. For decades the medical profession (or at least its organized officialdom) seemed to spend more of its time denouncing chiropractors and other "quacks" and tussling over the proper and legal "scope of practice" with nurses, midwives, and others than advancing medical knowledge. When acupuncture and acupressure, derived or adapted from ancient Oriental medicine, achieved a preliminary level of popularity in the United States, the impulse of many U.S.-trained physicians was to dismiss them as superstition or as examples of psychosomatic healing or a powerful placebo effect. Such attacks on alternative approaches to healing and health often have mixed motives. Most physicians genuinely believe they are acting in the best interests of patients by persuading them not to waste their time on approaches that won't work, which could be tragic or debilitating in the case of serious diseases. But they are also attacking economic competitors in the health promotion field, sometimes by asking the state to put them out of business or even in jail. Even if the physicians are right—that a given approach is useless or even harmful—the use of government power to prevent others from offering different ways of treating some diseases can be troubling. Used too often or too indiscriminately, such approaches can become a serious deterrent to innovation and scientific progress. Often enough in our history advances that later proved to be valid or beneficial have been dismissed or discouraged by the keepers of the official tablets.

The mention of Oriental medicine and acupuncture is a reminder that the European-American scientific tradition is not the only medical tradition extant in the world. Although Western influence and increased respect for and understanding of scientific methods have increased throughout the world, Chinese, Indian, Middle Eastern, shamanic, and other traditions are still alive and influential, and increasing numbers of American practitioners have come to believe that there is something to be learned from most of them. The use of certain medications in China or India, for example, may be the result of trial and error more than a rigorously applied scientific method, but it has been trial and error over thousands of years practiced on millions of people.

Asking whether a given substance has medicinal value, then, is more complex than one might at first realize. The question of proving whether or not a claim is true is also affected by one's underlying philosophical approach to matters of truth or proof, which can change over time and has done so within medicine. In the 19th century, for example, not only was it commonplace for researchers to try out new drugs on themselves, many took particular pride in it. Today hardly any medical researcher would do so, wary both of the possible hazards of potentially dangerous substances and of the peril of losing objectivity. Something has been gained in this shift, but it is possible that a bit has been lost also.

Many advances in medical practice begin with anecdotal information. Laboratory breakthroughs happen, of course, but sometimes doctors learn from patients who have tried some substance or practice that seems to show good results. When doctors come in contact with such information, the preferred course is to test it, preferably in a double-blind study in which as many variables as possible are eliminated or accounted for and neither the patients nor the administrators of the test know whether any given patient is receiving the medicine or substance being tested or an inert placebo. Good tests are not easy to design, and tests can be complicated by difficulties in isolating the true effects of a substance or not having enough subjects to make the test applicable to a broad cross section of the population.

In the case of marijuana, especially of smoked marijuana, the scientific difficulties are compounded by the fact that the substance has a recognizable psychoactive effect—making most of those who take it "high"—and a taste and aroma many Americans recognize from experience. An herbal mixture similar in taste and aroma to marijuana might not produce the psychoactive effect and make many of those who are test subjects reasonably sure they are not receiving actual marijuana, which could skew perceptions and the results of any test.

In addition, of course, with the substance being prohibited by federal law, it is difficult to procure marijuana of sufficiently reliable quality and consistency to make the results authoritative. The federal government maintains a marijuana plantation in Mississippi, which supplies marijuana at taxpayer expense to the eight patients authorized under federal law to use marijuana medicinally and for research projects. Since the early 1980s, the federal government has not allowed its marijuana to be used for tests on human subjects, except in a very few instances. Tests on animals and tests that involve applying either a marijuana extract or a purified or synthetic form of THC to cell tissue can be valuable and offer suggestions for promising research avenues, but they are seldom if ever completely applicable to human beings—especially since each person's biochemistry is unique and affected by anything from what he or she had for breakfast to one's mood that day.

Given all these difficulties, is it possible to say, in the light of modern scientific knowledge, that marijuana does or does not have medicinal value? One can judge from a preponderance of the evidence, but it is difficult to get a definitive yes or no answer that will satisfy all observers, even observers with a similar familiarity with scientific methods and the effects being tested.

In places where marijuana has been a long-term part of the culture, such as India, the matter is complicated by the fact that the substance has often been used for several purposes—as part of various rituals in religious observances, as an intoxicant, and as a medicine. It might not be all that important in the overall scheme of life or in the development of attitudes and practices conducive to health whether marijuana just makes patients feel good and forget their troubles or actually relieves specific symptoms through identifiable chemical or biological mechanisms. But it is important in determining whether marijuana has therapeutic value beyond a general "feel-good" attitude and in whether different dosages or different strains of the plant have markedly more or less beneficial effects.

Given all these difficulties, the evidence that marijuana has some therapeutic value for some people with serious or chronic physical illnesses is quite substantial.

In their invaluable 1997 book, *Marijuana Myths, Marijuana Facts*, Lynn Zimmer, Ph.D., and John P. Morgan, M.D., make a remarkable statement:

> Marijuana's therapeutic uses are well documented in the modern scientific literature. Using either smoked marijuana or oral preparations of delta-9-THC (marijuana's main active ingredient), researchers have conducted controlled studies. These studies demonstrate marijuana's usefulness in reducing nausea and vomiting, stimulating appetite, promoting weight gain, and diminishing intraocular pressure from glaucoma. There is also evidence that smoked marijuana and/or THC reduce muscle spasticity from spinal cord injuries and multiple sclerosis, and diminish tremors in multiple sclerosis patients. Other therapeutic uses for marijuana

have not been widely studied. However, patients and physicians have reported that smoked marijuana provides relief from migraine headaches, depression, seizures, insomnia and chronic pain.[156]

Lynn Zimmer is associate professor of sociology at Queens College, City University of New York. John Morgan is professor of pharmacology at the City University of New York Medical School. To prepare their book, they found and read every academic and medical research paper extant on the medical or therapeutic properties of cannabis. Their text was reviewed by a panel of seven people, including three medical doctors. Among them was Lester Grinspoon, M.D., of Harvard, who wrote (with James Bakalar) *Marijuana: The Forbidden Medicine* (published in 1993 by Yale University Press).

The brief paragraph quoted above includes footnotes with references to 35 different academic papers or books, from publications including *Annals of Internal Medicine, Journal of the American Medical Association, New England Journal of Medicine, Pharmacology Biochemistry and Behavior, Archives of Physical and Medical Rehabilitation, Journal of Clinical Pharmacology, Annals of Ophthalmology, Annals of Neurology,* and the like. They include complete particulars on the papers and studies so the interested reader can find and read these references.

The 1999 Institute of Medicine report commissioned by drug czar Barry McCaffrey after Arizona and California passed medical marijuana initiatives in 1996 looked into scientific studies of marijuana's alleged therapeutic properties with regard to pain reduction, migraine headaches, nausea and vomiting, wasting syndrome in AIDS patients and appetite stimulation in general, neurological disorders including multiple sclerosis, spinal cord injury, movement disorders including dystonia, Huntington's disease, Parkinson's disease, Tourette's syndrome, epilepsy, Alzheimer's disease, and glaucoma. The report summarized its conclusions as follows:

Advances in cannabinoid science of the past 16 years have given rise to a wealth of new opportunities for the development of medically useful cannabinoid-based drugs. The accumulated data suggest a variety of indications, particularly for pain relief, antiemesis, and appetite stimulation. For patients such as those with AIDS or who are undergoing chemotherapy, and who suffer simultaneously from severe pain, nausea, and appetite loss, cannabinoid drugs might offer broad-spectrum relief not found in any other single medication. The data are weaker for muscle spasticity but moderately promising. The least promising categories are movement disorders, epilepsy and glaucoma. Animal data are moderately supportive of a potential for cannabinoids in the treatment of movement disorders and might eventually yield stronger encouragement. The therapeutic effects of cannabinoids are most well established for THC, which is the primary psychoactive ingredient of marijuana. But it does not follow from this that smoking marijuana is good medicine.

Although marijuana smoke delivers THC and other cannabinoids to the body, it also delivers harmful substances, including most of those found in tobacco smoke. In addition, plants contain a variable mixture of biologically active compounds and cannot be expected to provide a precisely defined drug effect. For those reasons there is little future in smoked marijuana as a medically approved medication. If there is any future in cannabinoid drugs, it lies with agents of more certain, not less certain, composition. . . . The argument against the future of smoked marijuana for treating any condition is not that there is no reason to predict efficacy but that there is risk. That risk could be overcome by the development of a nonsmoked rapid-onset delivery system for cannabinoid drugs.[157]

The IOM report did acknowledge that "Patients who are currently suffering from debilitating conditions unrelieved by legally available drugs, and who might find relief with smoked marijuana, will find little comfort in a promise of a better drug 10 years from now." It therefore concluded that "Until a nonsmoked rapid-onset cannabinoid drug delivery system becomes available, we acknowledge that there is no clear alternative for people suffering from *chronic* conditions that might be relieved by smoking marijuana, such as pain or AIDS wasting."[158]

The IOM report also made reference to other recent reports on marijuana as medicine.

> Since 1996, five important reports pertaining to the medical uses of marijuana have been published, each prepared by deliberative groups of medical and scientific experts. They were written to address different facets of the medical marijuana debate, and each offers a somewhat different perspective. With the exception of the Health Council of the Netherlands, each concluded that marijuana can be moderately effective in treating a variety of symptoms. They also agree that current scientific understanding is rudimentary; indeed, the sentiment most often stated is that more research is needed. And these reports record the same problem with herbal medications as noted here: the uncertain composition of plant material makes for an uncertain, and hence often undesirable, medicine.[159]

It is interesting that the Health Council of the Netherlands, a country in which social and recreational smoking of marijuana and hashish is officially tolerated, should conclude that there is insufficient evidence to justify medical prescription of marijuana or THC in pill form. However, as the IOM report noted, the issue addressed was the relatively narrow one of whether the evidence warranted furnishing marijuana by prescription, not the broader question of whether more clinical trials were justified. "In contrast," the IOM report continued, "the American

Medical Association House of Delegates, National Institutes of Health (NIH), and the British Medical Association recommend clinical trials of smoked marijuana for a variety of symptoms. The NIH report, however, was alone in recommending clinical studies of marijuana for the treatment of glaucoma—and even then there was disagreement among the panel members."[160]

The question of whether there is a medical future for smoked marijuana may well be more controversial and open-ended than the IOM report intimated. The report acknowledged that the reason for its opinion was "not that there is no reason to predict efficacy but that there is risk."[161] But almost all medications involve a certain amount of risk, which must be balanced against the likelihood of success and the patient's general condition. A terminally ill, elderly cancer patient might well be less concerned about the risk of lung damage after 10 years of heavy use than a younger, healthier person who gets an occasional migraine headache.

In addition, as the IOM report acknowledged in its fine third chapter on consequences and risks of marijuana use, while marijuana smoke does contain many of the same harmful substances as tobacco smoke does, including known carcinogens, and there is laboratory and cellular research indicating that THC can cause cellular damage or disorders in petri dishes and in animals, so far studies of human marijuana smokers have failed to reveal evidence of debilitating bronchial disorders, although some minor bronchitis and chronic coughs have been reported. In one HMO, the IOM report noted, "the incidence of seeking help for respiratory illnesses was not higher in those who smoked marijuana for 10 years or more than in those who smoked for less than 10 years," although the incidence was higher for both groups than for nonsmokers. "There is conflicting evidence on whether regular marijuana use harms the small airways of the lungs," the IOM report noted, with one small-scale study showing such damage after one marijuana cigarette but a larger-scale, longer-term study showing no such damage among heavy users (three to four cigarettes a day for 10 years).[162]

The IOM report said:

> There is no conclusive evidence that marijuana causes cancer in humans, including cancers usually related to tobacco use. However, cellular, genetic, and human studies all suggest that marijuana smoke is an important risk factor for the development of respiratory cancer. More definitive evidence that habitual marijuana smoking leads or does not lead [note the avoidance of the term "cause"] to respiratory cancer awaits the results of well-designed case control epidemiological studies. It has been 30 years since the initiation of widespread marijuana use among young people in our society, and such studies should now be feasible.[163]

Major lung damage and bronchial disorders cannot be ruled out as possibilities from smoking marijuana. But so far only minor illnesses and irritations have been documented. Does it necessarily follow from that information that there is no medical future for smoked marijuana?

Richard Cowan, former executive director of NORML and now publisher of the Internet site MarijuanaNews.com, criticized the IOM report's devotion to what he calls the "single-molecule paradigm," the idea prevalent in modern Western medicine that the only "real medicine" is a single molecule, usually synthetically produced, whose dosage can be strictly regulated and controlled. That is the kind of drug the Food and Drug Administration is set up to evaluate. And there is little question that in many treatments the kind of control and predictability one gets with a pill that has precisely the same amount of the single active ingredient specified is desirable, although some might question whether the paradigm is more useful to the health of the patient or the convenience of the doctor. But in the case of smoked marijuana, there are other factors that require consideration.

In their *Marijuana Myths, Marijuana Facts* book, Zimmer and Morgan discuss the differences between smoked marijuana and the synthetic THC compound known as Marinol, available in the form of a pill. "This oral preparation of THC, dissolved in sesame oil, works for some patients. However, many patients find that smoked marijuana is more effective. For people suffering from nausea and vomiting, who are unable to swallow and hold down a pill, smoking marijuana is often the only reliable way to deliver THC. For nauseated patients, smoking marijuana has the additional advantage of delivering THC quickly, providing relief in a few minutes, compared to an hour or more when THC is swallowed."[164] (References to five scientific studies, from the *New England Journal of Medicine, Journal of Clinical Pharmacology, Clinical Pharmacology and Therapeutics,* and *Journal of Forensic Sciences,* are given to support these statements.)

Zimmer and Morgan go on:

> Smoking marijuana not only delivers THC to the bloodstream more quickly than swallowing Marinol, but smoking delivers most of the THC inhaled. When Marinol is swallowed, it must move from the stomach to the small intestine before being absorbed into the bloodstream. After absorption, orally consumed THC passes immediately through the liver, where a significant proportion is biotransformed into other chemicals. Due to metabolism by the liver, 90 percent or more of swallowed THC never reaches sites of activity in the body. Two hours after swallowing ten to fifteen milligrams of Marinol, 84 percent of subjects in a recent study had no measurable THC in their blood. By contrast, two to five milligrams of THC consumed through smoking reliably produces blood concentrations above the effective level within a few minutes.
>
> When THC is swallowed, the effects vary considerably, both from one person to another and in the same person from one episode of use to another. And because the onset of effect is an hour or more, patients using Marinol have

difficulty achieving just the effective dose. When THC is swallowed, the effects last longer—up to six hours, compared to one or two hours when marijuana is smoked. In other words, smoking marijuana is a more flexible route of administration than swallowing. Smoking allows patients to adjust their dose to coincide with the rise and fall of symptoms. For people suffering from AIDS or cancer chemotherapy, smoked marijuana provides rapid relief with lower overall doses of THC.

Another problem with swallowed THC is that the psychoactive side effects may be more intense than those that occur from smoking. When the liver biotransforms THC, one of the metabolites it produces is 11-hydroxy-THC, a compound of equal or greater psychoactivity. Some 11-hydroxy-THC is produced when marijuana is smoked, but its concentration seldom reaches psychoactive levels. With oral ingestion, patients experience psychoactive effects from THC *and* 11-hydroxy-THC, increasing the likelihood of adverse psychological reactions. There is also some evidence that one of marijuana's other cannabinoids—cannabidiol—modulates the psychoactive properties of marijuana. In a study of elderly patients, the large dose of oral THC needed to reduce nausea and vomiting produced severe psychoactive effects, reducing its utility as a medicine.[165]

That makes the flat statement "smoking is no way to administer a medicine" seem at least somewhat questionable. And practitioners seem to understand this, even if certain politicians do not. A 1990 survey asked oncologists to compare Marinol to smoked marijuana in terms of effectiveness. Only 28 percent of them believed they were familiar enough with both drugs to answer the question. Of these, 13 percent thought Marinol was better, 43 percent thought the two were equally effective, and 44 percent believed smoked marijuana was better.

Even so, smoking a medicine seems strange to most Americans. Zimmer and Morgan acknowledge as much:

> Smoking is a highly unusual way to administer a drug. Many drugs could be smoked, but there is no good reason to do so because oral preparations produce adequate blood concentrations. With THC this is not the case. Inhaling is a better route of administration than swallowing. Inhaling is about equal in efficiency to intravenous injection, and considerably more practical.
>
> Other than its illegality, the primary drawback of smoking marijuana is that it deposits irritants in the lungs. With prolonged high-dose use, this could cause pulmonary problems. However, with short-term use, there is little risk of lung damage. For terminally ill patients, the potential harm from smoking is of little consequence. Other THC delivery systems—for example, suppositories and aerosol sprays—have not been proven effective, but should be studied further. Given currently available options, smoking marijuana is the most efficient and effective way to deliver THC. It is also potentially the cheapest.[166]

Steve Kubby—who has been smoking marijuana medicinally for more than 20 years, believes he owes his life to it, and has discussed the matter with hundreds of other patients—believes smoking cigarettes (rather than pipes or water pipes) is the most effective and safest way to administer medical marijuana (at least for him).

> When you're using medical-grade marijuana, which is of higher quality and moister than what most people can get on the street, the marijuana itself acts as a filter, removing most of the harshness. I only smoke a cigarette halfway because I'm convinced most of the potentially harmful tars

and irritants are trapped in that [second] half and I would rather not ingest them. I know to a recreational smoker that might sound terribly wasteful, but I have a permanently life-threatening condition [adrenal cancer in remission, see chapter 5] plus high blood pressure, and this is a vital medicine for me, not a way to get high. I've tried a lot of different methods over the years and talked to doctors and other patients, and I'm convinced this is the best way for me to stay healthy.[167]

The American Cancer Society announced early in 2000 that it would finance studies into the feasibility of a THC "patch" similar to the nicotine patch many people use to help them stop smoking tobacco. This sounds as if it could be a promising avenue, but extensive tests and trials would be required before such a system would be available. The cancer society estimated that it would be several years before such a device would be available to patients in other than clinical-trial situations—if it pans out.

Meanwhile, what might be called "underground" medicine has developed a number of alternative methods of administration of which those who compiled the IOM report did not seem to be aware. It would be helpful to have open and peer-reviewed clinical trials of these and other alternatives before settling the question of the most effective way to administer THC, keeping in mind that each patient is an individual person and no one method is likely to be best for everybody.

Barry McCaffrey spoke at a seminar on drug policy at Chapman University School of Law in Orange, California on March 2, 2000, and repeated the widely accepted assertion that the future of marijuana as medicine does not lie in smoking a raw plant. Afterward I talked with Robert Schmidt, who said, "We've handled all of General McCaffrey's objections at our clinic. You've got to see what we've done."[168]

A few weeks later I visited Genesis 1:29's facility in a house and greenhouse in a working-class section of Petaluma, just north of San

Francisco Bay, and talked with Schmidt and people who helped at the clinic and to several patients. "We don't smoke here," Schmidt told me. "We vaporize. The cannabis is never burned but the patient gets the active ingredients."[169]

At Genesis 1:29 cannabis buds are placed in a bowl affixed through a glass tube that goes through a hole in the stopper to a chemical beaker with a glass tube on the side to which a flexible tube is attached. A heat gun is applied to the cannabis and the patient sucks through the tube. A smokelike vapor is ingested. "We use these in a hospital setting with excellent results," Schmidt told me excitedly. "There is almost no smoke and very little of the characteristic cannabis odor, so it doesn't bother or freak out other patients. The cannabis isn't burned, so most of the potentially harmful chemicals and compounds are not released. The 'spent' cannabis is still potent enough that it can be used for extracts and tinctures."[170]

Schmidt has also experimented with various methods (he wouldn't tell me the details, saying they're proprietary) of producing what he calls "honey oil," a thick syruplike extract that he says is a very concentrated form of THC and other compounds in cannabis buds. A few drops of this oil is put in a glass tube with a bulb at the end, usually with a hole in it, and a heat gun is applied while the patient sucks at the other end of the tube. The heat releases a vapor that can be taken into the lungs. This method of ingestion produces even less vapor and odor in the surrounding air than the vaporization method, and according to Schmidt the THC is so concentrated that most patients need only one or two "hits" to get the same amount of THC they might get from an entire cigarette.[171]

As experimental or "underground" medicinal methods are tested and either validated or falsified by researchers using standard scientific and clinical laboratory methods, it is more than possible that other methods of administration will be developed. During the 19th century cannabis was refined into various extracts and tinctures as well as pills and cigarettes. Whether the drug companies that produced them, many of which are still extant today, still have records showing how these compounds were produced or whether it would be useful to reproduce them through experiment and trial and error, I haven't met anybody who knows for sure. Other herbal medicines are readily available in tablet or capsule form that deliver standardized amounts of what are believed to be the active ingredients in products ranging from ginseng to St.-John's-wort. The methods used to make these herbal preparations might well be applicable to creating cannabis-based compounds. Researchers and clinicians have already made significant progress on other possible delivery methods. And it is still quite possible that for many patients simply smoking cannabis buds will prove to be the easiest and most effective way to ingest marijuana. A great deal more research is in order.

The issue of whether it is better to have cannabis in the form of a single molecule whose dosage can be closely controlled or by smoking or making a preparation from the whole plant or whole bud is also subject to debate. Many advocates of medical marijuana, like some advocates of "natural" or "organic" vitamins or compounds or herbal medicine in general, believe that the various compounds in the natural plant act synergistically to produce better healing results than a single-molecule THC preparation. This could be one of the reasons, in addition to the fact that smoking delivers THC to the bloodstream more rapidly than Marinol, that smoked marijuana achieves better results for some patients. I don't know of any scientific studies that would prove or disprove this thesis, although some studies have suggested that other compounds in the plant have a modulating effect on the psychoactive properties of THC. This is another area where scientific research would be desirable.

Based on the scientific research that has been done—much less than most medical marijuana advocates would prefer but still a substantial amount done with modern methods—there is little question that marijuana has therapeutic and medically beneficial effects for some patients. It is not a miracle drug or a cure-all, nor is it likely to prove to be the best available medication for all the maladies for which it might be indicated. However, as Zimmer and Morgan summarize the situation, "the question is not whether marijuana is *better* than existing medication. For many medical conditions there are numerous medications available, some which work better in some patients and some which work better in others. Having the maximum number of effective medications available allows physicians to deliver the best possible medical care to individual patients."[172]

CHAPTER SEVEN

It Didn't Start with George Soros's Checkbook

The widespread essentially recreational use of marijuana during the 1960s and 1970s led to a desire by many Americans who had been raised in an atmosphere in which the assertions of the 1930s film *Reefer Madness,* that marijuana might produce temporary sensations of pleasure but led inevitably to antisocial behavior up to and including unmotivated murder and serious harm to oneself, to know more about the qualities and dangers associated with the plant. If they couldn't stop their children from smoking the weed, at least they could find out about the effects and be prepared with either treatments or dissuasive information. Between 1966 and 1976 hundreds of research projects of varying degrees of quality, many sponsored by the government, were conducted into the effects of marijuana. Much of this material was summarized and put into perspective in a 1976 book, *Therapeutic Potential of Marijuana,* by S. Cohen and R. Stillman (Plenum Books). In 1973 Dr. Tod Mikuriya, a Berkeley psychiatrist, edited *Marijuana Medical Papers* (Medi-Comp Press), which traced the long history of cannabis use for medicinal purposes and reprinted original papers from Western scientists and physicians on marijuana, from studies published from 1839 to 1972.

Given that any summary necessarily misses subtleties and complexities, the general trend of this research suggested that marijuana might have therapeutic applications for asthma, glaucoma, nausea from chemotherapy, anorexia, and certain kinds of tumors. Evidence of relief or favorable anomalies were uncovered or developed in cases of epilepsy, Parkinson's disease, multiple sclerosis, dystrophy, and certain kinds of chronic pain. While many of the studies were incomplete or inconclusive, most medical authorities familiar with the literature agreed that further research, some involving larger numbers of patients and some with tighter controls or more direct comparisons with other medications, were warranted. In November 1975 a conference was convened by the National Institute on Drug Abuse (NIDA) that brought together most of the nation's leading researchers on medical marijuana at the beautiful state-owned Asilomar Conference Center in Pacific Grove, on the Monterey Peninsula in California. The scientists concluded that, considering the increasing quantity of hard evidence of therapeutic uses for cannabis, the federal government should fund more research. Dr. Raphael Mechoulam, who had been researching marijuana at Jerusalem/Tel Aviv University since 1964, ventured to suggest that by the middle 1980s cannabis and cannabis-based medicines might replace some 10 to 20 percent of all pharmaceutical prescription medicines, and that in time perhaps 40 percent of medicines (including patent medicines and over-the-counter preparations) would eventually contain some extract of the cannabis plant as an active ingredient.[173]

NIDA's recommendations were in line with recommendations of the National Commission on Marihuana and Drug Abuse, convened in 1970 by President Richard Nixon and headed by the former Republican governor of Pennsylvania, Raymond Shafer, which reported in 1972 that while marijuana was not entirely safe, its dangers had been exaggerated. It found no convincing evidence that marijuana use caused crime, insanity, sexual promiscuity, or an "amotivational syndrome" or that it was a stepping-stone to other drugs. Its recommendation was to retain the prohibition against cultivation and sale of marijuana but to eliminate state and federal criminal penalties for marijuana possession and use. Organizations such as the American Bar Association, the American

Medical Association, the American Public Health Association, the National Council of Churches, the National Education Association, and the New York Academy of Medicine specifically approved and endorsed (in some cases with minor reservations) the work of the Shafer commission. During the early 1970s government-convened commissions in England, Canada, Australia, and the Netherlands also concluded that the risk of marijuana use did not warrant criminal sanctions and that the potential therapeutic value of the plant warranted further research. In 1972 several years of research and compilation of materials by Edward M. Brecher and the editors of *Consumer Reports* culminated in the publication of *Licit and Illicit Drugs,* which analyzed the properties of a wide range of drugs from the standpoint of risk to the consumer. It noted that "Marijuana and hashish . . . are not addicting. Neither tolerance nor withdrawal symptoms have been reliably reported. The lethal dose is not known; no human fatalities have been documented."[174]

Many Americans were not pleased with the Shafer commission's recommendations and they were not pursued aggressively by the Nixon administration, which soon enough had serious problems arising from the 1972 re-election campaign that demanded virtually complete attention from top officials as America "wallowed in Watergate." In 1974, with help from Columbia University anesthesiologist and longtime anti-marijuana crusader Dr. Gabriel Nahas, Senator James Eastland organized Senate Judiciary Committee hearings explicitly designed to attack the work of the Shafer commission. Only witnesses who favored marijuana prohibition were invited to testify, and most of them accused the Shafer commission of ignoring demonstrated evidence of marijuana's physical, social, and moral dangers.

Witnesses testified that marijuana had a detrimental effect on motivation, personality, judgment, and intellectual capacity. The fact that THC electrolytes could be detected in the brain as long as a month after use, said some, showed that marijuana got "trapped" in the brain and made it possible that people who used marijuana only once a week were constantly intoxicated and subject to severe "flashbacks." Some said marijuana use had already led many college students into heroin addiction. Several witnesses had done experiments that seemed to show serious toxic effects or the potential for them, including brain damage, lung damage, and reduced testosterone levels. Many of these claims were based on giving very large doses of THC to laboratory animals or exposing human cells to concentrated THC in laboratory dishes, so findings like chromosomal abnormalities, damaged immune system indicators, hormone deficiencies, and the like were inferences (if it causes this much damage at high concentrations in a petri dish it simply has to cause some kind of damage at lower concentrations in human beings) rather than proven results based on tests in human beings. But most of the people who had done the tests were credentialed academics at respected institutions, so they commanded a certain amount of credibility. Many people no doubt came to believe that if this kind of damage was possible it would be downright irresponsible to conduct tests on human subjects and was a great human tragedy that millions of American young people were experimenting on themselves with no medical supervision at all.

Senator Eastland summed up the prevailing attitude among most of the witnesses toward the end of the hearings: "Our country has been caught up in a marihuana-hashish epidemic. If the epidemic is not rolled back, our society may be taken over by a 'marihuana culture'—a culture motivated by a consuming lust for self-gratification, and lacking any higher moral guidance. Such a society could not long endure."[175]

The Eastland hearings received more and more favorable publicity than the Shafer commission report. Combined with the continuing efforts of crusaders like Dr. Nahas and others, along with a request to the government in 1976 from a consortium of pharmaceutical companies that research into marijuana as medicine be turned over to these large established drug companies, the claims made at the Eastland hearings did much to shape the debate for the next decade. These factors also contributed to the fact that for the next 25 years almost all of the research approved by the federal government was designed to test or prove claims of damaging effects of marijuana rather than to test the possibilities of medical efficacy or therapeutic value. And since the federal government controlled the only legal source of research-grade marijuana, virtually no medical research was done. No respectable researcher wants to conduct an experiment or test, no matter how well designed, using marijuana bought off a street corner. Not only would quality control be difficult, the credibility of any results would be suspect—and would certainly be challenged vigorously.

Few of the dire effects of marijuana propounded during the Eastland hearings were subsequently proven or confirmed during the years of research that followed; indeed, Dr. Nahas, in December 1983, after Columbia University disassociated itself from his studies in 1975, and after the National Institutes of Health and the National Institute on Drug Abuse declined to give him any more grants for marijuana studies, renounced most of his old THC metabolite build-up and chromosome damage petri dish studies and extrapolations. Some of those studies are still cited by overenthusiastic drug warriors, however.[176]

While most government sanctioned or supported studies concentrated on trying to document specific harm done by marijuana during this period, however, social attitudes had changed to the point that President Jimmy Carter, in a speech to Congress in August 1977, could say: "Penalties against possession of a drug should not be more damaging to an individual than the use of the drug itself. Therefore, I support legislation amending federal law to eliminate all federal criminal penalties for the possession of up to one ounce of marijuana."[177] That would have left it up to the states to decide if they wanted to retain or adopt more severe penalties. But Congress was in no mood to entertain this proposal seriously, and introducing it early in his administration proved not to be a smart political tactic for Carter. His first drug czar, Peter Bourne, favored eliminating criminal penalties for marijuana but retaining a civil fine for possession or use and keeping sales illegal. During much of the Carter administration Robert DuPont, a holdover from the Nixon and Ford administrations, was in favor of legalizing possession of small amounts of marijuana for medical use. (He changed his mind after leaving office.)

By the end of Carter's term in office, however, the new drug czar, Lee Dogoloff, was actively and publicly concerned about what government studies showed was an increasing number of American teenagers smoking marijuana and recommended more stringent enforcement. Parents' groups (some funded or encouraged by federal law enforcement) were demanding more attention to the dangers of marijuana suggested by studies done by people like Gabriel Nahas. After Carter was defeated by Ronald Reagan in 1980, the Reagan administration escalated the drug war.

Even as official policy remained the same or hardened on medical use of marijuana, a few patients were using the courts to get access to marijuana legally. The effort began with Robert Randall. He had glaucoma at the age of 25, and in the early 1970s he was gradually going blind because of the intraocular pressure characteristic of glaucoma. One night he smoked a couple of marijuana cigarettes with friends and realized his vision was better—the "halos" around lights disappeared and he could see clearly. By 1975 he was smoking an ounce of marijuana a week and working successfully as a college teacher. To avoid the expense and risk of buying marijuana on the street, he started growing his own—four plants in the bathroom of his Washington, D.C., apartment.

One evening in August 1975, Randall returned from a short vacation to find his apartment ransacked and his plants gone. On the kitchen counter was a search warrant and a letter telling him to turn himself in. After doing so, he called NORML as part of his preparation for his trial. NORML referred him to scientists at NIDA, the FDA, and the DEA who were aware of research suggesting that marijuana could relieve the intraocular pressure of glaucoma for some patients, though not for all. Upset to learn that one hand of the government knew that marijuana was potentially useful for a disease that was otherwise difficult to treat while the other hand banned the plant and arrested people for possessing it, Randall decided to fight his case on the basis of medical necessity—a legal defense that had been tried only about a dozen times in the history of the United States, never successfully. It is based in the ancient common-law doctrine that sometimes it is necessary to break the law in order to prevent a greater harm being done; an example sometimes used is jumping over a fence and trespassing to save a child drowning in a pool. Randall's case was that breaking the law by smoking marijuana was necessary to prevent the greater harm and cost to society of going blind.

As journalist Dan Baum told it in his excellent 1996 book *Smoke and Mirrors,* "At the same time he was building his medical-necessity defense for his trial, Bob Randall filed a petition with the Department of Health, Education and Welfare to receive marijuana directly from the federal government's experimental pot farm at the University of Mississippi. After a one-day bench trial, the judge delayed delivering a verdict. HEW, worried that Randall would be acquitted on medical-necessity grounds without having a policy in place to deal with cases like this, told him that he could get government pot if he met certain conditions."[178]

HEW suggested he would have to be hospitalized or receive marijuana only in a hospital setting but dropped the idea when Randall reminded officials he would have to drive home from the hospital while high. HEW toyed with the idea of requiring that Randall have a huge safe for storage. As the judge continued to delay delivering a verdict, HEW offered to provide marijuana on the condition he not tell anybody. Randall's response was to talk to CBS News and the *Los Angeles Times,* which reported on the case.

As Dan Baum wrote, "HEW relented on November 12, 1976. Randall was handed a square tin containing three hundred long, straight-walled U.S. government-issue cigarettes, along with a promise that he could get more when they ran out. Twelve days later, the judge acquitted him of growing marijuana, on the grounds of medical necessity. It was the first time in U.S. history that anyone had beaten a drug charge on those grounds. Bob Randall was now the only legal marijuana smoker in the United States."[179]

HEW notified Randall in January 1978 that it was going to stop furnishing marijuana to him, and he had to file suit to keep it coming. The government's response was the establishment of a Compassionate Investigative New Drug (IND) program under the FDA to provide the legal and bureaucratic cover for what almost nobody in government really wanted to do. As other people with various illnesses learned about the program, some applied, but the criteria were very strict and from the end of the Carter administration through Ronald Reagan's two terms HEW (later changed to Health and Human Services) accepted only a handful of applications. Randall formed the Alliance for Cannabis Therapeutics in 1981 with help from a small grant from the Playboy Foundation. The organization tries to help patients qualify for the Compassionate IND, collects information on other diseases from which patients are getting relief through marijuana, and does educational work. Randall is still receiving about seven pounds of marijuana a year from the government, as are seven other patients. However, in the late 1980s, substantial numbers of AIDS patients, claiming that marijuana was the most effective way to counteract the extreme loss of appetite associated with AIDS and anti-AIDS drug therapies, known as "AIDS wasting syndrome," applied to the Compassionate IND program. In 1991, rather than deal with what could have been thousands of AIDS patients laying claim to free marijuana from taxpayers, the Public Health Service simply ended the program. Despite a flurry of criticism from newspapers and even from Bob Martinez, who was then the drug czar, the Public Health Service stuck by its decision. No new patients have been added since then.

The increase of both anecdotal stories and reasonably well-designed scientific studies in the 10 years preceding 1976 documenting possible therapeutic benefits of marijuana led a number of states to change their laws, permitting the medical use of marijuana. By 1980, 23 states had done so. These changes had little practical effect, however. Marijuana was still effectively prohibited at the federal level, and the federal government controls the ability of licensed physicians to write prescriptions legally and promised to challenge the prescription-writing privileges of any doctor who prescribed marijuana. This effectively made the state laws symbolic rather than efficacious.

In September 1981 Stewart B. McKinney, a moderate to liberal
Republican from Connecticut, introduced House Resolution (H.R.)
4198, a bill, as he put it in remarks on the House floor in November, "to
allow the controlled medical use of marijuana for the treatment of glaucoma and anticancer therapies. Since then, this measure has received the
cosponsorship of over 55 Members without regard to party or political
ideology."[180] Numerous physicians and many cancer and glaucoma
patients endorsed the measure. Among those who endorsed it was Newt
Gingrich, then recently elected to the House, who wrote in a letter to the
Journal of the American Medical Association in 1982 that "the outdated
federal prohibition" of medical marijuana was "corrupting the intent of
state laws and depriving thousands of glaucoma and cancer patients of
the medical care promised them by their state legislatures." Gingrich
went on to deplore "the hysteria over marijuana's social abuse" and
"bureaucratic interference" by the federal government, which in his
opinion prevented "a factual [and] balanced assessment of marijuana's
use as a medicant."[181]

With the "Just Say No" campaign of the Reagan administration years,
accelerated spending on drug war activities, and more intense interest in
other issues, the drug reform and medical marijuana movements became
relatively quiescent for a while. NORML continued to exist and to send
out press releases, but publicity was spare. Local groups organized a
debate on drug laws from time to time, and *Nightline* presented an occasional special or forum on whether the increased money devoted to the
drug war was bringing benefits in the form of fewer addicts or fewer
social problems. But drug law reform, while perhaps discussed rather
widely at a level that the media radar scopes miss, was not an especially
live part of the agenda; if anything, the mood among politicians was to
get tougher. The Omnibus Crime Bill of 1984 gave the federal government more power to confiscate (or "forfeit") cash, cars, boats, homes,
and other assets believed to be at least partly the proceeds of drug crimes
without a conviction or in some cases a formal charge being filed. Prison
terms for drug crimes were increased, including mandatory minimum
sentences for some relatively low-level drug crimes.

The media covered the drug war more heavily, with an emphasis on the dangers of drugs during a period when middle-class cocaine use was fashionable; one survey showed an increase in cocaine-related network news stories from 10 in 1980 to 140 in 1985, just before widespread awareness of crack cocaine occurred. The media also discovered raid footage and made "reality" programs about police activity, heavily slanted toward drug raids, an increasingly popular staple. The death of Maryland basketball star and Boston Celtics draft choice Len Bias of heart failure from cocaine poisoning in June 1986 led to the drug war being intensified even more. Tales of crack babies handicapped for life proliferated. Congress added more crimes to the list of those for which mandatory minimum sentences were provided. Drug war media coverage also focused mostly on African-American inner city areas. Although the vast majority of drug users are and always have been white, a University of Michigan research project showed that from 1985 onward the number of whites shown using cocaine dropped by 60 percent and the number of blacks shown using it increased by the same amount.[182]

Even as most of America seemed to have bought into the drug war with few if any reservations, however, an "underground" movement that would revitalize the drug reform movement was beginning to garner some attention in the mainstream. Jack Herer, a California businessman who had been active in the California Marijuana Initiative campaigns of the 1970s, had been encouraged by a few people—who told him that marijuana was hemp and that hemp was used to make rope and had been used to make clothes—to begin an intensive period of research into the nonintoxicating uses of hemp. (Anyone who has spent a few hours with Herer, who is constantly working, planning, selling, evangelizing, talking, and moving—and constantly smoking marijuana—would have a hard time believing that marijuana universally creates an "amotivational syndrome" that makes smokers sit around doing nothing.) What he discovered, over a period of years, was that hemp was an unquestionably useful fiber and long acknowledged as such ("canvas," for example, is derived from the word "cannabis") and that it had potential as an energy source, for making paper, and as a food. He also uncovered and systematized information known mostly to a few specialists about marijuana's medical uses. As I wrote in a column in 1988, "the history and useful aspects of hemp have been shoved down the American memory hole almost as effectively as knowledge was suppressed in the Dark Ages or erased in Orwell's *1984.*"[183]

Herer set about publicizing the information, first by compiling the information he had confirmed into a little booklet he had published called *The Emperor Wears No Clothes,* which has been updated and expanded almost every year since it first appeared in 1985. Several hundred thousand copies of the book have sold, and the sales—later supplemented by the sale of hemp clothing and hats—financed a growing movement. Herer did publicity stunts in Washington, D.C. (challenging the Smithsonian Institution to specify the "other fibers" in its displays on early American history, for example), and tours of college campuses. His persistence and charisma, along with the allure of knowledge the authorities didn't want one to know, attracted thousands of followers. Among them were Chris Conrad, who completely revised *Emperor* for the 1990 printing, formed an organization (Business Alliance for Commerce in Hemp, or BACH), and was soon writing books of his own. Lynn and Judy Osburn worked with Herer in similar ways. Before long some 500 local hemp activist groups had been formed. After a brief tussle with some older NORML members who thought Herer was exaggerating the potential industrial benefits of hemp and diverting attention from other aspects of the struggle, NORML embraced the hemp movement, which had reinvigorated the drug law reform movement, by about 1992.

Inspired in part by hemp enthusiasts, activists put a hemp/marijuana relegalization initiative on the Oregon ballot in 1986. It pulled 29 percent of the vote. A similar measure in 1990 in Alaska received a 45 percent affirmative vote. Drug Enforcement Administration Chief Administrative Law Judge Francis Young recommended that marijuana be taken off Schedule I in September 1988; his brief (a public document without a copyright) was quickly reprinted and had begun to be well known among drug reformers by 1990. In 1990 four measures to increase funding for the drug war were on the California ballot and all four failed, despite backing from prestigious law enforcement figures. In 1990, California government's Research Advisory Panel, a body of medical advisers created to advise the attorney general on controlled substance issues, recommended legalizing personal possession and cultivation of marijuana, as well as possession of hypodermic syringes, to reform aspects of the drug war that it believed were impossible to accomplish or medically unwise. Attorney General John Van de Kamp, a Democrat, repudiated the recommendations and refused to publish the panel's report. So the panel chairman, Dr. Frederick Myers of the University of California, San Francisco, medical school, published it at his own expense. The incident received considerable publicity.

For these and other reasons hemp activists believed the time was ripe to put a hemp legalization initiative on the California ballot. They began collecting signatures in 1991 for an initiative for the 1992 ballot. That initiative would have provided that "persons, 21 years or older, shall not be prosecuted, be denied any right or privilege, nor be subject to criminal or civil penalties for the cultivation, transportation, distribution, or consumption of: (a) Industrial hemp products . . . (b) Hemp medicinal preparations. (c) Hemp products for nutritional use. (d) Hemp products for personal use in private." After defining terms, it also provided that "Hemp medicinal preparations are hereby restored to the available list of medicines in California," called for regulation of recreational use along the wine industry model, and provided for "amnesty and clearing of all criminal records for all cannabis/marijuana related acts which are hereby no longer illegal." The legislature was to be authorized to enact legislation to regulate the use of hemp when driving or operating heavy equipment or in public places. It also would have provided that "No California law enforcement personnel or funds shall be used to assist enforcement of federal cannabis/marijuana prohibitions which conflict with this act," and further, that "The legislature, the Governor, and the

Attorney General are directed to challenge federal cannabis/marijuana prohibitions which conflict with this act," and would have created an advisory panel to study the feasibility "of making restitution to all persons who were imprisoned, fined or had private properties forfeited as a result of criminal or civil actions for cannabis/marijuana related acts which are hereby no longer illegal."[184] It would be difficult to imagine a more all-encompassing reversal of California's marijuana control policies.

This proposed initiative and its fate suggest some comments about California's initiative process in theory and in practice. The initiative process, begun in the teens as part of a wave of progressive-era reform under Governor Hiram Johnson and others, was intended to give the people a more direct role in creating legislation, partially as a result of the perception that the railroads and other big industries effectively controlled the legislatures of the time. In recent years it has been criticized widely both because it presents voters with too many confusing choices on complex issues where the outcome of voting one way or another is far from clear and because the process is said to have been captured by special interests that have realized that almost any proposition can be placed on the ballot with the deployment of enough money directed at the numerous professional signature-gathering firms (some of which also consult on wording, strategy, and campaign tactics). Such criticisms are worth consideration. I am not aware of any proposition that has made it to the California ballot without the use of paid professional signature gatherers since Proposition 13 (which limited property taxes) in 1978, except for those that are placed on the ballot through a vote in the legislature—usually "housekeeping" revisions and bond measures. (In 1994 Proposition 187, limiting government services including schooling to illegal immigrants—which was passed and substantially overturned in the courts—is a partial counterexample; it used very few paid signature collectors.) Thus although it is still theoretically possible, it is in practice quite difficult for a grass-roots organization with little money to place a measure on the ballot. The number that do make it to the ballot has grown in recent years, and analyzing them can be a chore. I have done it for a newspaper editorial page for 20 years, writing recommendations from a philosophical perspective rather than from a strictly pragmatic cost-benefit point of view, and I think I've gotten pretty good at it. But it is still a daunting chore to which I seldom look forward, requiring at least glancing familiarity with esoteric policy squabbles I could get along nicely not knowing about. And I still miss certain hidden, obscure, or ambiguous aspects of measures that become apparent after they are passed.

On the other hand, the initiative process does offer groups with little effective representation in the elected branches of government (for whatever reason, and they can be manifold and not necessarily sinister) an opportunity to put their concerns before the people or for the people to handle a policy priority that the legislature has neglected to address, either because of lack of political courage or because the complex dynamics of a legislative body influenced by entrenched special interests have paralyzed it. The California ballot has become more complex since interest groups have mastered the art of getting propositions on the ballot, and in some election years conflicting propositions reflecting radically different viewpoints have addressed the same or similar issues. Nonetheless, on balance, I have been favorably impressed by the ability of California voters as a whole to sort through these often confusing measures and the fog created by hysterical television ads on all sides and come to reasonable and defensible opinions—not always opinions that I agree with, but opinions that reflect at least some understanding of the stakes involved.

In politics, money is something of a proxy for popular support (though it's hardly a one-to-one ratio), so if a group cannot raise enough money to get a measure on the ballot it is probable that it doesn't have enough popular support to warrant serious consideration. And while spending a sufficient amount of money can almost guarantee that a proposition will make it to the ballot, meaning moneyed individuals and moneyed interest groups can put their measures before the voters, money doesn't guarantee that a measure will pass. The most recent example in California was a measure on the March 2000 ballot that would have reduced the majority required to pass certain kinds of school bonds from two-thirds to a simple majority. The proponents, including teachers' unions, most elected officials, and the most influential business groups, obtained the endorsements of most major newspapers and outspent opponents by a ratio of almost 23 to 1. The voters rejected the measure. Similar instances, not all of them quite so dramatic, occur almost every election year in California and in other states with initiative systems. Money can buy you ballot access but it can't buy everything in democratic politics.

The 1992 hemp initiative reflected the fact that it was written by people who had become convinced that the prohibition on hemp use was a grave and ongoing social injustice, a mistake of historic proportions requiring radical surgery to correct its ill effects. They wrote the initiative to reflect their considered opinion as to what needed to be done to set matters right—to correct as many as possible of the wrongs they perceived as having grown from the previous policy with one piece of legislation. So it was a sweeping proposal, attractive to those already convinced of the need to legalize the use of hemp but potentially off-putting to those not quite persuaded about the whole picture. Democratic politics in a politically diverse state or country is often a balancing act, reflecting the need to energize one's support base with proposals worth investing its time in while at the same time not activating too energetic an opposition base.

In addition, the initiative's proponents decided not to employ professional signature gatherers, preferring to rely almost entirely on voluntary efforts and grass-roots support. I remember talking to Jack Herer early in 1991 as he explained this decision. He reminded me that no initiative had qualified without paid signature gatherers since Proposition 13 and said that when this one did, it would be doubly big news. Whether this reflected miscalculation, hubris, or an inability or disinclination to spend the time and trouble necessary to raise large amounts of money I do not know. But it takes 536,000 signatures to qualify a measure for the California ballot, and most serious students of the process say it is prudent to collect at least half again that many to account for invalid signatures, people who sign who are not registered voters, people who sign twice, and people who are discounted for some other reason. By the end of the time allotted for signature gathering, the California Hemp Initiative had gathered between 400,000 and 500,000 signatures.

One can argue that it was not a wasted effort. It presented a thoroughgoing hemp relegalization proposal to millions of Californians; prompted discussion, debate, and thought about the issue; allowed those who advocated relegalization to present arguments and information about the historic uses of hemp to people who might never have listened if a ballot proposal were not being circulated; and gave valuable experience to thousands of activists. And it is quite likely that it did a great deal to prepare the ground for the eventual successful passage of Proposition 215.

Concern about drug policy, meanwhile, was not confined to the counterculture. On November 15 and 16, 1990, the Hoover Institution on War, Revolution, and Peace at Stanford University held a conference on drug policy that included more than two dozen of the top academic experts in the country, representing all sides of the issue. The Hoover Institution, endowed by former president and Stanford graduate Herbert Hoover, had long had a reputation as a conservative and especially an anticommunist think tank, having served as an academic refuge for dissident scholars from iron curtain countries for several decades—as well as something of a government-in-exile for Republican-oriented policy scholars when Democrats held the White House. (In fact, scholars from both major parties and a relatively wide section of the political spectrum have spent time as Hoover fellows, but the institution's reputation is decidedly conservative.) Milton Friedman, the libertarian Nobel Prize economist who was a senior fellow at the Hoover Institution, had been in favor of legalizing all drugs for many years. Former Secretary of State George Shultz, also a Hoover senior fellow, had also recently come out in favor of legalizing at least some drugs, in part because of what he saw as the adverse impact of prohibition on international relations. But for Hoover to host and publicize—it published a book and videotape based on the proceedings—a conference that took the idea of drug legalization seriously was a big step.

At the Hoover conference Dr. Lester Grinspoon, the Harvard psychiatrist who had been researching and writing about marijuana since the late 1960s, explained how he had begun in 1967 with "no doubt that it was a very harmful drug which was unfortunately being used by more and more foolish young people" but had become convinced it was "considerably less harmful than tobacco and alcohol" and three years later published a book, *Marihuana Reconsidered,* to explain why he had changed his views. "At that time," he told the Hoover conference, "I naively believed that once people understood that marijuana was much less harmful than drugs that were already legal, they would come to favor legalization. In 1971, I confidently predicted that cannabis would be legalized within the decade for people over 21. I had not yet learned that there is something very special about illicit drugs. If they don't always make the drug user behave irrationally, they certainly cause many nonusers to behave that way."[185]

He took the Hoover audience through the history and medical uses of marijuana, noting that "the medical ban produces absurd and appalling consequences. The most recent is the government assault on Kenneth and Barbara Jenks, a Florida couple in their 20s who contracted AIDS through a blood transfusion given to the husband, a hemophiliac." The Jenkses had discovered that marijuana alleviated nausea and stimulated appetite, so they grew two plants in their small trailer. After an informant's tip police burst in on them, confiscated the plants, and arrested them for cultivation. The judge rejected a medical-necessity defense. "Although he imposed essentially no punishment (they were sentenced to a year of unsupervised probation and five years of 'caring for each other')," Dr. Grinspoon explained, "they still have no way to obtain marijuana legally."[186]

In the spring of 1991 Harvard University researchers did a survey to which about a third of the country's oncologists—cancer specialists—responded. About half of them said they would recommend marijuana to their cancer patients. Almost all of those who responded that way went on to say that they had already done so, telling at least one patient that although illegal, marijuana could help alleviate the nausea associated with chemotherapy and if the patient could find a way to get it he or she would be well advised to do so.

Another development in 1991 may well have changed the direction of the drug reform movement for the next decade. On November 6, 1991, San Francisco voters approved Proposition P 136,492 to 35,732, a 79.3 percent yes vote. Proposition P, the brainchild of Dennis Peron, let the people of San Francisco "recommend that the State of California and the California Medical Association restore hemp medical preparations to the list of available medicines in California. Licensed physicians shall not be penalized for or restricted from prescribing hemp preparations for medical purposes to any patient."[187] Peron dedicated the victory to Jonathan West, his longtime partner, who had died of AIDS in 1990 but had found before his death that marijuana relieved some of the side effects of AIDS medications and restored his appetite.

San Francisco is a different kind of place, socially and politically. Not only had Proposition P been supported by California NORML and hemp activists, it was endorsed by all the city's newspapers, the Democratic Central Committee, Mayor Art Agnos, and other elected officials. No ballot argument was filed against it, although the chamber of commerce, the Republican Party, and people affiliated with the Partnership for a Drug-Free America had expressed opposition. After the initiative passed, city officials announced that they would treat marijuana like other AIDS medications and would allow patients with a prescription to grow up to six plants for their own use. The board of supervisors (San Francisco is both a city and a county in the identical geographical area) formally directed the police department to make marijuana law enforcement its lowest level of priority and to cooperate with certified patients.

It was not strictly luck or happenstance that made it possible for Dennis Peron to write a medical-marijuana initiative that almost 80 percent of San Francisco's voters would endorse. An activist for marijuana legalization and gay rights since the 1970s, he had made himself a fixture not just among gay people and drug reform activists but in City Hall and the corridors of power. Upon returning from a tour with the Army in Vietnam in the early 1970s, he plunged into San Francisco's hippie scene, campaigning in 1972 for Proposition 19, which would have legalized marijuana in California but did not pass, then opening a restaurant, The Island, that catered to the counterculture and featured a room upstairs where one could purchase and use marijuana before eating. He made friends and allies among the city's progay and generally promarijuana liberal and radical political figures, including state Senator George Moscone, who later became mayor; state Senator Milton Marks; and county Supervisor Harvey Milk, the first openly gay elected official in the country. Peron even ran for county supervisor and sponsored Proposition W, to virtually legalize marijuana, in 1979. (Proposition W received a 58 percent majority but because of state and federal law could only be advisory in nature.) Allies Milk and Moscone were assassinated by another county supervisor, Dan White, who used the notorious "Twinkies defense," in 1979.[188]

During the 1980s, Peron became an especially close associate of "Brownie Mary" Rathbun, who had become famous or notorious in the 1970s by being arrested for selling marijuana-laced brownies. At the time, the 58-year-old Rathbun was working as a waitress in an International House of Pancakes and selling the brownies to supplement her income; her husband had died and she had lost her only daughter to an auto accident in 1973. A sympathetic figure with a cheerful and indefatigable personality, she was popular with the city media. She received a 30-day suspended sentence and was required to do community service. Part of her community service involved working with AIDS patients at the dawning of awareness of the seriousness of the disease. After her community service requirement was completed, she continued volunteering at AIDS facilities and started to think of all of San Francisco's AIDS patients as "her kids." Over the years, as various people experimented, it was discovered that marijuana was useful to AIDS patients with what came to be called AIDS wasting syndrome, a loss of appetite and indifference to nutrition. Rathbun started supplying marijuana-laced brownies to her AIDS patients, whose number continued to grow. She was arrested again in 1982 while delivering brownies to a friend with cancer who was undergoing chemotherapy. The case attracted public attention and the district attorney dropped the charges. Shortly thereafter she became the first volunteer for the AIDS ward, Ward 86, at San Francisco General Hospital, and worked there two days a week—bringing brownies and doing whatever else needed to be done—for the next 13 years.

Proposition P had its origins in the arrest of Dennis Peron for marijuana possession on January 27, 1990. The police came at midnight and found four ounces, but it wasn't for sale. It was for his lover, Jonathan West, who was sick with AIDS, taking dozens of drugs, and finding marijuana useful to ease his nausea and restore his appetite. "When they found out that Jonathan had AIDS," Peron later wrote in *Brownie Mary's Marijuana Cookbook and Dennis Peron's Recipe for Social Change,* a little paperback published and sold to raise money for Proposition 215, "out came the rubber gloves and the AIDS jokes. When they found a picture of Harvey [Milk] and me hugging, they began a half hour harangue about how they hated that fag."[189] At the trial six months later, West took the stand to testify that the marijuana was his and that he was using it for AIDS. The charges against Peron were dropped. Peron had been arrested before and had spent a total of two years in jail on marijuana-related charges, but this arrest, when he wasn't selling marijuana at all but using it to alleviate West's pain, had a profound impact on him. Two weeks later West died. "It was his life and his death that inspired me and my friends," wrote Peron, "to collect thousands of signatures to get Proposition P, the medical marijuana initiative, on the November 1991 ballot."[190]

Shortly after Proposition P passed, Rathbun was arrested again, in Sonoma County, while baking brownies in a friend's kitchen. She became not just a local but something of a national media darling, appearing on *Maury Povich, Sally Jessy Raphael,* and other programs. Her defense attorney was J. Tony Serra, on whom the lawyer portrayed by James Woods in the 1989 movie *True Believer* was based. Before the case came to trial the San Francisco Board of Supervisors officially honored Mary Rathbun for her compassionate volunteer work, declaring August 25, 1992, Brownie Mary Day. At the trial the judge ruled that Rathbun had not been read her Miranda rights, so her statement that she was making brownies for AIDS patients was not admissible. The district attorney reluctantly dropped the charges. Immediately after that decision in Santa Rosa, Rathbun rushed to San Francisco, where a hearing on implementation of Proposition P was being held. Other witnesses included Kenneth Jenks from Florida, whose wife had just died; Amy Casey of Nurses for Social Responsibility; and Dixie Ramango, a multiple sclerosis patient in a wheelchair. One of the panel members, Angela Alioto, of one of San Francisco's most prominent and distinguished political families, told of how marijuana had helped her husband when he was dying of cancer four years before. Shortly thereafter the San Francisco Board of Supervisors passed Resolution 741-92, which states, in part, that "the San Francisco Police and the District Attorney shall place as its lowest priority enforcement of marijuana laws that interfere with the medicinal application of this valued herb."

The September 1992 national convention of NORML, held in San Francisco, focused almost exclusively on medical marijuana, with Robert Randall, Elie Muzeika, and other government-authorized cannabis patients as speakers, along with Dennis Peron. NORML's new executive director, Richard Cowan—who had first argued for marijuana legalization as a young conservative in William Buckley's conservative magazine, *National Review,* in 1972—embraced both the hemp and medical marijuana movements, whose relationships with NORML had sometimes been shaky in the 1980s, as essential elements of the overall drug reform movement. The convention received extensive local press coverage and some national press.

Shortly thereafter, buoyed by favorable publicity and the San Francisco supervisors' resolution, Peron founded the San Francisco Cannabis Buyers Club in a tiny apartment on Sanchez Street. At first Peron and only a few volunteers, mostly people with AIDS, worked together to buy marijuana on the black market in as large quantities as feasible and make it available to patients. They expected to be arrested and prepared to mount a full-scale medical-necessity defense. But the police didn't come and club membership kept growing. Soon they found a more suitable commercial location in early 1994, a 2,000-square-foot space above a bar at Church and Market Streets. Within a year and a half membership grew to 5,000 and the search for a larger facility began again. A five-story building at 1444 Market Street had been unoccupied for about 10 years. The Cannabis Buyers Club rented it, renovated it, and opened it in 1995.

Meanwhile, Proposition P was resonating elsewhere in the state. In August 1992 the Marin County supervisors voted in favor of changing state law so marijuana could be used legally with a doctor's prescription. In November Santa Cruz County passed an initiative similar to Proposition P with a 77 percent majority. In 1993 city councils in Morro Bay and in San Luis Obispo, in the Central Coast area, passed resolutions to restore marijuana to the list of approved medicines. Those resolutions came in response to the introduction in the legislature, by California State Senate Majority Leader Henry J. Mello of Watsonville, of Senate Joint Resolution (S.J.R.) 8, a joint resolution to be sent to President Clinton and relevant federal officials, notifying them that the California legislature wanted marijuana taken off Schedule I and restored to the list of medicines that could be legally prescribed by doctors. The California Medical Association, San Francisco Drug Abuse Advisory Board, the AIDS Prevention Action Network, the Gray Panthers, the San Francisco Board of Supervisors, numerous local Democratic clubs, a few local Republican organizations, several unions, and many of the state's newspapers endorsed S.J.R. 8. It passed in the assembly 47–20 and in the state senate 23–9 in August 1993, with a bipartisan majority. The next month Senator Mello wrote to President Clinton, HHS Secretary Donna Shalala, and others to inform them about the resolution and "to respectfully urge your personal review of the Drug Enforcement Administration (DEA) efforts to block marijuana's legitimate medical availability. The DEA's legal position, that marijuana has 'no accepted medical use in treatment in the United States' is clearly in error."[191]

The resolution had about as much impact in Washington as a stone dropped into a pond and sinking without so much as creating a ripple.

In 1994 Senator Milton Marks of San Francisco and Assemblyman Gil Ferguson of Newport Beach, a Republican usually viewed as the most right-wing member of the legislature, cosponsored S.B. 1364 to reschedule marijuana so physicians in California would be allowed to prescribe it. The bill passed in both houses of the legislature with bipartisan support in June. In September 1994, Republican Governor Pete Wilson, generally viewed as a moderate who was tough on crime, vetoed the bill.

In 1995 Democratic Assemblyman John Vasconcellos of San Jose in Silicon Valley sponsored Assembly Bill (A.B.) 1529, the Medical Necessity Defense Act, which would have provided a defense against marijuana possession, cultivation, and use charges for bona fide patients with cancer, AIDS, multiple sclerosis, and glaucoma with a recommendation from a doctor. This bill passed in both houses with bipartisan support. In October, Governor Wilson vetoed it.

In San Francisco the Cannabis Buyers Club continued to grow. In April of 1995 the Drug Enforcement Administration began enforcement activities designed to shut down the club by bringing in about 20 agents from around the country to conduct surveillance. The agency decided it would need about 50 officers for a proper raid and requested 30 officers from the San Francisco Police Department. The police, with backing from Mayor Frank Jordan (a Republican and former police chief) turned them down flat and advised them against the raid. Cannabis club members got wind of the intended raid and organized a rally and march at the federal building that drew about 500 people. The raid never occurred.

As the Associated Press reported, in one of many media stories about the club, "To join the club, you have to produce a photo identification and a doctor's letter certifying a condition that could be alleviated by pot. Members are issued a prosaic looking membership card (and if you lose it twice, you're out)." The club was decorated lavishly, with small tables and spaces suitable for socializing and talking. Dennis Peron said this was done purposely. "These people are very sick and they feel scared, and, you know, the first thing a sick person does is withdraw, and that's the last thing a sick person should do," he told a reporter from the magazine *Cannabis Canada*. "Sociability is part of the healing process."[192] To many who viewed television and other media coverage, however, the sociable atmosphere looked like a bunch of potheads using medical necessity as an excuse to have a pot party that never ended.

With every legislative effort to authorize the medical use of marijuana being vetoed by the governor, Peron and his allies decided that the only way to get medical marijuana legitimized was through the voter initiative process. So a group of activists began meeting around the kitchen tables at the buyers club, drafting and redrafting what they titled the Compassionate Use Act of 1996. Dennis Peron, John Entwhistle, Dr. Tod Mikuriya, California NORML chairman Dale Gieringer, Bill Panzer, and Scott Imler, who was later to form a medical cannabis cooperative in West Hollywood, all participated. "It was a more laborious process than many people realize," Peron told me in a recent telephone interview.

Senator Milton Marks—bless him—had authorized the legislative counsel's office to work with us on the project, and there were more than 20 drafts, each of which the legislative counsel's office went over minutely. We tried to combine what we had learned about what patients needed and how distribution could work from our own experience with the more tempered view the state lawyers brought to it. They helped us to understand the lines between state authority and the federal government's authority so we could avoid being trumped immediately by federal law. And while the wording of the initiative has been criticized, I think it's held up rather well. The feds have never challenged it in court because they know they would lose.[193]

In the end, however, there were two versions. They were very similar in most respects but, as John Entwhistle recalls, differed mainly in that the version Scott Imler and Dale Gieringer preferred did not have protection from prosecution and malpractice suits as specific as the version Entwhistle and Peron preferred. Both versions were filed the same day in the California secretary of state's office. The Peron-Entwhistle version was the one that finally made it to the ballot because the pair paid the $200 filing fee with a money order, while Imler and Gieringer paid theirs with a check.

The initiative was accepted by the secretary of state's office, then sent to the attorney general's office for an official title and summary. Dennis Peron and his allies, who had formed Californians for Compassionate Use to gather signatures and start to organize a campaign, wanted the official title to be the Compassionate Use Act. The attorney general's office insisted that it be called the Medical Use of Marijuana Initiative Statute, and that is how it appeared on the ballot. Under California law sponsors of an initiative have six months to collect the requisite number of signatures. The clock started running on December 1, 1995.

There is little doubt, as we have seen, that if the "suits from the East Coast" had not entered the process at a crucial time the Peron organization probably would not have gathered enough signatures to put Proposition 215 on the ballot. But Peron and others had done a great deal to lay the groundwork, to create a political atmosphere in which passage of such an initiative was possible. Scott Imler told me in an interview that although there were touch-and-go moments and he didn't feel absolutely confident until election night, the measure "passed largely because so much groundwork had been laid in the previous four years. There was Proposition P, and the state legislature had passed three different measures endorsing medical marijuana. By the time 215 got on the ballot most voters had heard of medical marijuana and had had time to think about it a bit. It was anything but a new idea coming at them out of the blue."[194]

CHAPTER EIGHT

Before Prohibition:
Medical Marijuana's History

To many Americans the idea of marijuana as medicine is novel—unfamiliar to the point of incredulity. But the plant has been used for therapeutic purposes in various ways, whether by inhaling the smoke or by preparing tinctures or oils, for thousands of years. Its therapeutic history is given in more detail in *Licit and Illicit Drugs,* published by Little, Brown in 1972, by Edward M. Brecher and the editors of *Consumer Reports*; in *Marijuana Medical Papers,* edited by Tod H. Mikuriya, M.D., and published in 1973 by Medi-Comp Press; and in the section on history in the 1972 report of the U.S. National Commission on Marihuana and Drug Abuse, commonly referred to as the Shafer commission, convened in 1970 by President Nixon and chaired by former Pennsylvania Governor Raymond Shafer. Most of the information in this chapter has been drawn from these three sources.

A Chinese treatise on pharmacology attributed to the Emperor Shen Nung, said to date from 2737 B.C.E. is usually cited as the first known reference to medical cannabis. Brecher says Shen Nung is a mythical figure and the date of the treatise is later than 2737 but that cannabis was certainly used therapeutically in China by the 1500–1200 B.C.E. period.[195] A reference in an Indian publication, the *Atharva Veda,* may date back as far as the second millennium B.C.E. Marijuana has been used in both

Ayurvedic (Hindu) and Tibbi (Muslim) medicine in India from ancient times to the present day. Cannabis was known in Persia several centuries before Christ. An Assyrian cuneiform dated around 650 B.C.E. but considered a copy of a much earlier document refers to using marijuana as medicine. An urn containing marijuana seeds and leaves was unearthed near Berlin, and archaeologists believe it dates from about 500 B.C.E.

Most historians believe cannabis was first used as an antiseptic and an analgesic in China and India and that knowledge of its properties became more widely spread in the Middle East around the fifth century A.D. The ancient Greeks and Old Testament Hebrews don't seem to have used cannabis for its medical or psychoactive properties, but they were surrounded by people who did. (The Ohio State Medical Committee report of 1860 contains this intriguing assertion: "Some high Biblical commentators maintain that the gall and vinegar, or myrhhed wine, offered to our Saviour immediately before his crucifixion, was in all probability a preparation of hemp, and even speak of its earlier use [Obstetric works]."[196] The Greek historian Herodotus wrote of the Scythians putting hemp on hot rocks in a closed room and breathing the vapor "that no Grecian vapor-bath can surpass."[197])

Knowledge of the plant's qualities spread gradually throughout the Middle East, Africa, and Eastern Europe. Arabic writers in the 13th and 14th centuries wrote of the social use of cannabis and unsuccessful attempts to suppress it. Hemp was widely grown for fiber used for linen and other fabrics in Europe, but there is little reference to the plant's intoxicating or medicinal qualities. The great French satirist and writer Francois Rabelais (1490–1553) did devote several chapters of his boisterous collection of picaresque tales featuring the characters Gargantua and Pantagruel to a full account of the uses of "the Herb Pantagruelion," which (accounting for the satirical exaggeration that permeates the entire work) bears great similarity to hemp.

When Napoleon's armies went to Egypt, military scientists and doctors investigated the widespread therapeutic use of cannabis in Egyptian medicine and became interested in its sedative and antiseptic qualities. (European doctors had previously used a hemp poultice to treat burns.)

The therapeutic use of cannabis was introduced into Western medicine in a more systematic way in 1839, when W. B. O'Shaughnessy, a 30-year-old physician serving in India and better known for his studies on intravenous electrolyte therapy in 1831, published a 40-page paper. He reviewed the plant's history in Hindu and Muslim medicine and told how, after animal tests, he had administered cannabis extracts to patients. He found that its analgesic and sedative properties made it useful for relieving rheumatism pain and stilling the convulsions of an infant. He also had success in quelling the muscle spasms of tetanus and rabies.[198] In France in the 1840s the writings of Drs. Aubert-Roche and Moreau de Tours drew wider attention to cannabis, and its use spread rapidly.

The Ohio State Medical Society convened a Committee on Cannabis Indica that published a report in 1860, which told of success in treating stomach pain, "childbirth psychosis," chronic cough, tetanus, bronchitis, inflammatory and neuralgic pain, epileptic seizures, and gonorrhea with hemp extracts. One doctor wrote, "I have used hemp many hundred times to relieve local pains of an inflammatory as well as neuralgic nature, and judging from these experiments, I have to assign to the Indian hemp a place among the so-called hypnotic drugs next to opium; its effects are less intense, and the secretions are not so much suppressed by it. Digestion is not disturbed; the appetite rather increased; sickness of the stomach seldom induced; congestion never."[199] Since, unlike opiates and morphine, it did not lead to dependency, it was viewed as a milder substitute for opiates and by 1889 was being reported as useful for treating opiate and chloral hydrate addiction. According to Russ Walton, M.D., who researched cannabis in the 1940s, more than 100 articles were published in the United States recommending cannabis for one disorder or another between 1840 and 1890. The *United States Pharmacopoeia* began listing Extractum Cannabis as a recognized medicine in 1850 and continued to do so until 1942. The *National Formulary* and the *Dispensatory* began listing cannabis in 1851, noting its use (from the 1851 *Dispensatory*) for "neuralgia, gout, rheumatism, tetanus, hydrophobia, epidemic cholera, convulsions, chorea, hysteria, mental depression, delirium tremens, insanity, and uterine hemorrhage."[200]

In Great Britain, Dr. J. Russell Reynolds, fellow of the Royal Society and physician in ordinary to Her Majesty's household, reported in *Lancet* in 1890 that he had been prescribing cannabis for 30 years and considered it "one of the most valuable medicines we possess."[201] Sir William Osler, professor of medicine at Johns Hopkins University and later regius professor of medicine at the University of Oxford, stated in his 1898 discussion of migraine headaches that cannabis "is probably the most satisfactory remedy" for the condition.[202] In the late 19th and early 20th centuries, Parke Davis, Squibb, Lilly, Burroughs Wellcome, and other leading firms sold cannabis preparations widely, mostly fluid extracts sold over the counter. Grimault and Sons marketed ready-made marijuana cigarettes as an asthma remedy.[203]

Medical use of cannabis declined in the early part of the 20th century, largely because of the wider availability of opiates (which are water soluble, whereas cannabis is not, and were easily injected following the introduction of the hypodermic syringe in 1856) and the development of synthetic analgesics like paraldehyde, sulfonal, the barbitals, antipyrine, and acetanilide. Although other medicines were regarded as superior or more convenient, the therapeutic value of cannabis was still recognized and doctors continued to prescribe or recommend it. In 1931 the chairman of the Investigating Committee of the American Medical Association noted that proprietary over-the-counter medications such as "Piso's Cure," "One Day Cough Cure," and "Neurosine" contained cannabis. In 1937 one authority listed 28 pharmaceuticals containing cannabis.[204]

That was the year, 1937, the Marihuana Tax Act, which effectively prohibited marijuana use, was passed. In that year the American Medical Association's committee of legislative activities reported as follows: "There is positively no evidence to indicate the abuse of cannabis as a medicinal agent or to show that its medicinal use is leading to the development of cannabis addiction. Cannabis at the present time is slightly used for medical purposes, but it would seem worthwhile to maintain its status as a medicinal agent for such purposes as it now has. There is a possibility that a re-study of the drug by modern means may show other advantages to be derived from its medicinal use."[205] Dr. William Woodward, the AMA's legislative counsel and the only physician heard at the 1937 hearings, opposed removing cannabis from the array of prescription drugs, although he was personally opposed to its use. "There are exceptions in treatment," he testified, "in which cannabis cannot apparently be successfully substituted for. The work of Pascal seems to show that Indian Hemp has remarkable properties in revealing the subconscious; hence, it can be used for psychological, psychoanalytic and psychotherapeutic research."[206] The *Journal of the American Medical Association* also vigorously opposed the tax act in a May 1, 1937, editorial.

The tax act, however, effectively eliminated cannabis from medical use as well as reducing, for several decades, recreational use. By 1941 cannabis was dropped from the *National Formulary* and *Pharmacopoeia*.

Prior to prohibition, then, marijuana had been used medicinally for thousands of years in various parts of the world, although it seems to have been used little if at all in European or American medicine until about the 1840s. Its properties were studied extensively and it was held in reasonably high esteem by physicians in the United States for much of the 19th century. Indeed, some authorities say it was the most used medicine, if one includes over-the-counter (or off the back of a gypsy wagon) patent medicine preparations. More widespread availability of opiates and synthetic analgesics decreased its popularity in the early part of the century, but in 1937 it was still used by a respectable number of doctors and patients. It is likely that some of the uses discovered, rediscovered, or inferred more recently, such as possible relief of glaucoma, use as an appetite stimulant, use to relieve nausea, and use in spasm disorders, would have been studied more extensively and systematically over the last 65 years or so if the Marihuana Tax Act had never been passed.

CHAPTER NINE

No Compromise—Why Is Opposition to Medical Marijuana So Fierce?

In his informative and entertaining 1996 history of the drug war, *Smoke and Mirrors: The War on Drugs and the Politics of Failure,* journalist Dan Baum notes that

> if anything is clear from the past twenty-five years of drug warfare, it is that marijuana—not crack, cocaine, or heroin—is politically the most important illegal drug. Precisely because it doesn't kill people who use it, spawn gun battles in city streets, enrich foreign drug lords, or inspire women to abandon their babies, marijuana separates drug policy for public welfare from drug policy for public relations. Without the marijuana ban, the country's "drug problem" would be tiny. There wouldn't be 11 million regular [defined by the government as once a month] users of illegal drugs in the United States, there would be 2 million. Of those, about 350,000 use cocaine every day. Along with half a million heroin addicts, these hard-core users are our real "drug problem": tragic, resistant to solutions, but statistically minuscule.

Heroin and cocaine are the scary drugs that keep the Drug War's home fire burning, but vastly more people are touched personally by a war on marijuana that yields few benefits. Lives aren't saved. Violent criminal organizations aren't disrupted. Instead, a lot of harmless potheads—and the generally peaceful growers who supply them—go to prison at enormous expense to the taxpayer. Diverting resources from that war to the treatment of our small but desperate population of drug dependents would be an act of medical logic and fiscal genius.[207]

In his afterword to the 1997 paperback edition, written after the passage of Propositions 215 and 200, Baum discusses the government's dilemma: "But either supplying marijuana or allowing the initiatives to stand unchallenged would slay the central myth of the War on Drugs: that marijuana is a lethal, addictive destroyer of souls with no medical value. For if marijuana is such evil, how could our government make peace with it? And if is not, then how do we justify confiscating pot smokers' houses and sending nonmedical users to prison for five years?"[208]

Whether you agree with Baum's attitude toward the overall drug war or not, his insight about marijuana is worth considering as at least a partial explanation of why federal and some state officials are so resistant to the idea that doctors should be able to recommend the use of marijuana even on terms similar to those on which they can recommend cocaine or morphine. The federal government spent more than $19.5 billion directly on the drug war in fiscal year (FY) 2000, and state and local governments spent at least that much again, probably a bit more, most of it on marijuana enforcement. If there weren't tens of millions of illicit drug users, would they be able to justify those kinds of expenditures? And if they let their guard down on marijuana just a little bit, even to the modest extent of allowing it to be used medicinally, would the laws against recreational marijuana use eventually, inexorably, be repealed as well? A lot of jobs, a lot of careers, a lot of emotional investments are at stake in the answers to those questions. The answers are far from clear; perhaps only experience will tell. But it's not difficult to understand that those whose jobs and careers hang on the answers, whose attitudes about marijuana and the proper role of government are too deeply embedded to change easily, would choose to play it safe—to assume the worst might happen if they allow even a tiny chink in the drug war defenses and so rush to plug the chink rather than welcoming the light it casts and the distinctions it clarifies.

In his compellingly readable little 1998 book, *Drug Crazy: How We Got into This Mess and How We Can Get Out,* Mike Gray, writer of *The China Syndrome* and *Angle of Attack,* makes a similar point in somewhat more colorful language:

> The coming engagement [over medical marijuana] promises to be bloody because the outcome of the whole war is at stake. Prohibition, as policy, can only ratchet in one direction. Each failure must be met with more repression. Any step backward calls into question the fundamental assumption that repression is the solution. Ultimately, every available gun will be brought to bear because marijuana is the pawl on the ratchet, the little catch that keeps the drum from unwinding. For sixty years, Harry Anslinger [the first federal antinarcotics chief, who served from 1934 to 1957] and his successors have put their backs to this wheel, laboring to hoist drug prohibition to the level of a national crusade. But if somebody jiggles that pawl and the drum slips, support for the current policy will plummet like a loose cage in a mineshaft, because it cannot sustain a serious evaluation.[209]

One could make a respectable argument for the other side, especially on the issue of medical marijuana. In light of the fact that physicians can

prescribe cocaine and morphine, the case for keeping doctors from prescribing marijuana becomes less compelling the more one investigates
it—and some 70 percent of the American people, when polled by rep-
utable pollsters, seem to agree.[210] As those who created the television ads
for Proposition 215 understood, the notion that very ill people, especially
very ill older people, should at least have the opportunity to try this
sometimes therapeutic agent, even if it turns out that it doesn't work for
them, can be appealing on a powerful emotional level. Where's the real
harm in it? People in wheelchairs and on crutches show up in court to
support medical marijuana activists accused of being mere drug dealers
and say to any media person who will listen: "Look, this stuff might not
work for everybody, but it works for me. My life would be much more
painful and difficult without it. Why are they so stubborn? Why do they
want to add the threat of arrest and jail to the pain I'm already suffering? They said we had to change the law, so we did. Why won't you
accept the verdict of the people and leave us alone?"

Few Americans can fail to be sympathetic and moved by such an
appeal.

So it's not impossible to imagine that somebody who believes the war
on drugs is a socially beneficial policy that must be continued might reason that the best way to maintain support for it is to eliminate from the
equation all these sympathetic victims, these sick and handicapped people who pull on peoples' heartstrings and cloud their rationality. If we
don't let them use marijuana under medical supervision, it is just possible that the public will start to think that if the only way to give them
relief from the nausea associated with chemotherapy is to legalize recreational use as well, maybe it's time to do that. It could be that resisting
the concept of compassionate use would prove more harmful over the
long term to the maintenance of the war on drugs than allowing a chink
in the armor. If those "stealth legalizers" are deprived of the ability to
wave wheelchairs and crutches and Grandma wracked by nausea at the
public, they won't have a prayer.

I can imagine supporters of the drug war reasoning that way, and
among the general public, obviously, some do think that way. But among

those responsible for waging the war, hardly anybody expresses such thoughts, at least not in public. Can it be that intransigence on the topic of medical marijuana can be traced strictly to bureaucratic turf protection and the desire not to have the budget cut by even a little bit? Or are other factors at work?

Lester Grinspoon and James Bakalar, colleagues in the Psychiatry Department at Harvard Medical School, discuss some cultural aspects of modern medicine in the chapter they contributed to the anthology *Dealing with Drugs,* published in 1987 by the Pacific Research Institute for Public Policy in San Francisco. They note that "different drugs are assigned to different social categories in different cultures. The spectrum includes magic, religion, medicine, recreation, disease, vice, crime, and madness. In modern industrial societies, we put great emphasis on keeping these categories separated, and that is one reason why psychoactive drugs are so difficult for us to deal with. For industrial societies, medicine or therapy is one thing, fun another, religious ritual still another—an attitude reflected in separate formal and informal institutions."[211] They note that the 19th century, when medical science was still struggling, sometimes fitfully, to emerge from being something of a medieval healing ritual and become a real science, combined with the rise of liberal individualism, "made the nineteenth century a great age of self-medication and competing medical authorities." Many of the proprietary medications, both those prescribed by doctors and those people used independently of doctors, contained opium, cocaine, alcohol, or cannabis, but little was understood about how they worked, and in many cases their real function was that they "actually reduced the pain while nature took its course, often toward a restoration of health."[212] As chemists and pharmaceutical companies in the decade surrounding the turn of the century learned to isolate ingredients or manufacture synthetic equivalents, however, such reliance on "raw" natural substances came to seem unpredictable and haphazard—almost primitive by comparison. "The promise of a materialist medicine based on the recognition of specific agents for specific diseases seemed about to be fulfilled.

Psychoactive drugs, with their nonspecific and merely palliative affects, became more suspect."[213] Such attitudes, they argue, are still predominant in most of the medical community and have come to be backed by the force of law.

So to most medical practitioners, who like to think of themselves as quintessentially scientific and rational, as these terms have been understood for the last century, the idea of marijuana as medicine, even among those few who have somehow learned (it isn't emphasized in medical school) that cannabis used to be widely prescribed, the idea of using an unrefined plant seems primitive. Add the fact that some patients want to use it medically by burning it and inhaling the smoke in an era in which sucking plant smoke into your lungs has been effectively (and perhaps, in the case of tobacco, justifiably) demonized and you have a resistance that might not be entirely rational but seems modern and progressive. Changing attitudes that are not entirely rational but include a fair amount of sometimes legitimate scientific knowledge is seldom easy.

In the first chapter of *Searching for Alternatives,* the book that grew out of the Hoover Institution's conference in 1990, UC Berkeley criminologists Gordon Hawkins and Franklin Zimring pointed out another complication. "Both the presumption in favor of liberty and the presumption in favor of continuity have deep roots in American culture. The sentimental enshrinement of personal liberty is reflected in all facets of American life from the Declaration of Independence to much popular music. The preference for preserving the status quo, and for known evils over those unknown, is reflected in such popular slogans as 'If it ain't broke don't fix it' and 'Why trade a headache for an upset stomach?'" They also note that "This clash of presumptions in relation to drug decriminalization differs from arguments about alcohol prohibition because in the case of the 'noble experiment' the prohibition involved never achieved the tenure and consequent venerability that could have led people to see it as a stable and continuous feature of an historically evolved, established tradition."[214] Few Americans are old enough to remember a time when marijuana was not illegal. Thinking seriously about upsetting that status, especially with memories of the 1960s, when marijuana use was popular and a venerable custom seemed to be overturned every other day can make many Americans powerfully uncomfortable.

A few years ago I addressed a drug reform forum at Chapman University in Orange, California, on the persistence of puritanism or modern variants in American culture as a factor not to be ignored in the drug reform debate. I did not necessarily mean by that term the tendency to worry, as H. L. Mencken famously put it, that someone, somewhere might be having a good time; I referred to a more generalized feeling that pleasure in life is or should seldom be unalloyed but should be accompanied by a price or by some pain or punishment. To many people, arguing that marijuana is not very harmful after all simply redoubles the desire to add a price in punishment to the putative pleasure and rebelliousness its use involves or symbolizes. There should be consequences for using a drug simply to make you feel artificially euphoric, and if nature has not been foresighted enough to build in as many natural negative consequences as might flow from using alcohol or tobacco, it's up to society to add some punishment. Thus the laws must be defended and perhaps strengthened.

Thomas Szasz, who teaches in the Department of Psychiatry at Syracuse University and has made a career of criticizing the profession of psychiatry from within, may have offered the most insightful comments on the phenomenon, as he has on many cultural issues. In his chapter of the 1987 Pacific Research Institute book, *Dealing with Drugs,* titled "The Morality of Drug Controls," he notes that sex as a central concern for most religions has lost much of its power and that the religious impulse in human beings has been secularized and in some cases transferred to the state as an object of veneration. As one result, in our modern world, "No longer are men, women, and children tempted, corrupted and ruined by the irresistibly sweet pleasures of sex; instead they are tempted, corrupted and ruined by the irresistibly sweet pleasures of drugs. Thus, youth's defiance of adult authority and, more generally,

man's defiance of societal conventions, is now enacted through cere-
monies of drug use, called 'drug abuse'; at the same time, the collective
celebration of the legitimacy and power of parental, societal, and scientific authority is now enacted through the counterceremonies of drug
control, called the 'war on drugs.'"[215] Szasz argues that the concept of
what constitutes a drug is at least as much political and cultural as it is
medical or scientific.

Szasz continues,

> in order to appreciate this, all we need to do is ask, for exam-
> ple, what is the difference between lithium as the third
> element in the Periodic Table of Elements and lithium as the
> now-fashionable "antipsychotic" medication? The difference
> between them is, of course, the same as between description
> and prescription, fact and value, science and politics. In
> short, while seemingly the word "drug" is a part of the
> vocabulary of science, it is even more importantly a part of
> the vocabulary of politics. This explains why there is no such
> thing—why, indeed, there can be no such thing—as a "neu-
> tral" drug. A drug is either good or bad, effective or
> ineffective, therapeutic or noxious, licit or illicit. Precisely
> herein lie the vast powers of drugs in modern societies. We
> deploy them simultaneously as technical tools in our fight
> against medical diseases and as scapegoats in our struggle for
> personal security and political stability.[216]

Throughout history, Szasz argues, groups have sacrificed scapegoats
as part of the effort to maintain social cohesion. "Perceived as the very
embodiment of evil, the scapegoat's actual characteristics of behavior are
thus impervious to rational analysis. Since the scapegoat is evil, the good
citizen's task is not to understand him (or her, or it) but to hate him and
to rid the community of him. Szasz argues that "the American 'war on
drugs' represents merely a new variation in humanity's age-old passion

to 'purge' itself of its 'impurities' by staging vast dramas of scapegoat persecutions. In the past, we have witnessed religious or 'holy' wars waged against people who professed the wrong faith; more recently we have witnessed racial or 'eugenic' wars waged against people who possessed the wrong genetic makeup. Now we are witnessing a medical or 'therapeutic' war waged against people who use the wrong drugs."[217]

That might not be a complete explanation for the take-no-prisoners—or should that be "make prisoners"?—attitude of many in charge of the drug war and others who support it enthusiastically toward what could be viewed as the minor, eminently rational, and certainly popular reform of allowing marijuana to be used for medicinal purposes. Medicalizing marijuana could be viewed not as the admission of a potentially promising therapy for some sick people but as the admission of the embodiment of evil into a holy sanctuary. There are certainly religious overtones, the rhetoric of the true believer willing to stand against Hell itself, in some of the statements and attitudes of those who oppose medical marijuana—and, to be fair, in some of the statements of those who support reform. Marijuana is not just a plant that has certain characteristics, some of which are understood well and some of which are not, but a sinister seductress of youth, a force of malignancy and oncoming chaos so powerful that any compromise with it is an admission of one's own weakness or ability to walk on the dark side—or, on the other side, the plant that can save the planet from human foolishness.

There is nothing in the Bible to justify such a determination to regard a plant as a center of sin and evil—indeed there are more passages urging believers to cherish and use all of God's creations, or that it is not what goes into a man's mouth but what comes out of it that is corrupting, than passages that would even suggest prohibition. Prohibition, if it is a religion, is a modern, secular religion; although many Christians and Jews might believe in it, it is not a Christian or Jewish belief.

The fact that scapegoats in the past—even in the rather recent past—have been changed in the cultural imagination from evil to neutral or even to positive suggests that "this too shall pass." It was only a little more than 50 years ago, remember, that intelligent people in Germany, widely viewed as the most civilized, tolerant, and socially advanced country in Europe, seriously believed that Jews were a social cancer that had to be excised for the nation to survive—and that Germans who didn't believe such nonsense were willing to put up with politicians and cultural leaders who spouted open and genuinely virulent anti-Semitism, a phenomenon that predated Adolf Hitler by decades. If anything, the pendulum has swung the other way, and in most modern Western countries the accusation of even a remotely credible hint of anti-Semitism is enough to ruin or marginalize a public figure. In the process of making this essentially healthy turnaround in attitudes, however, many Americans and Europeans have forgotten or have never been taught that it was not only knuckle-dragging Neanderthals from the backwoods (an image that itself reflects the apparently universal human impulse to demonize one's opponents) in Germany—or in France, Poland, Belgium, Italy, Russia, England, and the United States—who were anti-Semites. The most highly educated and intelligent classes accepted and bought into a "genteel anti-Semitism" that was considered (when it was considered) not as evil or bigoted but simply as part of the natural background of a modern, sophisticated culture.

It is possible that the fashion to scapegoat drugs will pass and that years from now people will look back on this interval in American history as one of those curious but inexplicable episodes of mass belief in an absurdity. If it doesn't pass—if arguments about drug policy are carried on in tones more appropriate to fervent religious believers than to impartial analysts, if drugs are viewed more as occasions of sin than as substances with costs and benefits, the argument about medical marijuana will not yield consensus, no matter how large the majorities that pass initiatives.

CHAPTER TEN

Taking the Cause National

Before we discuss initiatives, referenda, and legislative efforts in other states it might be helpful to discuss briefly some of the cultural differences within the medical marijuana reform movement and the drug reform movement more generally. These differences have sometimes created friction and impeded progress and have sometimes been used creatively to broaden the support for medical marijuana. They are important here because since 1996 two rather distinct types of political action have been used to place medical marijuana initiatives on ballots, resulting in two rather different types of initiatives.

It is easy to speak of two general types of activists with perhaps some subtypes, but it's not easy to think of satisfactory labels, which may reflect my own lack of creative imagination or may reflect the fact that the groups defy easy stereotypes. "Suits" and "tie-dyes" seem dated, as do "suits" and "hippies." One could speak of those who work primarily within the system compared to more grass-roots, bottom-up organizations or personality types, while recognizing the complication that some who seem most firmly ensconced within the system (including a few drawing paychecks as legislative aides) have more profoundly subversive attitudes toward the system than some scruffy-looking activists who still take civics-book pieties seriously. There are those who believe that if you are serious about success rather than mere posturing you need to cut your hair, shave or trim your beard, put on a suit and tie, and blend in with the culturally conservative (however radical their ideological politics) types who inhabit the political realm, and there are some who genuinely feel most comfortable wearing relatively formal clothes and being middle-class Americans who happen to have strong views on drug laws. Others believe that the larger goal has to do with loosening up the culture so that suits and ties don't matter, so the objective is to be true to yourself and if that means some short-term battles are lost, at least one has lived as an example of what might be. Some with this attitude have thought it through on a fairly deep level while others are in an essentially adolescent *epater les bourgeoisie* (scandalize the middle-class) mode.

Within the medical marijuana reform movement, these general tendencies have found expression in the campaigns run by Americans for Medical Rights, funded largely by George Soros and other wealthy people, and campaigns that grew within a state and either needed little outside assistance or even resisted outside assistance from an organization perceived as an expression of corporate culture and corporate interests. This does not necessarily mean that all those who worked with AMR were "suits" and all the others were grass-roots outsiders. Some people straddle the tendencies, wearing suits when it seems appropriate but not when it doesn't seem necessary, and every successful referendum has happened in part because of people putting aside cultural differences and working together on the goal of the moment. In some of the states in which little outside help was needed the operation was done mainly by "suits." But even as there were two types of successful campaigns, they tended to put forward somewhat different models when it came to writing the actual initiatives.

The Colorado Levellers, who would not be displeased to be called at least the "non-Soros" if not the "anti-Soros" faction, speak of the "therapeutic" and the "law enforcement" models on their Web site (www.levellers.org). They describe the therapeutic model as "modeled on the ideas embodied in the California Compassionate Use Act (CCUA—Prop. 215) passed by California voters in 1996. These initiatives were written by the local grass-roots patients and patient advocates and put the needs of the patient first." By the Levellers' reckoning the initiatives in Washington, D.C., and Washington state fit this model. The others—those of Alaska, Colorado, Oregon, and Nevada—"were written by Americans for Medical Rights to appease law enforcement concerns about the CCUA. Since this model diverges so greatly from the California model, many patients have serious concerns about these initiatives," the Levellers claim.[218]

The Levellers—who have said a flawed or imperfect initiative is better than none at all and urged people to support all of them—asked four questions about the different initiatives:

1) *Does the initiative allow patients to possess and cultivate an adequate supply of medicine?* The City Council of Oakland, California adopted a standard of six pounds of cannabis and 144 plants as necessary to maintain an adequate supply for patients. This was based on the amount of cannabis currently supplied by the federal government to eight patients in the Investigative New Drug program.

2) *Does the initiative allow for legal distribution to patients?* Legal distribution is important to protect patients from having to obtain their medicine from the black market.

3) *Does the initiative protect patients who are not registered with the state?* Many of the initiatives that follow the law enforcement model require a patient to register with the state to receive protection of the law. Many civil libertarians and AIDS patients are concerned that the confidentiality of the registry is not guaranteed and that law enforcement would use the registry to target medicinal cannabis users for harassment.

4) *Is the initiative a constitutional or statutory law?* Constitutional amendments are much harder to change than statutory laws are [and in general more difficult to qualify for the ballot].[219]

Actually, as we have seen, the Oakland guidelines contemplate 144 plants, only half of them flowering, as an outside limit for an indoor planting, not as the minimum "necessary to maintain an adequate supply." The assumption is that a great many if not most patients will require considerably less (especially since, as a study by California NORML Executive Director Dale Gieringer strongly suggests, the cannabis supplied by Northern California clubs is measurably more potent and effective than the cannabis supplied by the federal government). Still, the point is worth considering. If the criteria on which the Oakland guidelines are based are valid, while a limit of three or six plants might provide an adequate supply for many if not most patients, it will almost certainly not supply an adequate quantity for some patients—and the patients whose quantity needs are greatest are almost certainly going to be those who will have the most adverse responses if they are deprived of cannabis. It is also worth noting that while plant or possession limits are fairly straightforward in that they are numbers, in some of the initiatives for which the Levellers say the answer is "no" to the questions about distribution or protection of patients who are not registered with the state, others might justifiably respond "maybe" or "yes, but perhaps not adequate in practice."

Before discussing the initiatives that came after 1996, let's explore the Arizona experience, which was a case in itself.

––––––––––

Arizona is generally viewed as an extremely conservative state politically (although the Udall brothers, Morris and Stewart, and Bruce Babbitt, who may not have been standard-issue liberals but were hardly conservative, have found electoral success in the state). Yet Arizona's drug reform initiative, passed in 1996 and reaffirmed by the voters in 1998, was noticeably more far-reaching than the California initiative or than any of the subsequent initiatives passed in other states. Perhaps that is due in part to the fact that in Arizona, to a great extent, conservatism is expressed (as was embodied in the Arizona political figure best known nationally, Barry Goldwater) as individualistic and freedom-oriented, fiercely independent, and with more of a "leave us alone" orientation than with a desire to have government supervise any aspect of peoples' lives. Perhaps current Senator Jon Kyl does not fit this category (especially on the drug reform issue), but Sam Steiger, who was a U.S. senator from Arizona through most of the 1970s and later ran as an outright Libertarian, certainly did.

A good deal of the groundwork for Arizona's drug law reform was laid by the exploitation (with court approval) of the anomalies of a law passed in 1983 as part of a conservative state legislature's effort to get tougher on drug users and drug dealers. The heavily Republican legislature that year passed a marijuana tax law, amounting to $10 per ounce, to give courts another way to impose punishment on marijuana users and raise revenue. The legislators also added a dealer licensing provision with a $100 per year fee so that convicted dealers could be assessed on top of whatever other punishment was imposed in court. At the time a few legislators questioned whether the law might be interpreted as a form of legalization or at least legitimization of marijuana and marijuana dealing, but the objections were brushed aside. The legislature passed the law and Democratic Governor Bruce Babbitt, later to be a semiserious presidential candidate and secretary of the interior, signed it. Then the law, while used a few times to impose extra punishment, was all but forgotten until 1990.[220]

In that year Bill Green, an aerospace engineer at Allied Signal and a casual marijuana user, tested positive in a company drug test. He was forced to undergo random urine tests for the next two years and became upset at the prospect. So, believing that his use of marijuana did not affect his ability to do his job or to be an otherwise law-abiding citizen, he formed an Arizona chapter of NORML. For one of the first newsletters he produced, he began to research the state's drug laws in order to provide accurate information to NORML members. He stumbled across the licensing provision and at first couldn't believe what seemed to be the implications. "When I first read the law I thought, OK, I see this, but I didn't think you could really do it," he later told James Sterngold of the

New York Times.[221] But he obtained an application, sent in his money, and received a dealer's license and a sheet of stamps, with instructions that one be affixed to every one-ounce bag of marijuana sold.

Green was succeeded as state NORML chairman by Peter Wilson, who was concerned that with as high a profile as he had it might be dangerous to get a marijuana dealer's license, but he did so anyway. It brought no repercussions for several years, and when Wilson came to the attention of law enforcement it was almost by accident. His wife, since deceased, had ailments and conditions that made her violent at times. One night he had called the police to help subdue her, and she blurted out that he was hiding a supply of marijuana. The police searched and found a few ounces, but when he showed them his license they simply returned it to him. He was arrested four days later. His attorney, W. Michael Walz, argued that the charges that had led to the arrest amounted to double jeopardy, since the tax and license fee, which Wilson had already paid, were punitive in themselves. The local magistrate handling the case, John R. Barclay, a Republican, after reading the law, agreed and dropped the charges. This was in early 1995.

The state appealed that decision, and the case traveled back to the state superior court, which sent it along to the state court of appeals. The court of appeals sent it back to the magistrate with instructions to reconsider it. The magistrate said he was inclined to reaffirm his original decision but sent it back to the superior court. The superior court sent it back to magistrate Barclay, saying it disagreed with his double-jeopardy ruling and asking him to reopen the case. He said that as far as he was concerned the case was closed and he would only throw it out again if somebody actually forced him to reopen it. "Anyone with one neuron left of legal knowledge knows that if they want to try this case they will have to bring it to a grand jury or refile it," he told reporters.[222] He insisted that he was simply enforcing the statute as written and that if higher-ups in the system wanted a different outcome they would have to get the statute changed.

All this legal wrangling took almost 18 months and received an increasing amount of publicity both inside Arizona and to a lesser extent in other parts of the country. That gave the legislature the opportunity and a certain amount of pressure to change the law, but it declined to do so. A bill to repeal the licensing law was introduced early in the 1996 legislative session but went nowhere. State Senate President John Greene, a Republican, called the repeal attempt "a stupid bill," commenting that "it made lawmakers nervous to vote on it."[223] As far as he was concerned the current law was fine and sooner or later the courts would correct the current interpretation.

This wink-and-nod attitude toward state-licensed casual marijuana use may have reflected a more general tolerance toward marijuana use among the general populace and electorate of Arizona that elected politicians might not have wanted to acknowledge openly but had to be aware of. Wilson's lawyer, W. Michael Walz, told James Sterngold in 1996 that this climate of opinion was one of the reasons he had focused much of his legal practice on marijuana defense cases. "It was easier to be successful in this area because juries just aren't interested in convicting people on this stuff," he said.[224]

The attitude that putting people in jail might not be the most effective or humane way to deal with drug abuse problems wasn't confined to those who made up Arizona's jury pools. A group of about two dozen Phoenix leaders in a variety of fields and professions—doctors, lawyers, educators, clergy members, businesspeople, judges, and politicians—had begun meeting in 1995 and conducted polls and focus groups to test public opinion and to try to craft a reform that would meet with voter approval. The members found that almost none of the general population wanted to legalize drugs but that substantial majorities would endorse a strategy that put users into treatment programs rather than in jail or prison. They noted that by some measures, with the "do drugs, do time" program in full swing, drug use had gone up substantially in Arizona schools over the previous four years. As John Norton, who serves on the executive committee of the Goldwater Institute, a conservative think tank, put it, "The only way to conquer the drug problem is by persuading people that it is against their own self interests to use drugs. You will never get them to do that with a sledgehammer."[225]

Phoenix attorney Marvin Cohen, former Secretary of State Dick Mahoney, and John Sperling, president and CEO of the Apollo Group, a Phoenix holding company for educational institutions, including the University of Phoenix, contributed money and advice to the effort. Phoenix physician Jeffrey Singer became an enthusiastic supporter and spokesman. As an initiative measure that would, in the opinion of this group, improve the situation by reducing harm and also receive support from Arizona voters was crafted, Sperling gave the first installments of what would eventually be $480,000 to the campaign. Later, after the initiative qualified for the ballot, out-of-state donors such as George Soros ($430,000) and Ohio insurance company owner Peter Lewis ($330,000) would give substantial amounts. But it seems likely (at least in retrospect) that while the out-of-state donations certainly didn't hurt, the initiative might well have succeeded in Arizona without out-of-state help. Its backers were substantial members of Arizona's political and business establishments who were able to persuade former Republican presidential candidate Senator Barry Goldwater to be honorary chairman of the campaign, while former Democratic Senator Dennis DeConcini was an adviser, spokesman, and counselor for the campaign. And while other sectors of Arizona's leadership classes, especially those in law enforcement, would oppose this reform, enough money and influence coalesced behind what would become Proposition 200 that, combined with grassroots efforts from NORML and others, the reform would be treated as a serious rather than a frivolous or utopian proposal.

The proposal developed had several facets. First, it allowed some 116 Schedule I drugs, including marijuana, heroin, LSD, and certain analogs of PCP and ecstasy, to be recommended by a doctor to a patient with a serious or terminal illness—if the doctor provided serious scientific evidence to support the proposed treatment and had a second doctor to agree in writing that the treatment was appropriate under the circumstances. Since the prescription system is controlled at the federal level, the initiative did not seek to alter it. The initiative encouraged without mandating that state and local governments facilitate distribution systems, although it was apparent to all that at least some patients would have to get the prescriptions "filled" on the streets for at least a while. Patients who used, possessed, or received Schedule I drugs under this doctor recommendation system would be immune from state criminal penalties.

The initiative also made serious changes in the penalty system for drug use and possession in cases where no doctor's recommendation protected people from prosecution. A first or second offense for "personal possession or use of a controlled substance" would bring required treatment for substance abuse problems rather than incarceration. Second-time offenders could receive additional sanctions, such as "intensified drug treatment, community service, intensive probation, [and] home arrest," but could still not be incarcerated.[226] The proposition also made possible, through an appeals process in the probation system, the early parole or early release of prisoners currently in the state prison system who had been convicted of drug offenses that did not involve violence. Those who had previously been convicted of violent offenses would not be eligible for probation, but a person previously convicted of a felony offense that involved sales but not a violent act would still be eligible.

Opponents of the proposition, mostly law enforcement organizations, were able to raise only about $5,100 to conduct a campaign. In November 1996 Proposition 200 passed by a margin of almost two to one. Although the governor in Arizona is empowered to veto an initiative and although Republican Governor Fife Symington said he believed that "Proposition 200 is a thinly veiled attempt to legalize drugs at the expense of public safety," he continued: "I decided not to exercise the governor's veto authority because there are other avenues available through the Legislature and the courts to address the threats it poses." House Majority Leader J. Ernie Baird was disappointed. "I wish he would have vetoed it" despite the two-thirds voter majority, he told reporters. "While legislators are interested in making changes, right now they have no idea what those changes might be. But something has to be done. If we legalize drugs, it will be the end of society as we know it."[227]

Joe Arpaio, sheriff of Maricopa County, a former Drug Enforcement Administration agent who had long cultivated an image as "the toughest sheriff in America" was beside himself at the prospect of having to enforce a law with which he disagreed so profoundly. "I still believe drug peddlers should be put away as long as possible," he said. "Believe me. I'll find a way around it," he said, demonstrating his profound commitment to the sacred concept of the law as it is written rather than to the law as he would prefer it to be. "But we have to see how it all shakes out first."[228] U.S. Senator Jon Kyl continued to insist that Arizona voters had been "duped" (as they presumably had not been when they had voted for him) by expensive and misleading advertising and had not understood the true ramifications of the measure.

By the following April the legislature had gathered itself sufficiently to reprimand the deluded voters. It passed House Bill (H.B) 2518 and S.B. 1373, which nullified key provisions of Proposition 200. H.B. 2518 required that the federal government approve the medical use of marijuana before Arizona physicians would be allowed to prescribe it or any other Schedule I drug under the terms of Proposition 200. S.B. 1373 reinstituted incarceration as punishment for drug possession and other drug offenses for which Proposition 200 had prescribed penalties other than incarceration. Persons placed on probation could be incarcerated as a result of a positive drug test. In other words, the previous punitive regime was restored.

Republican state Senator John Kaites, chief sponsor of the bills, defended them as being consistent with the voters' true will. "Does it make it tougher to distribute heroin in Arizona?" he asked rhetorically. "The answer is yes. But it still allows for the medicinal use of marijuana as long as it gets FDA approval. That just makes sense." The assumption, of course, was that notoriously independent Arizona voters would be perfectly pleased to wait for their desires to become effective until an unelected agency in Washington that had previously shown no interest in studying marijuana, let alone approving it, decided to take action. In Washington, the White House Office of National Drug Policy was pleased: "The Legislature of Arizona has taken a very responsible course of action, requiring FDA approval of any drug before it is declared to be medicine, as required by law," it said in an official statement.[229]

Sam Vagenas, a key supporter of Proposition 200, was not so pleased, criticizing the Legislature as "gutting what the voters approved. This is the ultimate act of political arrogance, killing it before it has a chance to take effect," he told Reuters.[230] Before long, in cooperation with some of the original sponsors of Proposition 200, Vagenas and others organized a group called The People Have Spoken to circulate petitions to put these two bills on the ballot to let the voters decide if they wanted them to become law. Because of the way Arizona law is written, H.B. 2518 became Proposition 300, which required federal approval of marijuana before Schedule I drugs could be prescribed; a yes vote would be to approve what the legislature had done, while a no vote would be to make Proposition 200, as passed by the voters in 1996, effective. S.B. 1373 became Proposition 301, which restored prison as an option for drug offenses including possession. Former Arizona Attorneys General Grant Woods and John A. LaSota, along with Judge Rudolph J. Gerber of the Arizona Court of Appeals, joined The People Have Spoken in urging a no vote. The Arizona Pharmacy Association, the Center for Arizona Policy, the Arizona Christian Coalition, and the Arizona Association of Chiefs of Police urged a yes vote.

By voting yes, Arizona voters could admit that they had gone too far and that the legislature was wiser and more prudent than they were. By voting no, they would tell the legislature, "We really meant it; now stop obstructing the will of the people in what is supposed to be a democratic political system." In November 1998, Arizona voters rejected Proposition 300 by a 57–43 margin. Proposition 301 was defeated by the same margin. The people had told the legislature to stop obstructing.

For a number of reasons, including hemp organizing in the 1980s and early 1990s and other activities outlined in chapter 7, some kind of organized constituency for medical marijuana was in place in most U.S. states by 1996, when California and Arizona passed their initiatives. Some were organizations more in hope and rhetoric than in reality, while some had already made contact with sympathetic state legislators or legislative aides, along with organizations of physicians and civic groups. As Dave Fratello of Americans for Medical Rights explained to me later, however, the condition or strength of activist groups was one of the last factors AMR took into consideration when choosing states in which to launch medical marijuana initiatives for the 1998 election. And while AMR representatives spoke boldly about the will of the voters and how the establishment would be unable to resist the inevitable voter-driven wave of the future, in private they allowed themselves to wonder whether some of the critics were right—that California might have been a fluke that could not be repeated because they had caught the opposition off guard. They therefore approached initiatives in other states systematically and somewhat cautiously. Nobody knew in late 1996 and early 1997 that by November of 1998 American voters would be prepared to approve almost any initiative that had "medical marijuana" in the title, almost independently of what the details were.

The main factors AMR looked at were, first, whether the state even had an initiative process (only 31 do), then whether the state's voters, based on polling and other measures, would be receptive, then whether a campaign could be run for a reasonable cost. This last factor ruled out several larger states such as Michigan and Illinois, even though other factors looked favorable, and Florida, even though a state-based marijuana reform movement was already quite active in the state. Other states were ruled out where it was judged that extraneous factors or special political circumstances would make a campaign especially difficult. Thus Montana and Arkansas had favorable polling ("When a majority of self-identified born-again evangelical conservative Christians registered as Republicans favor medical marijuana before any campaigning has been done you've got to feel good about your chances," Dave Fratello told me[231]) but were dropped for other reasons.

By about the middle of 1997 Americans for Medical Rights had decided to launch medical marijuana initiatives in Alaska, Colorado, Nevada, and Oregon. An independent effort was underway in

Washington, D.C. The organization conducted polling and focus groups in order to craft propositions that would meet the stated concerns of voters and other interest groups such as law enforcement. "You bet we consulted with law enforcement," Dave Fratello told me. "Most of the Pacific Northwest is deeply conservative in the rural areas and heavily supportive of law enforcement. If we hadn't been able to at least neutralize law enforcement opposition I doubt we would have had a realistic chance."[232] In Washington state an active drug reform coalition was already in place and in a position to put a fairly broad initiative similar to Arizona's on the ballot in 1997.

The Alaska initiative, Proposition 8, offers an example of the kind of proposition Americans for Medical Rights put together. It mandates the Department of Health and Social Services (DHSS) to establish a confidential registry of medical marijuana patients. Certain state and local law enforcement agents would have access to the registry, but only to enough information to enable them to verify that a person with a registry card is actually registered. To be registered, a patient is to submit written documentation confirming that the patient has a debilitating condition and would benefit from marijuana, along with the name, address, date of birth, and social security number of the patient, and with the name, address, and telephone number of the doctor. Proposition 8 authorized the use of marijuana medicinally for the following "debilitating medical conditions": cancer, glaucoma, HIV/AIDS, cachexia, severe pain, severe nausea, seizure disorders, spasticity disorders, or conditions that are later approved by the Department of Health and Social Services. Once the DHSS receives a registry application it has 30 days to verify information, then 5 days to issue an identification card. If the card is not issued within 35 days it is deemed approved unless the patient is otherwise notified. Patients are required to update their registry information each year and to return the registry card if he or she no longer has a disease or condition for which marijuana is indicated.

Patients under the Alaska initiative are allowed to possess no more than one ounce of marijuana and to grow no more than six plants, with a maximum of three of them flowering. The initiative also says that a patient or caregiver who is not in the registry cannot be "penalized in any manner" for an offense "related to medical marijuana" if he or she has a doctor's diagnosis and recommendation and does not possess excessive amounts. Registered patients have firmer, more automatic protection. Physicians who recommend marijuana cannot be penalized. Nonmedical use of marijuana remains explicitly prohibited. Property associated with medical use of marijuana "shall not be harmed, neglected, injured, or destroyed" while in possession of the state, and property associated with medical marijuana cannot be seized by forfeiture. Registered patients are not allowed to use marijuana "in a way that endangers the health or well-being of any person," to use marijuana in public, or to sell or distribute marijuana to anybody who does not have a registry card or doctor's recommendation. Insurance companies are not required to reimburse for medical marijuana, nor does medical marijuana use have to be accommodated in places of employment, on or within 500 feet of school grounds, in a school bus, or near a community center or youth center. A patient who is a minor must have the written consent of a parent or guardian, and the DHSS is required to set up a procedure whereby new diseases or conditions may be added to the list of those for which marijuana use is permitted.[233]

This initiative is clearly more restrictive than the California version in ways that seem to have more to do with political negotiations or accommodating the interests of people whose knowledge is incomplete or who insist on controls for the sake of control than science or experience. The limitation on the amount of marijuana and the number of plants that can be possessed at any one time might well be enough for most patients, but it would clearly not be adequate for some. It is difficult to discern anything resembling an objective rationale for it.

The listing of specific diseases for which marijuana can be recommended is also a departure from the normal patient-physician-pharmacist relationship. In the federal controlled substance system, drugs are usually approved for a specific disease, and a pharmaceutical company may not advertise them to be used for another disease without getting a second approval, which is less expensive than the original application but still costly and time-consuming. But a doctor may prescribe an approved drug for any disease or condition for which he or she believes it may be helpful; indeed, sales of a few pharmaceuticals are greater for off-label uses than for the primary indication. Presumably a licensing board might pay attention to a physician who had a pattern of prescribing medications in ways for which there is no scientific evidence or in clearly inappropriate or dangerous ways, although even this is far from certain. But in general, a licensed physician is not subject to second-guessing from any government agency as to which medications are appropriate for which disease; the matter is kept between doctor and patient and within the medical community.

In some ways the establishment of a medical registration system within the state health department, despite possibly valid concerns about privacy or collection of information that might facilitate harassment, is an improvement over the California system. Despite more liberal rules on paper, in California marijuana has remained by default the concern of law enforcement agencies; Senator John Vasconcellos's implementation legislation would have created a voluntary registry in the Department of Health Services, but it did not pass and four years later law enforcement is the branch of government that has most contact with medical marijuana patients. The Alaska initiative also provides a certain protection for patients against governmental foot-dragging by treating an application as automatically approved if the card is not received in 35 days. The protection of property against being destroyed or forfeited, while implied under the California law and becoming the general practice after three years or so, could also be seen as an additional protection for patients. The protection for nonregistered patients against legal penalties would probably not be as automatic or as easy as for registered patients, but that might be considered an acceptable trade-off. For the Colorado Levellers to categorize it as no protection is not quite accurate. The initiative has no provision for distribution.

The initiative in Washington state was crafted by a group formed by Rob Killian, M.D., in the Seattle area, which clearly had ambitious plans to reform drug policy on a somewhat broader scale. The group got I-685, a measure modeled on the Arizona initiative, onto the ballot in 1997. It would have allowed physicians to recommend any Schedule I drug, including heroin, so long as they had scientific research to justify the recommendation and a second doctor's approval. It also had similar provisions to Arizona's about incarceration: first- and second-time nonviolent drug offenders would have been offered treatment rather than imprisonment, and those currently in prison on nonviolent drug charges would have been released. Washington voters were not ready for this approach and rejected I-685 by a 60–40 margin in November 1997. But exit polls showed considerable support for medical marijuana; 46 percent of those who voted against I-685 said they would support an initiative confined to medical use of marijuana. Seeing that kind of support, two state senators, Democrat Jeanne Kohl of Seattle and Republican Bob McCaslin of Spokane, cosponsored S.B. 6271 in the 1998 state legislative session. When it became obvious the bill was not likely to pass the legislature, Dr. Killian and his organization, Washington Citizens for Medical Rights, created an initiative substantially the same as S.B. 6271 and (with help from Americans for Medical Rights) qualified it for the November ballot.

The initiative began by reaffirming that nonmedical use of marijuana, along with growing, selling, or purchasing it, is still illegal. Fraudulent tampering with records to achieve medical status illegitimately was made a class C felony. Initiative 692 created an affirmative defense in court against charges of violating the state's marijuana laws. It also specified a list of disorders for which marijuana use was approved: cancer, HIV, multiple sclerosis, epilepsy, seizure disorders, spasticity disorders, intractable pain, glaucoma, or "any other medical condition duly approved by the Washington state medical quality assurance board," for which a petitioning system was set up. Patients would not be allowed to possess more than a 60-day supply of marijuana, but no quantity or plant-number limits were specified. A doctor's recommendation was required to be written, and qualifications for primary caregivers (who were required to have a written designation from a patient) were established, including being older than 18 and "responsible for the housing, health, or care" of a patient. It provided that physicians who recommend medical marijuana "shall not be penalized in any manner, or denied any right or privilege." The initiative also protected patients' property from forfeiture and also specified that people could not be criminally prosecuted just for being "in the presence or vicinity of medical marijuana." Public use or display of medical marijuana was prohibited, as was any use that endangers others by use of a motor vehicle. Health insurance companies were exempted from being required to reimburse for marijuana, and schools, places of employment, and other locations were not required to accommodate medical use if they chose not to do so.

The nonnumerical limits on supplies clearly showed a stronger concern for the interests of patients than for the convenience of law enforcement, as did the provisions on property and protection from seizure. The closer definition of "primary caregiver" seemed to be designed to avoid some of the mutual confusion that came in the wake of the California initiative. The protection for those in the vicinity of medical marijuana is a potentially important safeguard nobody else seems to have thought of. The limited disease list is more restrictive than the California initiative's.

The Washington state initiative was a case where the essential initiative was crafted and the support formed by people in the state with Americans for Medical Rights providing money and help at key junctures. The Washington, D.C., initiative provides a fairly clear example of AMR generally being kept out of the process and for the most part purposely. As early as November of 1996 ACT-UP (AIDS Coalition to Unleash Power), the militant gay group and sponsor of an initiative that had already collected 12,000 signatures, was protesting what it took to be AMR's plans to sponsor a separate initiative. "I am angered that the California-based Americans for Medical Rights would actively undermine the efforts of D.C. AIDS activists working to qualify a medical marijuana initiative in our community," said Steve Michael on November 11. "The AMR crowd has hired a K Street PR firm and is currently calling on community groups throughout the District of Columbia to convince people to support their effort. . . . This has been a long and draining campaign. I have been frustrated by the leadership of the drug policy movement time and time again. With a few exceptions they've ignored our requests for help, even the simple things, like postage, printing, signs. Volunteers. We've been left twisting in the wind."[234] The initiative being circulated at that time, Initiative 57, ultimately failed to get enough signatures to qualify for the 1997 ballot.

ACT-UP-DC came back with Initiative 59, with slightly different wording. The campaign submitted 32,000 D.C. voter signatures (16,997 required, including at least 5 percent of the voters in five of the city's eight wards) to the D.C. Board of Elections and Ethics on July 6, 1998 (original organizer and campaign director Steve Michael had died of AIDS on May 25). The board disqualified more than 4,600 signatures from one petitioner and ruled on August 5 that the number of signatures was "statistically insufficient." Initiative 59 organizers challenged the city in superior court and on September 2, 1998, the board admitted it had erred in the original signature count (including not counting Steve Michael's signature). On September 3, Superior Court Judge Ellen Segal Huvelle ruled that thousands of signatures that had previously been disqualified should be counted, which opened the way for Initiative 59 to be placed on the November ballot—and on a collision course with Georgia Republican Congressman Bob Barr.

In its final form, Initiative 59 affirmed the right of patients with "HIV/AIDS, glaucoma, muscle spasms, cancer, and other serious or chronic illnesses" to "obtain and use marijuana for medical purposes" if a licensed physician had determined that it is "medically necessary" and recommends it. The recommendation could be written or oral. Patients would be allowed to designate up to four persons, including relatives, licensed health practitioners, friends, or partners, as "primary caregivers" for the purposes of the act. Primary caregivers and patients would be protected from prosecution under the District's Controlled Substances Act. Patients and caregivers were to be allowed to grow "a sufficient quantity of marijuana" to assure a patient's medical supply without interruption. The initiative noted that use of medical marijuana could not be employed as a defense in a "crime of violence, the crime of operating a motor vehicle while impaired or intoxicated, or a crime involving danger to another person or to the public" and prohibited distribution to nonmedical users. It also authorized D.C. residents to set up nonprofit corporations, under existing city laws, to cultivate, purchase, and distribute medical marijuana to patients and caregivers.

The initiative directed the director of the Department of Health to submit to the city council within 90 days a plan for the "safe and affordable distribution of marijuana" to all patients enrolled in Medicaid or in the federal government's Ryan White Act–funded programs for AIDS treatment who need medical marijuana. It also required the mayor—by delivering a copy of the passed initiative within 30 days to the president and Congress—to convey the sense of the people of the nation's capital that the federal government must develop a legal medical marijuana distribution system with all deliberate speed. As is the case with every official action in the District of Columbia, Congress has the final say, so the initiative included a provision stating that Congress was authorized to review the act and if Congress did not act within 30 days of passage the measure would take effect and become law.

This was the first initiative to deal so directly with the questions of supply and distribution that have bedeviled patients in California since 1996. Patients were authorized to "obtain and use," a key and liberalizing difference. It declined to put a number on what a "sufficient quantity" would be, leaving that for patient and doctor to determine. And, while it bought into what is probably ultimately a self-defeating but apparently pervasive prejudice against profit-making entities in health care, it did authorize nonprofit corporations for distribution and even required the city government to make an effort to help obtain marijuana and funding through federal government programs.

Colorado's Initiative 19, presented as a constitutional rather than a statutory amendment, represented an effective collaboration between Americans for Medical Rights and local activists that encountered unexpected complications because of official opposition and foot-dragging. "Marty Chilcott, a psychiatrist who worked with cancer patients was on our target list but he contacted us first," said AMR's Dave Fratello.[235] Along with AMR and Luther Symons, Chilcott used the AMR model— almost identical to the Alaska initiative except that it allowed for possession of two ounces rather than one ounce—and began collecting signatures in the spring of 1998. Local activists had written a Compassionate Therapeutic Cannabis Act that was more like the California law, but it was never circulated.

Coloradans for Medical Rights (CMR) submitted 88,815 signatures to the secretary of state's office (54,242 were required for ballot status) on July 7, 1998. On August 6, after using a random sampling technique, Secretary of State Vikki Buckley ruled that only 47,960 signatures were valid. CMR appealed that decision after commissioning an independent review that found Buckley's sampling technique was flawed. On September 10, Denver District Court Judge Herbert Stern ruled that sampling errors had been made and that the initiative could be placed on the ballot without a line-by-line signature count. Buckley appealed that decision to the state supreme court, which ruled on October 5 that the initiative should not get automatic ballot status but that the secretary of state would have to perform a line-by-line count. On October 17 Buckley announced that there were only 51,904 valid signatures, almost 3,000 short of the required number. Since the ballots had already been printed, Initiative 19 was to be placed before the voters, but if a final determination concluded that there were not enough signatures, the vote would not be counted. That could be viewed as odd. The ostensible purpose of requiring a certain number of signatures is to determine if there is sufficient potential support to warrant placing a measure before the voters, but if a measure gets a majority, that question of potential support would seem to be moot or irrelevant; but that was the ruling.

Nevada's Question 9 was drafted as a constitutional amendment by Americans for Medical Rights with some help from local activists. It differed rather significantly from the usual AMR model in that it not only didn't have limits on the number of plants or quantity of marijuana a patient could possess, it required the state legislature to authorize "appropriate methods for supply of the plant to patients." It included the usual disease list with a provision for "other conditions approved pursuant to law for such treatment."

In Nevada a constitutional amendment requires two votes in successive elections to become effective. Nevadans for Medical Rights began collecting signatures in March 1998 and turned in 74,466 signatures (46,764 were required for ballot status, including a minimum quantity from each county) in July. The first count showed the campaign was 7 signatures short in Lyon County and 36 short in Nye County. But the secretary of state did a more thorough sampling and on August 3 determined that signature-counting errors had been made on the first pass and that the initiative would be on the November 1998 ballot.

In late 1997 and early 1998 Oregonians had the opportunity to consider at least five different ballot measures related to marijuana and other illicit drugs. The first was a referendum on H.B. 3643, a measure passed by the state legislature to re-establish criminal penalties for marijuana possession in Oregon. Oregon had been one of the first states to "decriminalize" marijuana possession back in 1973, when it made marijuana offenses a noncriminal violation punishable by a fine of $500 to $1,000. H.B. 3643 would have made marijuana possession a "class C" misdemeanor punishable by up to 30 days in jail, a $1,000 fine, and loss of one's driver's license. Citizens for Sensible Law Enforcement, organized by Jeff Sugarman and David Smigelski, collected more than 90,000 signatures to put the measure on the ballot, then reconstituted itself as No on 57 to urge that the voters reject the reimposition of criminal penalties. The Oregon Association of Chiefs of Police set up a campaign committee, Oregonians Against Dangerous Drugs, to urge a yes vote.

In the meantime, Floyd Landrath, a Portland resident who is director of the American Anti-Prohibition League, was circulating a petition that would allow the state to regulate but not to prohibit adult possession and use of controlled substances, require the repeal of criminal laws inconsistent with the measure, and provide for the release of some inmates whose prior conduct was made legal. Another petition drive was underway for an initiative that would permit the sale of marijuana to adults through state liquor stores and eliminate laws against marijuana except for driving under the influence. Paul Loney and Douglas Stanford of Portland had been promoting this concept for several years. Another proposal would have permitted people 21 years or older to manufacture, possess, and consume cannabis in private but would not have affected laws prohibiting delivery of marijuana. Yet another proposal would have made it legal for medical practitioners to prescribe or provide any herbs, seed-bearing plants, and marijuana to patients. Stephen Sedlacko of Eugene was a major force behind these latter two proposals.

The version crafted in association with Americans for Medical Rights was filed on March 3, 1998, by Portland doctor Rick Bayer. It included a registry system to allow registered patients to possess, deliver, or produce marijuana and had the usual disease list, with a provision for adding other diseases by petitioning the Oregon Department of Human Resources. It provided an affirmative defense in the case of arrest for patients who were not on the registry and set limits of (1) one ounce of marijuana at a location where marijuana is not produced, or (2) three mature plants, four immature plants, and one ounce of usable marijuana per mature plant at a location where marijuana is produced. Patients would be required to renew their registration annually and would be prohibited from driving under the influence, smoking in public, delivering marijuana to somebody without a registry card, or delivering marijuana "for consideration" to anyone, including registry cardholders. The proposal specified that a patient could have only one designated primary caregiver (to be exempt from marijuana laws) at a given time.

The campaign was probably helped by the widely publicized trial in Portland of Craig Helm, a 48-year-old multiple sclerosis patient and former truck driver. He said he had begun using marijuana when a prescription for the painkiller Baclofen failed to calm the muscle spasms in his legs and doctors wanted to surgically implant a pump that would feed the drug continuously into his spinal column. He was arrested with eight plants in his yard. The Medical Marijuana Defense Fund, coordinated in part by Portland NORML, one of the country's more active chapters, flew in a doctor from Virginia to attest to the medical efficacy of marijuana, and Helm's neurologist testified that she would prescribe marijuana if it were legal. The jury found him guilty of marijuana manufacture and possession on April 28, 1998, and he was sentenced to two years of probation and two $100 fines. The trial, which occurred as petitioners were gathering signatures for the Medical Marijuana Initiative and other proposals, probably helped to acquaint many Oregonians with some of the arguments for medicinal use of marijuana.

With that kind of essentially positive publicity and with money, advice, and professional help from Americans for Medical Rights, Oregonians for Medical Rights (OMR, with which Sugarman and Smigelski of No on 57 were also associated) submitted 97,648 signatures to the secretary of state's office in July, with 73,261 being necessary to qualify for the ballot. Signatures in Oregon are checked by scientific sampling. The sampling showed that OMR's signatures had a validity rate of 79 percent and since 75 percent was the required validity rate, on July 10 the proposal was declared qualified as Measure 67 on the November ballot.

In addition to these successful initiative campaigns, petition campaigns to place various versions of a medical marijuana law on the ballot were conducted, largely by local groups without help from Americans for Medical Rights, in Florida, Arkansas, Massachusetts, and Maine. None of these campaigns succeeded in placing an initiative on the state ballot, although a measure was qualified and passed in Maine in 1999, but all increased local awareness of the issue.

American officialdom was well aware of these efforts but at first it seemed as if federal drug warriors would play little role in opposing them actively or personally. On September 30, 1997, drug czar General Barry

McCaffrey testified before a House subcommittee on crime and, as Reuters reported, "dodged lawmakers' calls to campaign against various state laws allowing the medical use of marijuana, saying the American people must decide." "I am not in charge of America," McCaffrey told the subcommittee. "I'll provide information for the debate, leaning heavily on the scientific-medical community. I'll inform them of the federal law. I'm not America's nanny. The American people are perfectly capable, when they are exposed to the facts, of making up their own mind."[236] He said he did not plan to travel to Florida, Arkansas, and other states to campaign personally against the initiatives. Nobody seemed to think it the least bit odd that elected members of Congress should be begging an appointed federal official in charge of setting and recommending federal policies to intervene actively and aggressively in the political process whereby state policies are set through a direct vote of the people.

At the same hearing, Roger Pilon, director of the libertarian-leaning Cato Institute's Center for Constitutional Studies, offered scholarly and thoughtful testimony on the implications of the medical marijuana movement for the constitutional system of federalism. Under the federalist system set up before the Constitution, the state governments clearly had authority to regulate medical practices and the only justification for the national government to intervene would have to come from Congress's power to regulate interstate commerce. But especially since interstate commerce in marijuana was illegal, there was no way a doctor and a patient within one state making decisions on using a plant could even affect interstate commerce. "There simply is no power under the Commerce Clause, or under any other clause of the Constitution," said Pilon, for the federal government to regulate how state governments dealt with marijuana as a medicine.[237] Nobody paid Pilon any attention, least of all Republicans on the subcommittee who three years earlier had promised solemnly that with the Contract with America they would preside over a massive "devolution" of power from the national government to the states and to the people.

In addition to pending voter initiatives, legislation relating to medical marijuana or industrial hemp was introduced by elected legislators in a number of states in 1998. In Hawaii, Representative David Tarnas introduced H.B. 2403 to "ensure that seriously ill patients are not penalized . . . for obtaining and using marijuana strictly for medical purposes." In Iowa, Representative Ed Fallon introduced H.B. 422 to "authorize research into the use of marijuana for medicinal purposes." In Massachusetts, Senator Richard Moore introduced S.B. 473 to authorize "the Department of Health to approve the experimental use of marijuana in the treatment of additional disease entities, including AIDS." In New Hampshire, Representative Tim Robertson introduced H.B. 1559 "to allow a person to possess and cultivate marijuana for personal use when it is prescribed by a physician," In New York, Assemblyman Richard Gottfried sponsored A.B. 6407 "to allow the medical use of marijuana for a serious medical condition under the supervision of a licensed practitioner," and in Wisconsin, Representatives Frank Boyle and Tammy Baldwin sponsored A.B. 560 "to move THC from Schedule I to Schedule II . . . and establish a medical necessity defense to THC-related prosecutions."[238]

In Kansas, Senator David Corbin sponsored Senate Concurrent Resolution (S.C.R.) 1605 to "request the Department of Housing and Commerce to form a task force to investigate and research the viability of industrial hemp as an alternative crop." In Iowa, Representative Cecelia Burnett and others proposed H.B. 402 to "provide for research regarding the production and marketing of industrial hemp," while in Minnesota, Senator Roger Moe has S.B. 1181 to "classify industrial hemp as an agricultural product subject to regulation and registration by the commissioner of agriculture." In New Hampshire, Representative Tim Robertson proposed 1576-FN-A to "permit the development of an industrial hemp industry in New Hampshire," and likewise in Vermont, Senator Hull Maynard Jr. offered S.B. 285 "to permit the development in Vermont of an industrial hemp industry." Later Kentucky farmers would file suit to be allowed to grow industrial hemp; the U.S. Justice Department immediately opposed the suit, and Barry McCaffrey traveled to Kentucky to explain that he had determined that there was no real economic future for industrial hemp and it would be a tragedy even to consider legalizing it. (A federal court later dismissed the suit on the grounds that the farmers had no standing to sue because they were not hemp growers.)

None of these proposals were passed into law in 1998, and few received much discussion or publicity. But at least some elected officials in the country were seeking actively to legalize or authorize nonrecreational use of marijuana or hemp—and doing so through standard, established legislative methods.

As it became obvious that at least some initiatives would qualify for the ballot, however, supporters of the current drug laws became concerned. On February 26, 1998, Florida Republican Representative Bill McCollum introduced H.R. 372, which would put Congress on record as disapproving of state initiatives to legalize medical marijuana, which was described as a "dangerous and addictive drug." On March 30 Cheryl Miller, a 51-year-old multiple sclerosis patient, used medicinal marijuana with the help of her husband in the offices of California Republican Representative Jim Rogan, a supporter of H.R. 372. She was arrested and charged with possession. In early June, Drug Enforcement Administration chief Tom Constantine and former drug czar William Bennett traveled to Florida to oppose the initiative in that state. And on June 17 Barry McCaffrey warned the Senate Foreign Relations Committee that "There is a carefully camouflaged, exorbitantly funded, well-heeled elitist group whose ultimate goal is to legalize drug use in the United States. . . . Through a slick misinformation campaign, these individuals perpetuate a fraud on the American people, a fraud so devious that even some of the nation's most respected newspapers and sophisticated media are capable of echoing their falsehoods."[239]

On August 5 a plan by two Republican congressmen to require drug testing of House members and their staffs, as the Congress thought was appropriate for ordinary citizens, was quashed by the House leadership. On August 6, Representative Bob Barr took time out from his campaign to get President Clinton impeached to introduce an amendment to the

Washington, D.C., budget to provide that "None of the funds contained in this act may be used to conduct any ballot initiative which seeks to legalize or otherwise reduce penalties associated with the possession, use, or distribution of any Schedule I substance under the Controlled Substances Act, or any tetrahydrocannabinols derivative."[240] In other words, the votes for Initiative 59 could not be counted. Cosponsor Dennis Hastert, Republican of Illinois, now speaker of the House, said he supported the measure because he was concerned about the safety of constituents who came to visit the nation's capital.

H.R. 372 was softened into House Joint Resolution (H.J.R.) 117, which declared that it was the "sense of the Congress" without being a binding law, that marijuana is a dangerous and addictive drug and that Congress is unequivocally opposed to the legalization of marijuana for medical use. On September 16, 1998, with no hearings and very little debate, the House passed this joint resolution by a margin of 310–93. The *Orange County Register* editorialized the next day: "In essence, the House stuck its finger in the eye of California and Arizona voters who recently passed initiatives to make marijuana available to patients with the recommendation of licensed physicians. Even more important, it told thousands of patients and their doctors—who believe that marijuana can alleviate their conditions, often with less serious and dangerous side-effects than 'standard' prescriptions—that Congress is pleased to see them continue to suffer or to obtain relief only at the price of becoming criminals."[241] One patient had proven that point on September 16. Renee Emry Wolfe, a multiple sclerosis patient from Ann Arbor, Michigan, who had sought to discuss the issue with Representative McCollum, began to suffer spasms while in his office. She lit a marijuana cigarette for relief and was promptly arrested.

By October, law enforcement and the drug war hierarchy were fully engaged in a campaign to oppose the state initiatives. On October 18, police chiefs from the nation's 52 largest cities, convening in Salt Lake City, went on record as officially opposed to all the medical marijuana ballot initiatives. "Decisions about medicine in our country should be

based on science, not popular votes," said Charles Ramsey, the
Washington, D.C., police chief and the police association president.[242]
That same day Hoover Adger Jr., M.D., of the Office of National Drug
Control Policy, told the annual convention of the American Association
of Pediatrics that "If pot is a medicine, teens will rightfully conclude that
it's good for you. That sends the wrong message."[243]

Barry McCaffrey had told Congress a year before that he would provide information and let the people decide. But in October 1998,
although he still didn't campaign personally, his office was busy sending
surrogates to states with initiatives and distributing op-ed articles on the
theme that no change should be made in the marijuana laws until a great
deal more scientific research was completed. "No one argues that people
should eat moldy bread instead of taking a penicillin capsule,"
McCaffrey argued in one article. "If components of marijuana other than
THC are found to be medically valuable, the current scientific process
will approve those components for safe use."[244] He didn't mention that
for years he had argued that any claim that there was any medicinal value
associated with the marijuana plant at all was a "cruel hoax."

On October 26 Donald Vereen of the ONDCP, campaigning in
Oregon against Measure 67, said that the determination of the validity
of medical marijuana claims should be left to federal health officials. "We
don't want something determined to be a medicine because a bunch of
people voted on it," he concluded. On October 29 the Clinton Justice
Department announced that it would defend Congress's right to bar the
counting of votes on the District of Columbia's Initiative 59. That same
day ads made by the Drug Free America Foundation starring former First
Lady Barbara Bush began appearing in states with medicinal marijuana
initiatives. "Now is not the time," Mrs. Bush pleaded, "to send the message to our young people that marijuana is 'medicine.' It is not. It is a
dangerous, illegal drug."[245] Former presidents Gerald Ford, Jimmy
Carter, and George Bush all issued statements denouncing the state medical marijuana initiatives and urging voters to oppose them.

In the end, however, although most elected officials and law enforcement representatives were united in their opposition, there was little if

any grass-roots opposition to the medical marijuana initiatives. On November 3, 1998, Arizona voters voted down Propositions 300 and 301 by a 57–43 margin, which meant that they reaffirmed 1996's Proposition 200 and, in effect, told the state legislature to stop obstructing their will. In Alaska Proposition 8 passed by a 58–42 margin. In Colorado Initiative 19 passed by a 57–43 margin, even though it was understood at the time that the vote would not count unless a federal court overruled the secretary of state's decision that the initiative had not legally qualified for the ballot. In Nevada 59 percent of the voters approved of Question 9. In Oregon, Measure 57, the referendum on reimposing criminal penalties and jail time for marijuana possession, lost by a 33–67 margin, while Measure 67 won by 55–45. In Washington state Initiative 692 passed by a 59–41 margin and carried in every county. And although the votes on Washington, D.C.'s Initiative 59 were not counted, an exit poll paid for by Americans for Medical Rights showed that 69 percent of the voters said they had voted for it. In Minnesota, Reform Party candidate Jesse Ventura, who had made the failure of the war on drugs something of a campaign theme and had talked about reintroducing industrial hemp as a Minnesota crop, unexpectedly won the governor's race. None of the 93 members of Congress who had voted against H.J.R. 117, the anti–medical marijuana resolution, was punished by the voters for taking that stand.

I wrote in the *Orange County Register* of December 7, 1998 (in an article reprinted on the WorldNetDaily.com news site), that

> This election showed that when it comes to the drug war, the American people no longer trust their government or the two major parties. . . . the voters, in the face of the usual alarmist rhetoric about how any softening of the drug laws in the name of compassion would lead to chaos (and congressional refusal even to count the votes in Washington, DC), voted for every single reform measure. In short, the only clear message to emerge from the 1998 election was one

of respect for freedom and personal dignity, of confidence in
the judgment of individuals and their doctors over the mandates of the state.

All the media missed it. Almost two years later, it is unclear how good
a prophet I was. The voters still seem to favor allowing the medical use
of marijuana, but it is not clear that it is a high enough priority for most
voters that they will hold elected officials accountable for trying to sub-
vert or nullify their votes.

Implementation has hardly been uniform or easy in any of the states
that passed medical marijuana initiatives. When Measure 67 actually
became effective in Oregon, Dr. Rick Bayer, who led the initiative drive,
commented that "it will be imperative that the patient educate the doctor. That education won't be coming from Eli Lilly or Merck."[246] Law
enforcement and prosecutors warned that they expected a flood of
phony medical excuses from recreational pot smokers. The Oregon
Medical Association advised its members not to write recommendations
for marijuana. In Washington, Joanna McKee, who had been involved in
a Green Cross patient co-op before I-692 passed, said she had gotten
calls from at least 100 people since the election who had been sick for
some time but were still worried about getting in trouble if they tried to
acquire marijuana for medical use. In late December a semiparalyzed
Tacoma man with AIDS was arrested for cultivation of three plants
because police said he did not have his doctor's recommendation available, but prosecutors declined to press charges. By January, 1999, the
Grants Pass Daily Courier reported that a "haze of uncertainty" still
hangs over medical marijuana patients because of questions about distribution, noting that an Oregon Department of Justice spokesman was
clear in his mind that "the law doesn't allow you to buy it or for it to be
sold to you."[247]

In Hawaii, however, Governor Ben Cayetano announced in
December 1998 that he would push for a law to legalize the use of
marijuana for medical purposes. "We need to be at the forefront of

treatment," governor told reporters.[248] Hawaii, home of an active hemp movement, authorized a test growing of industrial hemp in 1999 and in April 2000 became the first state to remove criminal penalties for the medical use of marijuana through the state legislature rather than by a voter initiative.

A bipartisan medical marijuana bill made some progress in the Maryland legislature in 2000, and Chuck Thomas of the Marijuana Policy Project in Washington, D.C., said he expected it to pass in 2001. In Maine, voters approved a medical marijuana initiative similar to the Americans for Medical Rights model (illness list, possession limited to one ounce and three flowering plants), but patients expressed frustration over the difficulty of acquiring medical marijuana except on the black market. In March 2000 state Senator Anne Rand, a Democrat from Portland, introduced a bill to have the state distribute marijuana plants confiscated from those arrested for recreational use to patients who are legally entitled to use it for medicinal purposes. But she said she doubted if it would pass so long as possession of marijuana remains illegal under federal law.

In March 1999 Democratic Representative Barney Frank of Massachusetts introduced the Medical Use of Marijuana Act, which would set aside federal controls on marijuana so that states can set their own policies. The bill would reschedule marijuana from Schedule I to Schedule II, making it legal to prescribe. No hearings have been held on the bill. A March 1999 Gallup poll showed that 73 percent of Americans would "vote for making marijuana legally available for doctors to prescribe in order to reduce pain and suffering."[249]

On April 20, 1999, the Arizona Supreme Court reported that a state program as authorized under Proposition 200 to divert nonviolent drug offenders into treatment saved the state $2.5 million in its first fiscal year of operation. Some 77 percent of the probationers tested drug-free after completing the program.

By November 29, 1999, the Associated Press, in a story on the aftermath of I-692 in Washington state, found a 67-year-old former paratrooper willing to talk about how marijuana eased the pain of a tumor in his lower back but unwilling to have his real name used because of uncertainty about whether law enforcement would target him since a friend brought the marijuana to him and some law enforcement agencies still considered that illegal distribution. Although the state had officially added Crohn's disease, a painful bowel disease, to the list of illnesses for which marijuana could be prescribed, authorities were wrestling with the question of what constituted a 60-day supply of marijuana under pressure from prosecutors to provide firm guidelines so they would know whom to arrest and whom to leave alone. And most physicians were still reluctant to recommend marijuana because of uncertainty about possible legal repercussions from the federal government.

On May 22, 2000, the *New Yorker* published a long article by renowned investigative reporter Seymour Hersh on General Barry McCaffrey's service in the Persian Gulf War in 1991. A two-star general at the time, General McCaffrey had led the famed "left hook" infantry maneuver that placed American troops in a position to cut off retreating Iraqi troops. But Hersh suggested strongly, based on on-the-record comments from military personnel, that two days after top American officers ordered a cease-fire, McCaffrey had ordered a four-hour assault on retreating Iraqi troops that was wholly disproportionate to any threat. McCaffrey insisted that the Iraqis fired first and he was still proud of the victory his troops had achieved. Whether the controversy will have any effect on McCaffrey's credibility as a drug warrior or on his lobbying for more money to fight drug traffickers and guerrilla insurgents in Colombia, a country wracked by a decades-long civil war, is unclear.

In early June 2000 the organization behind Americans for Medical Rights in California announced that it had qualified a measure for the November ballot that would divert nonviolent drug offenders into treatment programs rather than incarcerate them, at least for the first two offenses. McCaffrey immediately criticized the initiative, saying it would gut the promising avenue of using special drug courts to deal with drug offenders by eliminating the option of incarceration as a spur to be serious about treatment. Dave Fratello said preliminary polling showed the initiative had a solid chance to pass, but the campaign had just begun.

In brief, medical marijuana has been accepted by voters in every state where it has been on the ballot, and pressure is building on the federal government from a number of directions to change its policies. But the federal government at the official level resists change obdurately and, in large part for that reason, implementation remains spotty in the states where voters have approved medical marijuana.

CHAPTER ELEVEN

What Does Federal Law Really Say?

Marijuana or cannabis is regulated at the federal level of government by the 1970 Controlled Substances Act, which provides a spectrum of "schedules" for prescription drugs, from outright prohibition of use to uses that require extensive recordkeeping by pharmacists to relatively unrestricted use by prescription. Over-the-counter drugs that can be obtained without a prescription can also be described as "unscheduled" drugs.

When the Controlled Substances Act, written by attorneys in what was then the Bureau of Narcotics and Dangerous Drugs (BNDD), was passed, cannabis was included on Schedule I, the most restrictive schedule. But during hearings on the bill in Congress, Department of Justice witnesses told Congress that "the medical profession" would be responsible for scheduling decisions in the future. The deputy chief counsel of the BNDD (the precursor to the present Drug Enforcement Administration) told the House subcommittee considering the bill that "this basic determination . . . is not made by any part of the federal government. It is made by the medical community as to whether or not the drug has medical use or doesn't."[250]

With this in mind, what are the criteria for placing drugs into the various schedules? The Controlled Substances Act spells them out, providing (21 U.S.C. Sec. 812 (b)) that certain findings must be made about a drug before it can be placed in a given schedule.

For Schedule I, the most restrictive schedule, on which heroin, LSD, and marijuana are now placed, the criteria are as follows:[251]

(A) The drug or other substance has a high potential for abuse.

(B) The drug or other substance has no currently accepted medical use in treatment in the United States.

(C) There is a lack of accepted safety for use of the drug or other substance under medical supervision.

For Schedule II, which includes methadone, morphine, methamphetamine, cocaine, and, until recently, Marinol, the criteria are as follows:

(A) The drug or other substance has a high potential for abuse.

(B) The drug or other substance has a currently accepted medical use in treatment in the United States or a currently accepted medical use with severe restrictions.

(C) Abuse of the drug or other substances [sic] may lead to severe psychological or physical dependence.

These are the criteria for Schedule III, which includes anabolic steroids and now Marinol:

(A) The drug or other substance has a potential of abuse less than drugs or other substances in Schedules I and II.

(B) The drug or other substance has a currently accepted medical use in treatment in the United States.

(C) Abuse of the drug or other substance may lead to moderate or physical dependence or high psychological dependence.

Schedule IV includes Valium and other tranquilizers, with these criteria:

(A) The drug or other substance has a low potential for abuse relative to the drugs or other substances in Schedule III.

(B) The drug or other substance has a currently accepted medical use in treatment in the United States.

(C) Abuse of the drug or other substance may lead to limited physical dependence or psychological dependence relative to the drugs or other substances in Schedule III.

Schedule V includes codeine-containing analgesics. Its criteria are:

(A) The drug or other substance has a low potential for abuse relative to the drugs or other substances in Schedule IV.

(B) The drug or other substance has a currently accepted medical use in treatment in the United States.

(C) Abuse of the drug or other substance may lead to limited physical dependence relative to the drugs or other substances in Schedule IV.

With all those "relative to other drugs and substances" phrases, these are obviously not airtight scientific definitions, and the placement of a substance on one schedule or another will obviously involve a certain exercise of discretionary judgment. Many people familiar with the effects of cannabis might be forgiven for wondering whether the substance meets the criteria for any of these schedules. In March 1972, shortly after the Controlled Substances Act came into effect, the National Organization for Reform of Marijuana Laws petitioned the BNDD to remove marijuana from the list of scheduled drugs entirely or to place it on Schedule V, where it would be subject to only minimal controls. The BNDD director refused, NORML went to an appeals court, which ordered the agency to consider the matter "on the merits," and thus began a years-long legal battle whose issues were finally summarized best in a September 6, 1988, Opinion and Recommended Ruling by Francis L. Young, then the chief administrative law judge of the Drug Enforcement Administration, from which all direct quotes in the following section are drawn.

By the time the matter was in Judge Young's hands, the parties had stipulated that the issues had been narrowed down to whether marijuana should be on Schedule I or Schedule II. Judge Young recommended that it be placed on Schedule II, so it could be prescribed by physicians under controlled circumstances, noting that "the evidence in this record clearly shows that marijuana has been accepted as capable of relieving the distress of great numbers of very ill people, and doing so with safety under medical supervision. It would be unreasonable, arbitrary and capricious for DEA to continue to stand between those sufferers and the benefits of this substance in light of the evidence in this record."[252] The administrator of the DEA, political appointee John Lawn, declined to accept Judge Young's recommendation (without even attempting to refute Judge Young's reasoning or to demonstrate in which particulars he was incorrect), a federal appeals court affirmed the DEA decision this time, and rescheduling advocates gave up on this particular effort. But the evidence and legal reasoning in Judge Young's recommendation are worth examining. They suggest strongly that under federal law as it now stands, not only does marijuana not belong on Schedule I, but keeping it there amounts to systematic defiance of the law.

The issue can certainly be considered more broadly, but as it came before Judge Young it was, as he put it, "narrowed to whether or not marijuana has a currently accepted medical use in treatment in the United States, and whether or not there is a lack of accepted safety for use of marijuana under medical supervision."[253] Those are questions that can be answered by a preponderance of the evidence, and Judge Young, who had heard from the best experts that advocates from the two sides could muster during at least 15 full days of hearings over more than 10 months, including vigorous cross-examination at every step, proceeded to lay out the evidence as it was known to him.

He also discussed the question, the answer to which is not necessarily as obvious as might seem at first blush, of what constitutes "currently accepted medical use in treatment in the United States." Noting that Justice Department witnesses, when the act was under consideration, assured Congress that "the medical community" rather than the government, would decide what was and wasn't a useful drug, he went on: "No one would seriously contend that these Justice Department witnesses meant that the entire medical community would have to be in agreement on the usefulness of a drug or substance. Seldom, if ever, do all lawyers agree on a point of law. Seldom, if ever, do all doctors agree on a medical question. How many are required here? A majority of 51%? It would be unrealistic to attempt a plebiscite of all doctors in the country on such a question every time it arises, to obtain a majority vote."[254]

Judge Young found help, however, in the way courts have handled medical malpractice cases. In deciding whether a medical procedure or practice is actionable as malpractice, they determine (see *Hood v. Phillips,* Texas, 1976) whether a "respectable minority" of duly licensed physicians supports a certain procedure or treatment. That term is not precisely defined, of course. One decision in the Sixth Circuit (*Chumbler v. McClure,* 1974) tried to define it more carefully: "Where two or more schools of thought exist among competent members of the medical profession concerning proper medical treatment for a given ailment, each of which is supported by responsible medical authority, it is not malpractice to be among the minority in a given city."[255] That "respectable minority" criterion is not quite as precise as you might like in a scientific experiment or mathematical formula, of course, and using it argues by analogy that the rule that applies to malpractice should work for determining a "currently accepted medical use." But the law, for all the chest-beating about being a predictable yardstick, is seldom all that precise and in practice often uses analogies. I haven't heard anyone offer a better criterion.

Judge Young then made another important point. The statute—the instrument that gives the Drug Enforcement Administration whatever legitimate power it holds—doesn't give the DEA the power to tell doctors what they should or should not accept as being medically useful or potentially beneficial. "It is not for this Agency to tell doctors whether they should or should not accept a drug or substance for medical use. The statute directs the Administrator merely to ascertain whether, in fact, doctors have done so."[256] If even a "respectable minority" of them have, a substance has no place—under the law as written—on Schedule I.

In applying the "respectable minority" test, Judge Young was willing to make judgments based on the evidence he had available. He cited dozens of cases involving dozens of doctors, for example, in concluding that marijuana has an accepted medical use in relieving nausea and vomiting often brought on by cancer chemotherapy and in relieving symptoms of multiple sclerosis and spasticity brought on by other conditions including hyperparathyroidism and spinal injuries. In his discussion of glaucoma, however, while acknowledging that his doctors believe that marijuana has helped glaucoma patient Robert Randall, the first patient (since 1937) to receive marijuana legally from the federal government, Judge Young concluded that the petitioners had not furnished him enough evidence from enough doctors to establish "that a respectable minority of physicians accepts marijuana as being useful in the treatment of glaucoma in the United States.

"This conclusion is not to be taken in any way as a criticism of the opinions of the ophthalmologists who testified that they accept marijuana for this purpose," he continued. "The failure lies with petitioners. In their briefs they do not point out hard, specific evidence in this record sufficient to establish that a respectable minority of physicians has accepted that position."[257]

When it came to the question of whether there was "a lack of accepted safety for use under medical supervision," Judge Young ruled that there was no question that marijuana would be a safe treatment, even for glaucoma. His reasons for so deciding deserve to be quoted at length. These numbered paragraphs come under the heading "Findings of Fact," meaning that after both sides presented their best case and their best experts, these facts emerged undisputed from the fray:

3. The most obvious concern when dealing with drug safety is the possibility of lethal effects. Can the drug cause death?

4. Nearly all medicines have toxic, potentially lethal effects. But marijuana is not such a substance. There is no record in the extensive medical literature describing a proven, documented cannabis-induced fatality.

5. This is a remarkable statement. First, the record on marijuana encompasses 5,000 years of human experience. Second, marijuana is now used daily by enormous numbers of people throughout the world. Estimates suggest that from twenty million to fifty million Americans routinely, albeit illegally, smoke marijuana without the benefit of direct medical supervision. Yet, despite this long history of use and the extraordinarily high number of social smokers, there are simply no credible medical reports to suggest that consuming marijuana has caused a single death.

6. By contrast aspirin, a commonly used, over-the-counter medicine, causes hundreds of deaths each year.

7. Drugs used in medicine are routinely given what is called an LD-50. The LD-50 rating indicates at what dosage fifty percent of test animals receiving a drug will die as a result of drug induced toxicity. A number of researchers have attempted to determine marijuana's LD-50 rating in test animals, without success. Simply stated, researchers have been unable to give animals enough marijuana to induce death.

8. At present it is estimated that marijuana's LD-50 is around 1:20,000 or 1:40,000. In layman terms this means that in order to induce death a marijuana smoker would have to consume 20,000 to 40,000 times as much marijuana as is contained in one marijuana cigarette. NIDA-supplied marijuana cigarettes weigh approximately .9 grams. A smoker

would theoretically have to consume nearly 1,500 pounds of marijuana within about fifteen minutes to induce a lethal response.

9. In practical terms, marijuana cannot induce a lethal response as a result of drug-related toxicity.

10. Another common medical way to determine drug safety is called the therapeutic ratio. This ratio defines the difference between a therapeutically effective dose and a dose which is capable of inducing adverse affects.

11. A commonly used over-the-counter product like aspirin has a therapeutic ratio of around 1:20. Two aspirins are the recommended dose for adult patients. Twenty times this dose, forty aspirins, may cause a lethal reaction in some patients, and will certainly cause gross injury to the digestive system, including extensive internal bleeding.

12. The therapeutic ratio for prescribed drugs is commonly around 1:10 or lower. Valium, a commonly used prescriptive drug, may cause very serious biological damage if patients use ten times the recommended (therapeutic) dose.

13. There are, of course, prescriptive drugs which have much lower therapeutic ratios. Many of the drugs used to treat patients with cancer, glaucoma and multiple sclerosis are highly toxic. The therapeutic ratio of some of the drugs used in antineoplastic therapies, for example, are extremely toxic poisons with therapeutic ratios that fall below 1:1.5. These drugs also have very low LD-50 ratios and can result in toxic, even lethal reactions, while being properly employed.

14. By contrast, marijuana's therapeutic ratio, like its LD-50, is impossible to quantify because it is so high.

15. In strict medical terms marijuana is far safer than many foods we commonly consume. For example, eating ten raw

potatoes can result in a toxic response. By comparison, it is physically impossible to eat enough marijuana to induce death.

16. Marijuana, in its natural form, is one of the safest therapeutically active substances known to man. By any measure of rational analysis marijuana can be safely used within a supervised routine of medical care.[258]

To be placed on a schedule other than Schedule I, however, marijuana would not have to be one of the safest substances known. It would simply have to be safe enough to be used under medical supervision. Toxic substances that make one's hair fall out or can cause liver failure or death with only a slight overdose are routinely used under medical supervision, and many patients owe their lives to them. Legally, then, marijuana doesn't have to be any safer than them to be disqualified from remaining on Schedule I.

Another question revolving around legal issues often arises in discussions of medical marijuana. To be accepted as a medicine, some say, marijuana would have to be submitted to the Food and Drug Administration and go through the entire battery of tests required of a new drug a pharmaceutical company wants to market. Since it is a complex plant rather than a single molecule—the kind of drug the FDA is set up to evaluate and that modern medicine tends to prefer, for not entirely illogical reasons—the testing procedure could be even more complex than for most new drugs. The usual cost for bringing a single-molecule new drug through the FDA approval process is "$200–$300 million, depending on the method and year of calculation," according to the 1999 IOM report. After clinical testing in three phases, which usually takes about five years, comes the FDA approval process. "In 1996 the median time for FDA review of an NDA [new drug application], from submission to approval," says the IOM report, "was 15.1 months, a review period considerably shorter than that in 1990, when the figure was 24.3 months."[259] Getting marijuana approved by the FDA could be even more expensive since clinical tests might have to include extensive testing for abuse potential, and since marijuana can't be patented, no drug company is likely to incur the expense. That's the way medicine is handled in the United States, and on balance we're better—safer, less likely to be accidentally poisoned by a drug released without sufficient testing—for it. Bringing marijuana into the mix is a pipe dream.

Aside from the question of whether relying solely on single-molecule drugs that can be given in precise doses is the only way to promote health and well-being—a premise that advocates of a healthy lifestyle including proper diet and exercise or of herbal medicines (or in some cases of a spiritual foundation) would dispute with a fair amount of evidence—the question of FDA approval for marijuana is irrelevant under federal law. The FDA was established in 1935 by the federal Food, Drug, and Cosmetic Act, in part (under Section 505) to determine the safety and efficacy of synthetically formed new drugs. Marijuana is not a new drug—it was used therapeutically 2,000 years before the birth of Christ—and it is a plant, not a synthetic substance.

Judge Young dealt with this issue in his recommendation because the government had argued that FDA interstate marketing approval should be the criterion for "currently accepted medical use" and that since marijuana didn't have approval, it wasn't accepted. Judge Young reminded the DEA that it had made a similar argument in a previous case dealing with the scheduling of MDMA ("ecstasy") and the First Circuit Court of Appeal had overruled it. "Thus it is appropriate for the FDA to rely heavily on test results and scientific inquiry to ascertain whether a drug is effective and whether it is safe," Judge Young wrote. "The DEA, on the other hand, is charged by 21 U.S.C. Sec. 812(b)(1)(B) and (2)(B) with ascertaining what it is that other people have done with respect to a drug or substance: 'Have they accepted it?;' not 'Should they accept it?'"[260]

In its wisdom, the federal government has chosen to regulate marijuana under the Controlled Substances Act of 1970. As we have been discussing, under the scheduling system established by that act, marijuana, by almost any legal or common-sense understanding, does not

qualify to be placed on Schedule I. It would be easy to find honest disagreement as to whether marijuana, based on its pharmacological
properties and safety characteristics, belongs on Schedule II, III, IV, V, or
any of the act's schedules at all. But there is no scientifically or legally
defensible basis for keeping it on Schedule I. The numerous difficulties it
might face in gaining FDA approval if it were a new synthetic substance
are not legally relevant.

If that law is supposed to mean what it says—if the words mean anything comprehensible to an ordinary mortal and are to be used as a
reliable guide to action rather than as an inconvenience to be finessed—
you really have to wonder. Who is breaking the law—the people who
keep marijuana on Schedule I or those who want doctors to be able to
prescribe it and to allow patients to use it under medical supervision?

The status of Marinol, manufactured as a capsule containing THC in
sesame oil and approved by the FDA in 1985 for the treatment of nausea and vomiting associated with cancer chemotherapy, could have some
bearing. The drug was developed with the encouragement of the government and with pivotal research support from the National Cancer
Institute. It is taken orally and, as noted, appears to be effective for some
patients but not as effective as smoked marijuana for other patients. In
1992 the FDA approved Marinol (also called by the generic name dronabinol) for the treatment of anorexia associated with weight loss in
patients with AIDS. According to the Institute of Medicine report, "the
FDA's review and approval of Marinol took about two years after the
submission of the NDA, according to Unimed [the holder of the NDA].
To obtain approval for Marinol's second indication (through an efficacy
supplement), the FDA required two more relatively small Phase III studies. The studies lasted three years and cost $5 million to complete."[261]

When it was commercially introduced in 1985, Marinol was placed
on Schedule II, a scheduling decision having been made by the DEA even
before FDA approval. Many doctors are reluctant to prescribe Schedule
II drugs (which are defined legally as having "high potential for abuse"),
not only because they involve more paperwork and can carry a stigma

for some but because many doctors believe prescribing "too many" Schedule II drugs (especially opioids) can bring unwelcome attention from drug enforcement agencies. But Marinol encountered no delays in marketing due to scheduling. It was recently moved to Schedule III, for drugs legally defined as having "some potential for abuse." Prior to this change, Unimed had estimated that its sales would increase 15–20 percent as a result of rescheduling. Although Unimed cannot promote Marinol for uses other than those approved by the FDA, physicians are free to prescribe it for other purposes (what are referred to as "off-label uses"). The IOM report estimated that 5 to 10 percent of Marinol is prescribed for other uses, much of it "thought to consist of Alzheimer's patients drawn to the drug by a recently published clinical study indicating Marinol's promise for treatment of their anorexia and disturbed behavior."[262] Unimed is now doing research to support FDA approval for this use also.

Marinol is synthesized in a laboratory rather than being extracted from the cannabis plant. Its manufacture is complex and expensive because many steps are needed in the purification process. The IOM report also notes that it has certain shortcomings, especially relating to determining the proper dosage and controlling adverse side effects.

> The poor solubility of Marinol in aqueous solutions and its high first-pass metabolism in the liver account for its poor bioavailability; only 10–20% of an oral dose reaches systemic circulation. The onset of action is slow; peak plasma concentrations are not attained until two to four hours after dosing. In contrast, inhaled marijuana is rapidly absorbed. In a study comparing THC administered orally, by inhalation, and intravenously, plasma concentration peaked almost instantaneously after both inhalation and intravenous administration; most participants' peak plasma concentrations after oral administration occurred at 60 to 90 minutes. Variations in individual responses is highest for oral THC and bioavailability is lowest."[263]

This is an interesting result, considering that one of the reasons most present-day physicians prefer single-molecule pills to herbal medications and especially to raw plants is their belief that with pills, dosage and bioavailability can be more precisely and reliably calibrated and regulated. However, in the case of THC as compared to raw marijuana, the reverse is true, at least according to this study and to widespread anecdotal reports.

The IOM report continues: "Marinol's most common adverse events are associated with the central nervous system (CNS): anxiety, confusion, depersonalization, dizziness, euphoria, dysphoria, somnolence, and thinking abnormality. In two recent clinical trials, CNS adverse effects occurred in about one-third of patients, but only a small percentage discontinued the drug because of adverse effects. Lowering the dose of dronabinol can minimize side effects, especially dysphoria (disquiet or malaise)."[264]

As of early 1999, when the IOM report was issued, Marinol sales were estimated at about $20 million per year. The market has been growing at about 10 percent per year, mainly because of "increasing use by HIV patients being treated with combination antiretroviral therapy. Marinol appears to have a dual effect, not only stimulating appetite but also combating the nausea and vomiting associated with combination therapy. Unimed is supporting a Phase II study to examine this combined effect and, with promising results, plans to seek FDA approval for this new indication."[265] If rescheduling increases sales by 15 to 20 percent a year and the market could continue to grow at 10 percent a year on top of that, sales could approach $100 million a year in a few years. By pharmaceutical company standards, however, this is not a large market. Unimed, aware of some of the drawbacks involved in oral administration, is researching a deep lung aerosol, nasal spray, nasal gel, and sublingual preparation as possible alternatives. The cost of developing any new method to the point of getting FDA approval is estimated at between $7 and $10 million for each new formulation.

The price of Marinol for anorexia in AIDS is about $200 per month. The IOM estimates that this makes it less expensive than marijuana cigarettes if a patient uses two or more cigarettes a day but more expensive if the patient uses one cigarette a day or less (at current black-market or cannabis-club prices). If marijuana were to become commercially available with the same restrictions applicable to other Schedule II or Schedule III drugs, the price would probably decline. Some patients, of course, can grow it at home for very little financial investment, but not all are able to do so. Marinol has a cost advantage for some patients because most health insurance covers it, whereas as of this writing no known health insurance company covers the cost of medical marijuana. In addition, Roxane (which markets Marinol for Unimed) sponsors a patient assistance program to defer the cost of Marinol to indigent patients who are uninsured.

The placement of Marinol on Schedule III, however, raises serious questions about where raw marijuana would be placed if the decision were made objectively, taking into account relative benefits and risks. As Lynn Zimmer and John Morgan point out in *Marijuana Myths, Marijuana Facts,* and as the IOM report acknowledges more implicitly, the apparent risks of Marinol may well be more pronounced than the risks of smoked marijuana. Marinol is associated with more adverse psychoactive effects and takes longer to achieve effectiveness, which makes regulating dosage somewhat more difficult. If Marinol is actually somewhat riskier and less effective than smoked marijuana, shouldn't smoked marijuana be on the same schedule or perhaps on Schedule IV or V?

John Gettman, who just received his doctorate in public policy and regional economic development from George Mason University in Virginia (and who is a former national director of NORML), has asked the same question. On July 11, 1995, he filed a petition to remove marijuana and THC from Schedule I, without specifying which schedule they should be on. The DEA acknowledged his petition and formally accepted it on July 22, 1995. It was referred in December 1997 to the Department of Health and Human Services, which is mandated under the Controlled Substances Act to conduct a study taking therapeutic value, abuse potential, and other factors into account and convey a recommendation. The petition was probably accepted because it raises different issues than were considered in the petition Judge Young responded to. Whereas the earlier petition's filers had stipulated that marijuana had the kind of serious abuse potential that would warrant placement on Schedule I or Schedule II, Gettman's petition alleged that the abuse potential of marijuana was so slight that placement on either of those schedules was not warranted. "The law requires three criteria to require the DEA to take a rescheduling petition seriously," he told me in May 2000. "There must be new information that was not previously on the record, new information not considered in the prior proceeding, and new information that throws new light on old information from a prior proceeding. The discovery, after Judge Young's recommendations, of specific cannabinoid receptors in the brain, satisfies the first and third criteria. The fact that this petition focuses on abuse potential, which was specifically excluded from the prior proceeding, satisfies the second."[266]

Gettman told me his petition had been filed a few months after Unimed filed to have Marinol moved from Schedule II to Schedule III, and it has tracked the Marinol rescheduling petition with a lag time of six months to a year. He considered objecting to the rescheduling of Marinol in March 2000 because of what he views as clear scientific evidence that Marinol carries more known risks than smoked marijuana but decided to let the normal bureaucratic procedures take their course. As of June 2000 no decision had yet been rendered on his petition, and his impression was that it was "sitting on a shelf somewhere in HHS collecting dust,"[267] with official HHS investigations and evaluations yet to begin. While a recommendation from the Department of Health and Human Services is seldom reversed in rescheduling matters, the administrator of the Drug Enforcement Administration has final rescheduling authority.

A recommendation from the Department of Health and Human Services would ultimately have to be signed off by the HHS secretary. The current HHS secretary, Donna Shalala, might have a difficult time doing so. She has been notable as an opponent of recreational marijuana use and also of medical use. During the flurry of federal hand-wringing after the passage of California's Proposition 215 and Arizona's Proposition 200, she said that "all available research has concluded that marijuana is dangerous to our health." Wire services said she claimed "the drug harms the brain, heart, lungs and immune systems of users, limits their learning, memory and judgment, and contains cancer-causing compounds."[268] That is the standard litany of the "reefer madness" line in the 1990s, and to put it charitably it is not solidly supported by reliable scientific research.

Shalala was quoted in *Prevention Pipeline* in 1995 as saying "we have to roll up our sleeves and get busy educating all Americans about the dangers of marijuana use." In an August 18, 1995, article in the *Wall Street Journal* she made a number of claims about marijuana dangers that, as we have seen, are dubious. Among them are "Marijuana can put a serious choke-hold on long-term users who try to quit," which could be true depending on what "put a serious choke-hold" means in clinical terms, but most authorities acknowledge that serious addiction problems are rare. "Young marijuana users are less likely to achieve their academic potential, which detracts from national productivity," she also wrote,[269] which might be qualified enough to have merit, although most studies show that college students who smoke marijuana have the same grades as students of similar demographic makeup who do not smoke marijuana.

However, the issues related to drug scheduling are narrower than the issues surrounding recreational use and/or legalization of marijuana. Almost all prescription drugs have side effects, some of them quite serious. The question of whether marijuana could be safely prescribed by a physician for symptomatic relief of serious or debilitating illnesses, even if it has all the side effects attributed to it by some critics, is different than the question of whether it should be legalized for recreational use. It could be answered affirmatively and in good conscience even by those who prefer to take the cautious approach of believing allegations about adverse side effects until they are proven wrong.

The scheduling system also affects, as the Institute of Medicine noted, the possible development of medications from or based on other cannabinoids in the marijuana plant besides THC that might have some therapeutic value or modulating impact on the effects produced by THC. Under current law, any cannabinoid found in the plant is automatically controlled in Schedule I. (If the plant were to be rescheduled, of course, the constituent cannabinoids would presumably be rescheduled also.) Even when research is to be done in lab dishes or on animals, therefore, any researcher studying cannabinoids must submit the research protocol to the Drug Enforcement Administration, which can issue or deny a registration. If the research is allowed, the DEA will require additional security arrangements. "However, the regulatory implications are quite different for cannabinoids *not found in the plant*," notes the IOM report. "Such cannabinoids appear to be unscheduled unless the FDA or DEA decides that they are sufficiently similar to THC to be placed automatically into Schedule I . . . Thus far, the cannabinoids most commonly used in preclinical research appear to be sufficiently distinct from THC that they are not currently considered controlled substances by definition."[270] But the cost of developing new cannabinoid drugs, even from novel cannabinoids, might well be higher than the ordinary cost of developing new drugs, which, mostly because of regulatory costs (as the IOM reports), are in the $200–$300 million range. Unless the regulations are changed, it will be extremely expensive to bring new cannabinoid drugs to market—and virtually impossible if marijuana remains on Schedule I.

CHAPTER TWELVE:

Frontier Journeys

Reporting on medical marijuana issues has given me an opportunity to visit and interview numerous patients, activists, growers, and distributors around California and to understand some of the dreams and plans these agents of social change have. I have discussed Marvin Chavez in chapter 4 and Steve Kubby in chapter 5. In this chapter I would like to share some of what I have learned from several of the more remarkable pioneers in this field.

It is hard to imagine what the medical marijuana landscape would be like—indeed, one wonders if it would be a live issue even now—without the study, research, work with patients, and vision Dr. Tod Mikuriya of Berkeley has put into the issue for about 35 years. He began researching marijuana's therapeutic qualities when he was in charge of marijuana research at the National Institute of Mental Health (NIMH) in the 1960s. He was a consultant to the National Commission on Marihuana and Drug Abuse (the Shafer commission) in 1972, by which time he had become something of an authority on the history of marijuana's medical uses. The book he assembled and published in 1973, *Marijuana Medical Papers,* which reprinted in their entirety some two dozen of the most significant medical studies and papers published in the United States and Europe from 1839 to 1972, did a great deal to increase awareness of the fact that for a considerable period of our history cannabis had been an accepted and widely used medication.

I had met Dr. Mikuriya at events and had brief conversations a few times over the years, talked with him extensively on the telephone, and exchanged numerous e-mails. But the first time I had the opportunity to visit him in his home office in Berkeley and discuss issues in depth was in March 2000.

UC Berkeley and the small section of the city near the university are surrounded by hills, some of them quite steep. It doesn't quite require a four-wheel-drive vehicle to negotiate the road to Dr. Mikuriya's house, but it is a long, steep, and winding drive from the San Francisco Bay side of the hills, past houses ranging from modest to spectacular with sweeping views of the bay to the west. His consulting and research rooms are in the lower levels of the house, with living quarters above, at street level.

Dressed casually but with quiet elegance, Dr. Mikuriya welcomed me to his dining room table, where we talked for several hours. His voice is quiet and deep, bespeaking the authority that comes with knowledge and experience. A throaty chuckle emerges from deep within him from time to time as he uses a phrase he knows is a bit extravagant ("a Thin Blue Line Coven of lawbreakers actively trying to put this law to death" or "what we need at the Department of Justice is some serious ethic cleansing"), and his eyes twinkle as he glances to see whether his companion appreciated the excursion. I had seen him only once on a witness stand, but I would not want to have been the attorney trying to question him or make him look like a zealot. With his large but trim frame (he plays tennis very competitively several times a week), his short, dark hair just graying around the edges, and his deep voice—which he seldom raises but can modulate from patient explanation to mildly impatient exasperation to withering scorn quite effectively—he exudes self-confidence and authority.

Nonetheless, the attorneys try. There's a thick file full of radical and unsupportable statements or claims Dr. Mikuriya has supposedly made in previous trials that makes the rounds from one district attorney's office to another when he is scheduled to testify either as an expert witness or as a patient's doctor. Each time, he patiently but persistently insists that they get the quotes right, that his statements be explained and put in context. It gets tiresome, he told me, "and it's a good thing I've been consistent from one testimony to another. Otherwise they would have succeeded in discrediting me. That they have failed so far is not for lack of trying."[271]

He said a little later,

> What concerns me is that so many people in law enforcement and prosecution seem to be incapable of allowing the statements of the voters into their consciousness. I don't know what they really think, but they act as if they imagine that if they ignore Section 11362.5 in the course of their pot busting activities, it will just go away. When I was in charge of marijuana research at NIMH in 1967, I got a chance to observe that government bureaucracy. To me, it looked as if lateral communication was not permitted; if you wanted to communicate with somebody in another department you had to go all the way up your chain of command and down his rather than just picking up the phone or having lunch. That means change comes slowly if at all, and it's more likely to be based on a decision or attitude of a superior who didn't quite understand the problem than on the objective facts. I see a lot of that in government at all levels. There are exceptions, but I see a lot of it.

Dr. Mikuriya, who has spent a good deal of his life researching medical marijuana and trying to communicate what he has learned outside a small circle of researchers and drug reform enthusiasts, was involved from the beginning, when he and others sat around Dennis Peron's kitchen table suggesting revisions and arguing fine points of law and trying to describe and understand the relationship between caretakers and patients. When Proposition 215 passed (after sending an e-mail to a large list of correspondents urging them to refer to "Section 11362.5 of the California Health and Safety Code" rather than "Proposition 215" to stress and implant the fact that it was the law now, not some proposal, and that it was the duty of the government to obey the law), he shifted his psychiatry practice in Berkeley so he could see more patients whose conditions might be alleviated by marijuana used medicinally. As one of the few physicians in the state willing to recommend marijuana—even though he had been personally ridiculed by name by drug czar Barry McCaffrey shortly after Section 11362.5 passed for claiming marijuana could cure all kinds of unlikely ailments—he soon had patients from all over the state, with a wide variety of ailments. This made him potentially vulnerable to criticism as a "Dr. Feelgood" eager to prescribe marijuana to anyone with a reasonably plausible story and collect a fee. He was well aware of the possibility and if anything, he says, it has made him more cautious and conservative than might sometimes be warranted.

The license from the state to practice medicine, given almost exclusively to people who have earned a doctor of medicine degree from an accredited medical school, is generally held on what might be called good behavior. As is the case with most state-licensed professions, there is very little proactive supervision of doctors by state medical boards; they operate almost exclusively on the basis of complaints from patients and occasionally from insurance companies or others in the health-care field. Whether this is because licensing is really designed to protect licensees from competition and criticism, as some argue, or because state medical boards are chronically understaffed and underfunded, as others would say, is neither here nor there. The fact is that in the ordinary course of affairs, unless you have a lot of complaints, it takes quite a bit more than a few malpractice suits to earn closer scrutiny from a state medical board. And since most doctors act responsibly and conscientiously most of the time and have more important things to do than process paperwork and answer to bureaucrats, perhaps that's not so bad.

Since he has been identified as an advocate of allowing marijuana to be used medicinally, Dr. Mikuriya has received attention from the medical board. "They came to me a bit more than five years ago," he said to me, "and told me there was talk that I was doing a number of things outside the customary scope of practice. They investigated and couldn't find anything that would justify disciplining me but said they would keep the file open. That five years was due to expire last August [1999], but the Napa district attorney made an inquiry regarding one of my patients with multiple sclerosis. Again they took no disciplinary action," he sighed, "but the file is to be kept open a while longer." He shrugged his shoulders. "To me the litmus test for a real doctor is whether you're willing to go out on a limb for your patients. There's always a price to be paid when you follow the science instead of the fashion, especially when some results differ from some official line. But you can live with yourself and sleep well at night."

Having spent so much time in courtrooms in the last few years, Dr. Mikuriya has some mordant comments on trial procedures, especially the mechanisms for determining what kind of testimony and what kinds of defense will be allowed. "When you hear the term *de limine* [the Latin used when testimony or evidence is ruled inadmissible] it really means 'Can we *not* talk?'" he chuckled.

> Let's not let the jury know there's an Oakland club that has a cooperative relationship with the city, that it has guidelines for quantities based on rational and empirical criteria, that nobody has challenged them. Let's make sure that kind of information isn't communicated across county lines so people can learn what works and what doesn't. If possible, let's not even let the jury consider that California voters authorized the medical use of marijuana because we know the guy isn't really sick, that it's just a ruse, and 11362.5 is neither material nor relevant. There may be reasons for clamping down on the free flow of information so tightly in the judicial system, but that system simply won't permit the

kind of unrestricted flow of information characteristic of science that is so critical to moving toward an empirically based system of making cannabis available to sick people. Fortunately the Internet has no such clamps on information.

Since the state government has not acted positively, Dr. Mikuriya believes it's time to practice what he calls "proactive structuralism"—creating structures where they don't exist, building community-based entities to fill the vacuum created by government inaction. Once these new structures are built, they will become the status quo and mainstream by default. The best example in the state, he believes, is the Oakland Cannabis Buyers Cooperative, for which he is a medical adviser who gives regular seminars to patients and prospective patients. He takes only a little credit for the fact that it is, in his opinion, the most tightly run and professional cannabis outfit in the state; he thinks Jeff Jones deserves most of the credit. The admission rules are clear and carefully explained, then scrupulously enforced. The quantity guidelines are based on the amount of cannabis the federal government furnishes to patients in the Compassionate IND program; that might not be scrupulously scientific, but it's hard to say that it's in conflict with federal policies. He hopes that Alameda County will contract with the club to be the official provider of medical marijuana services for the county, from checking recommendations to issuing identification cards emblazoned with the county seal to furnishing cannabis of consistent quality, perhaps even growing it. "That would solve a problem for the county that the county really doesn't know how to solve just yet," he said. "And that's what we should be thinking about as we build these structures and institutions: how we can solve problems for officials who are willing to address them rather than creating problems for them." Not that he's opposed to making problems for people who have already shown their hostility; he's talking with his lawyers about civil suits against prosecutors who have kept him on the stand for days, away from his medical practice, to deal with spurious accusations. But the real key to success, he insists, is moving ahead with constructive projects.

He has formed a company, Classic Pharmaceuticals, whose main but not sole purpose is to return cannabis products and formulations to the U.S. formulary and to develop new cannabis-based medicines and formulas. It is now seeking to have the right to the names from the days when large pharmaceutical companies made cannabis-based patented medicines, "grandfathered" to Classic Pharmaceuticals, so it can make those formulations and use those names. He is also optimistic about new products. He says the company is very close to being ready to license a monoclonal antibody testing kit, and other products are in the works.

In addition to being involved with the American Medical Marijuana Association formed by Steve Kubby, he is starting a Medical Cannabis Association (MCA), with Robert Raich, who has been an attorney for the Oakland club, as corporate counsel. Among other projects, he's hoping the MCA will be able to register particular names, along with characteristics and empirical descriptions, of different strains and varieties of cannabis, so there can be uniform and science-based standards. It is important for cannabis practitioners and researchers to follow the ISO 9000 international standards for quality assurance, he says. Following those standards will assure that cannabis products will be compatible with FDA procedures and with international trade treaties and protocols.

"We are still just beginning to explore the possible therapeutic uses of cannabis," he told me.

> But we know enough now to be reasonably sure that cannabis is the safest immune-modulator and analgesic known to medicine. It seems to have antispasmodic effects on both smooth and skeletal muscles, which is unusual. It is a safe and effective bronchodilator. I believe, though I'd like to see more research, that it is effective for gastrointestinal disorders because it controls stomach muscle spasms. But we do know that in most patients it promotes normal digestion

and acts as an appetite stimulant, which is the opposite of what the opiates do. I see numerous avenues of research and treatment just in these qualities alone.

From early on I have been asking patients to pay attention and to tell me whether they feel the medical, physical changes or the mental, psychological effects first when they take cannabis. Almost all of my patients tell me they feel the physical changes, whether pain relief or end of nausea, before the mental changes kick in. Some of them take a little more and get that "high," but many are grateful they don't have to and they don't. That leads me to at least consider the possibility that we should be thinking of cannabis as a medicine first that happens to have some psychoactive properties (as many medicines do) rather than as an intoxicant that happens to have a few therapeutic properties on the side. One of the ways people without experience develop misperceptions, I believe, is that they think it's like their favorite legal drug, alcohol, when in fact the effects are quite different.

Treating as many different patients as he does allows Dr. Mikuriya to learn, sometimes at first from patients' self-administered experiments, about therapeutic effects on a wide range of ailments. One patient, for example, has a rare congenital blood disorder called Burger's disease. This patient gets relief from the spasms in his blood vessels in 17 seconds. This and other experiences have caused Dr. Mikuriya to consider the possibility that there are cannabinoid receptor sites (chemically speaking, rather like locks waiting for the right key to open them) not only in the brain, where they were discovered and characterized in the late 1980s and early 1990s, and in the immune system, where their function is hardly understood at all, but also at peripheral sites in some muscles. He would love to do the research to discover if his hypothesis is true or have somebody else do it.

"What seems to be the case—and again this is preliminary," said

Dr. Mikuriya, "is that many of the conditions for which cannabis is indicated are mostly chronic and often very painful, but not lethal. The range of usefulness and the presence of receptor sites suggests that cannabis could play a role in the maintenance of good health—the fact that it is a powerful antioxidant is suggestive here also. But we'll need a great deal more research before we can say anything like that with anything approaching the level of confidence I would like to see."

It occurs to me that cannabis preparations are likely to be relatively inexpensive compared to many prescription medications. But if they're useful for a wide range of chronic conditions, the market should be extensive enough that an appreciable number of people could make quite a bit of money producing them, even if competition is effective and profit margin is only modest.

The best way to get to Lake County from the San Francisco Bay Area is to drive through the Napa Valley, California's premier winery region. I hadn't been through the area in about 15 years when I drove up in June 1999 to visit Dennis Peron and John Entwhistle at their medical marijuana growing facility outside of Middletown. I was amazed at how many more vineyards had been planted, how many more small wineries had been established since last I had been there. From Napa through Yountville, Rutherford, St. Helena, and on through Calistoga at the northern end of the valley, it almost seemed as if there is not an acre of ground in the valley and on the hillsides that is not either planted in grapevines, home to a winery, or a small town filled with espresso lounges, tasting rooms, and antique stores.

When I got to The Farm, as Peron and Entwhistle call it, some 12 miles of narrow road and a few miles of dirt road off the main street, I found that they have been thinking about the valley about 25 miles of twisting mountain roads south of their location. "Someday . . . someday this valley will be as well known for growing medical marijuana as the Napa Valley is for wine grapes," Entwhistle said. "I hope I live to see the day." The two have visited more than a dozen wineries, taking tours and talking to those in charge of the vines, hoping to pick up information on growing, adapting to the seasons, storing, and processing the finished product that would be applicable to their own project.

The Farm is a modest start to such a dream. The two have leased 20 acres on a gentle, wooded hillside with a small pond still large enough for swimming and paddling slowly in a rowboat. The house is a modest four-bedroom affair, comfortable but hardly luxurious. Peron and Entwhistle grow marijuana for themselves and for perhaps a dozen other people, most of whom provided seeds or seedlings and come up some weekends to help out, paying a rental fee for the separate plots in which their plants are grown. Marijuana plants line the walkway from the driveway to the door. A couple of small greenhouses contain seedlings, and in the several acres between the house and the lake are little plots, each on the order of a good-sized vegetable garden in a suburban home, for the different clients or members of the cooperative, with plants from small bushes to tall stalks. Most are surrounded by wire fencing to keep animals out. All told, there were 400 to 500 plants in various stages of development.

Peron and Entwhistle don't believe in keeping secrets, from their neighbors or anybody else. Next to the lake is an old concrete slab— what's left of what might have been a boathouse or a small guest house years ago—about 20 or 30 feet square. The two have cleared the over-growth and painted it white, with the red cross overlaid with a green marijuana leaf that has become something of a symbol of the medical marijuana movement. "That's so the helicopters can't miss it," Peron tells me. They did have an all-day visit from Drug Enforcement Administration agents, who scoured every inch of the property without making an arrest or filing charges. "We just explained what we were doing and why and tried to make friends," Entwhistle said to me.

In the evening they like to sit on the patio overlooking the pond and— between swats of mosquitoes—drink a little wine and talk about what they have learned that day and what they have to do the next day. On weekends it can be a party atmosphere if a lot of people have come up from the city to help out. On weekdays it's the two of them or sometimes some neighbors.

Dennis Peron grew up in Long Island and spent most of his life in San Francisco, the most prototypically urban city in California. John Entwhistle grew up in New York City, then moved to San Francisco. For these two urbanized gay men, running a farm has been a ground-up—literally—learning experience. "We didn't know how to adjust a lawn-mower or how to get a weed whacker to start," Entwhistle said as he tried to explain to me (without much luck) the subtle differences between male and female marijuana plants in the early stages. They like to uproot all the males if possible, not only because the females produce the largest and most THC-rich buds but also because they believe a renegade male in a plot can wreck all the females.

Their hope is to learn more about farming each year and gradually expand the scope of their operations so that they can grow the strains most suited to the climate or to particular diseases. At the same time they experiment with the effects of different strains and ask the members of their cooperative to do the same, so they can learn whether there are really some strains of cannabis more suited to treat certain diseases than others. As they learn, they are gathering material for a book, not only on their own experiences but also on what they have learned about farming and growing. "As we develop techniques that solve the various problems we discover in growing on an increasingly large scale," Entwhistle told me, "I can see us becoming consultants, to speed up the learning curve of others who get into the business."[272]

When I called them almost a year after my visit, they sounded even more content with the direction their life has taken. "We have fallen in love with our 20 acres," Entwhistle said to me. "Growing up in the city I always dreamed of something like this, a little plot of land. I was also curious whether our brand of politics could be transplanted from the city to a rural area, to a place like Lake County that is basically run by the sheriff and a board of supervisors, without much infrastructure, where everybody knows everybody else. So far, so good." Last summer, when

they saw lights late at night around the perimeter of their property several times and worried that people were crawling around getting ready
to steal their crops, the called the sheriff's office, said "this is the marijuana farm," and asked if they could send somebody up to check things
out. The sheriffs did so, and the problems stopped. When neighbors
came by, they would help the two men learn how to use their equipment.
Now people from the area bring a Bobcat or a riding mower over and
volunteer to help with the chores for a few hours. "The place looks like
a golf course now," Entwhistle said. "You wouldn't recognize it. When
we had 8,000 patients, as we did toward the end at the cannabis club,
that's just too many people to be social and real with. Here we can spend
time with a few people at a time and really get to know them."[273]

The more they think about it, the more Peron and Entwhistle think
the analogy to a vineyard is a good way to look at growing medical marijuana. The plants require care and attention to produce most effectively
and also require understanding and respect for the weather, the soil type,
and the variations that each season brings for best results. The next step
will be growing in much larger quantities. They believe it will be a challenge. They will have to learn how much can be done with mechanized
equipment and how much will still have to be done by hand. Storage will
be a problem, especially since cannabis tends to lose potency in almost
any kind of storage situation. Eventually they hope to have to figure out
what kind of equipment will be necessary to deal with large-scale processing. "Another way to envision the business is as something like
bottled water companies," said Entwhistle. "It starts out with boutique
bottlers selling to a small clientele, and then some hotshot businessman
will figure out it's possible to sell to a larger market and get costs way
down. Our goal is to keep doing things that are absolutely legal so you
can apply real business techniques rather than being troubled by the dis-
tortions and violence that go along with a black market."[274]

"We're working very hard," Peron told me, "but it's good, healthy
work and overall I feel a sense of relaxation and enjoyment unlike
anything I've felt before. It's almost like a soldier coming home after the

war is over and decompressing. The war we had to fight in the city wasn't always a physical war, but it was a real war and we were the targets. It cost a lot and created a lot of stress. Now the combat part is over, at least for us, and we can get on with doing something productive and building a positive legacy with the rest of our lives."[275]

Robert Schmidt would understand the almost mystic bond between people and the land that Dennis Peron and John Entwhistle have come to feel. The self-styled "Emperor of the Emerald Triangle" seldom talks about any subject for very long before getting around to expressing his opinion that the country started to decline when we abandoned the farm, especially the family-sized farm, as the basis of society, sometime in the 1930s.

> The industrial revolution was valid enough because it was based on things people needed. But somewhere around World War II, when Americans got used to building things like bombs that were meant to be destroyed when they were used, or products that sank to the bottom of the sea before getting to our Allies, we stopped thinking about widgets based on necessity and got into widgets based on short-term marketing. We left the farms and went into the martini era in the 1950s. We purposely suppressed a useful plant like hemp. And we forgot that everything comes from the earth and the earth needs to be nurtured."[276]

Schmidt was telling me all this while sitting at a desk inside a modest house—perhaps 2,000 square feet—in Petaluma that has been mostly gutted inside and turned into a marijuana growing room, laboratory, and office. This is Genesis 1:29, taking its name from the verse in the Bible that reads "For I have given you every herb bearing seed, which is upon the face of all the earth, and every tree, in the which is the fruit of a yielding seed; to you it shall be for food." Schmidt thinks God's authority, that we are to consider every herb a gift from him, trumps the government's. At age 49, however, he's ready to take the government into account and pursue his plans to make medical marijuana more widely available to patients who can benefit from it in a scrupulously legal as well as an ethical fashion.

He wasn't always ready. He is frank and open about the fact that one of the reasons he knows a lot about marijuana and the marijuana trade is that he used to be a large-scale smuggler of marijuana and other drugs for quite a few years beginning in 1970. Perhaps he got into it because he loved flying airplanes, perhaps because he liked living on the edge. He is not an intellectual; his conversation, even about spiritual matters, is punctuated with casual profanity. He smuggled drugs and he served time in prison for it. "I did it the wrong way for a long time, I paid for it, I've learned from my mistakes," he said earnestly. "Now, understanding as I do the beneficial aspects of this herb, I want to do it the right way."

The Genesis 1:29 Mission Statement describes the organization as

> a nonprofit foundation operating a botanical nursery for the specific purpose of cultivation and distribution of medicinal herbs such as Echinacea and clinical cannabis. The spirit of the Genesis program is to produce the finest organically grown, chemical and pesticide free herbs for medicinal purposes.
>
> Genesis is a pilot program established in 1998 and has operated successfully and lawfully within State guidelines established by Proposition 215, by complying with public health and safety codes 11362.5 paragraph C including 11357 and 11358.
>
> Genesis provides an alternative to the so-called cannabis clubs by providing product and service directly to the patient through home delivery, eliminating public safety risks.
>
> Patient's medical records and histories are privileged and private.
>
> Genesis requests that physicians allow or permit, not nec-

essarily prescribe to patients who are seen on a regular basis, to evaluate the benefits of our program for their individual needs. We are not doctors. Patients and doctors acting irresponsibly in the program will not be allowed to participate, to protect the needs of others.

Later in the day Pamela Byrd, a dignified black woman, explained to me how she handles patient intake and recordkeeping. Two summers ago she met "Duke" Schmidt when she was taking "speed" and her brother was dying of AIDS. He suggested a doctor who would recommend cannabis to help her get off speed. Then, since she worked at a medical center doing scheduling for four doctors, he offered her a job.

When a prospective client first comes to Genesis, she explained, he or she is given one of the Genesis standard forms, which includes the wording "recommend or approve" and requires a physician's signature. This is a Genesis form the organization requires over and above the letter a physician might write on his or her own letterhead. Byrd then calls the doctor, discusses the case, and gets confirmation that the recommendation is valid. Handling the paperwork and verification ordinarily takes about seven days, she said, but if there's an obvious and visible problem and they have the physician's recommendation, they will dispense (not sell) a small amount of cannabis pending final verification. Most doctors, she said, will issue a recommendation good for six months that needs to be renewed. She generally approves of that arrangement because it provides some assurance that the doctor and patient see one another fairly regularly.

Genesis was serving fewer than 12 patients when she started two years ago and now has about 80 on its books in the Petaluma area, said Byrd, and perhaps a dozen more in the Lake Tahoe area. "We're meeting a good bit of the need here, and doing it in an aboveboard and ethical fashion," she told me. "It's hard to know how many patients in the area could benefit from cannabis but won't even consider it because of stereotyped attitudes. But we're helping the people we can help, one patient at a time, and it feels good."

The house in Petaluma contains not just a lot of marijuana plants and some laboratory facilities but four large dogs, three iguanas, and at least two cats. Schmidt says the humane society has come to know, in the four years or so he has been in the house, that he will take almost any animal that would otherwise be put to sleep. A greenhouse is attached to the rear, filled with cannabis plants—about 100, most in the 8- to 10-inch high range when I visited in March—and a smaller adjunct to the greenhouse with perhaps 100 seedlings. While these plants are used for medicine, they're not the totality of the organization's supply. Schmidt said he has contracts with 31 different growers up and down the Emerald Triangle. "We don't pay as much as they might get on the black market and we're tough on quality control," he said. "But it can be a steady business with less risk that can make a grower feel proud of what he's doing. As more informed distributors get involved and as more growers learn how to produce for medicinal uses, I see us getting the price down substantially, for extremely high-quality medical cannabis."

Genesis, while being careful about confidentiality, is keeping detailed records on its patients, including how much cannabis they use and what they say about the effects on their conditions. "We're not doctors, but we've learned some of the questions to ask," said Schmidt. "And we're not scientists, but we believe we have the raw material for a number of potentially valuable studies when somebody qualified has the time and the interest to do them." A former pharmaceutical lab manager who works for a major pharmaceutical firm in Silicon Valley is intrigued enough to be working part-time with Genesis, conducting state-of-the-art lab tests on the cannabis products Schmidt has spent the last several years developing through trial and error. He believes some of the formulations are on the verge of being ready to apply for patents.

Robert Schmidt first approached me and others at a Chapman University forum on drug laws in Orange, California, saying that he had the answers to drug czar Barry McCaffrey's oft-stated objection that sticking a big "doobie" in a patient's mouth is no way to administer medicine in the modern world. When I visited he showed me the second bed-room, full of vials, beakers, and other laboratory paraphernalia. "We don't smoke here at Genesis," he said. "We vaporize." That means applying a heat gun to the bowl of cannabis and having the patient suck the vapor released, which apparently contains enough of the therapeutic chemicals to be helpful without burning up the cannabis buds. There is much less smoke than with ordinary smoking, which, Schmidt said, makes it more low-key, less potentially disruptive, and more acceptable in a hospital setting. He also makes what he calls "honey oil," a thick, syrupy substance almost the viscosity of motor oil, which also releases a vapor when heat is applied. Schmidt wouldn't tell me exactly how he makes it ("That's proprietary; I think I've found methods better than what they used in the 19th century when liquid cannabis products were commonplace"), but it is apparently extracted from the whole bud and has an extremely concentrated THC content. Not only does it produce almost no smoke and very little odor when heated, patients can get as much THC as from a marijuana cigarette in just two or three draws. He showed me vials that have four distinct colors, each one, he says, with subtly different properties and effects on individual patients. He thinks a good bit of the future of medical cannabis is in extracts like these, if they are made with sufficient purity and quality control such that delivery of THC and/or other substances can be assured with more precision than is possible even with fairly uniform and high-quality raw herbs.

Genesis was originally organized as two sister organizations, a coop-erative distribution service to serve patients and a for-profit company to license whatever patents are granted to formulas Schmidt and others develop. The for-profit company would then make payments to the non-profit arm to sponsor more research. I heard the business plan change subtly during the day I spent there, as Schmidt spoke to his patent attor-ney, one of his partners, somebody who is trying to find some venture capital, and Robert Jack, head of the cannabis distribution set-up in Calaveras County. Like any start-up, it will probably continue to change as circumstances change and as new opportunities present themselves and yesterday's certainty becomes tomorrow's bittersweet memory of what might have been. This is new territory being charted, and pioneers have to be flexible without being inconstant. And most new ventures fail even in established lines of business.

I went with Schmidt, with the patient's permission in advance, as he delivered a packet of medical marijuana to a man confined to a hospital bed in his family room, which had a television set mounted on a bracket high up on the wall, just as in a hospital room. A friend was staying with him and opened the door. The patient and Schmidt were obviously well acquainted, and they talked for several minutes about how different strains of cannabis had slightly different effects on chronic back pain, at a level of detail far beyond my ken. "I think you'll find this quite effective," said Schmidt. "It's a blend of the two kinds that have worked best, picked fresh this morning. Let me know how it works." On the way back home he tells me they are trying to keep the same kind of records the FDA uses to evaluate an Investigative New Drug application.

A few weeks after I visited, Schmidt called my office, very excited. "I have cannabis out in pill form and it works. Not just the isolated THC, but an extract of the whole plant, suspended in olive oil and encapsulated. We've had seven patients on it for two weeks—those who wanted to gave it a try—and they've had almost exactly the same results as with vaporized cannabis or the honey oil." Then he told me about his experience the last few days with Ford Motor Company, from whom he's applied to lease a tractor. "They called and asked how much cash I had on hand." He told me. "I said, 'Oh, about $39. And I need to make a payment of $7,000 next week and I have $12,000 a month overhead that I'm not sure I'll make this month.' I figured I had torpedoed myself. A couple of hours later they called and said. 'A balance sheet like that just proves you're really a farmer. You've got the lease.' I think Ford has sold some new tractors to the hemp industry in Canada over the last year or so and sees a market in this country if a hemp and medical marijuana industry takes root."

EPILOGUE

On Wednesday, June 14, 2000, Peter McWilliams's housekeeper came to work and found McWilliams in the bathroom, dead. He had apparently choked on his own vomit. In my weekly column for WorldNetDaily.com on June 23, 2000, I wrote the following:

> Perhaps the word "murder" is too strong. But there is little question that author and publisher Peter McWilliams died in large part because of an overdose of government—one that could have been ameliorated by several specific people at specific times during the process of his interaction with what some call the justice system. His early death at the age of 50 was morally attributable—whether or not it would be appropriate or useful to have formal charges filed or not—to the federal government, War on Drugs branch.
>
> By the time he contracted AIDS in 1996 Peter McWilliams had a varied and mostly successful career as a writer and publisher. Beginning with how-to books on personal computing in the late 1970s through *How to Survive the Loss of a Love* and *Life 101* and *Life 102,* he had about a half dozen books on the *New York Times* bestseller list at various times. His magisterial *Ain't Nobody's Business If You Do* was an eloquent and masterfully documented plea for

an end to laws against actions that harm nobody but the person who does them.

When he was diagnosed with AIDS and non-Hodgkins lymphoma in March 1996, he hadn't smoked marijuana in years, though he had long been in favor of ending criminal penalties against those who did. But he had heard and read that marijuana seemed to control the nausea that in most patients follows standard medical treatments for AIDS and cancer. He tried it, then became an active campaigner for Proposition 215, then on the California ballot. . . .

With state law authorizing the treatment that he found most effective and with the wherewithal to grow it at home, Peter McWilliams might have been home free. But he wanted, as was his wont, to do more. So he made an arrangement with another patient, Todd McCormick, for Todd to grow different strains of marijuana, experiment to determine the effects of different strains and different dosages on different diseases, and write a book about the results. If marijuana, after more than 60 years of federal prohibition, was going to become a medicine again (it was the most-prescribed drug, by some accounts, by American doctors during the 19th century after being rediscovered by British doctors in India), Peter wanted to play a part in developing systematic, scientific evidence about its medicinal properties. Peter gave Todd a large advance so he could rent a large, old, and largely gutted house in Bel Air as a greenhouse.

But although their activities were perfectly legitimate under state law and neither state nor local law enforcement officials bothered them, Todd and Peter came to the attention of federal officials. First Todd was arrested and charged with cultivation for sale as the "Bel Air Mansion Pot Grower." Peter defended Todd and eventually began to explain that he had financed the growing operation as part of a research program for a book. For his trouble and honesty, he was arrested on December 17, 1997, as a "drug kingpin," and federal agents confiscated a wide array of his property, including his computers, one of whose hard disks contained the book he was writing at the time. More complete information on all aspects of the case is still up at Petertrial.com.

His financial situation at that point was nowhere near as strong as it had been at various times in his life. His mother and brother had to mortgage their homes to make his bail. One of the conditions of bail was that he not smoke marijuana. Federal Judge George King would not even entertain a medical-necessity argument. Since his loved ones' homes were at stake, Peter abided by the order. But he paid a heavy price.

His viral load at the time of his arrest was down to undetectable levels. By November 1998 his viral load had soared to more than 256,000. In 1996, when he had developed the AIDS-related cancer, the viral load had been only 12,500. The government continued to administer urine tests. Unable to work because of the disease and the toll taken by the court battle, he was forced into bankruptcy.

He did develop various regimens, including prolonged bed rest and frequent soothing baths, that enabled him to keep his medications down for as long as an hour and a quarter. His viral load came down, but he was considerably weakened and wheelchair-bound most of the time. Still, he looked forward to going to court, presenting the information about his use of medical marijuana to a jury, being vindicated, and striking a blow for freedom.

Last November, however, Judge King ruled that at the trial no information would be allowed to be presented to a jury about his illnesses, about the fact that the government's own research (most recently summarized in the March 1999

Institute of Medicine report commissioned by the drug czar) showed that marijuana was efficacious in the treatment of the diseases, or even that California had a law that authorized certified patients to grow and use marijuana. It was to be a pot-growing case under federal law, plain and simple, with Peter cast in the role of financier and kingpin.

It is likely that this outrageous decision would have been overturned on appeal, especially since the Ninth Circuit federal appeals court had ruled in September that lower federal courts must be open to medical-necessity pleas even under federal law. But Peter and Todd were almost out of resources and very sick. They took a plea bargain. Peter hoped his incarceration could be served under house arrest, especially since there would be no way he could stick to the strict regimen that was permitting him to keep his medicine down (in the absence of the ability to use a medication proven effective as an antiemetic) while in prison. A prison sentence would have amounted to a death sentence.

On Sunday, June 11, there was a fire in his home that destroyed his computers, including the book he had been writing about his ordeal that he had wanted to be his last salvo against the marijuana laws. He was depressed and wouldn't talk to anybody for several days. The following Wednesday, he choked on his own vomit in his bathroom. If he had been allowed to use marijuana he would almost certainly have been able to control the nausea that led to his death.

Through all of this, Peter retained a remarkably cheerful and optimistic outlook. He never succumbed to hate, and in the e-mail messages he was still able to send and receive prolifically, he often reminded his friends and supporters not to give in to the desire to seek vengeance. "My enemy is ignorance," he would say, "not individuals." During the dozens of phone conversations I had with him during the last couple of years he never once sounded as if he were complaining or seeking sympathy. His health situation was what it was, and the only thing was to understand it, accept it, deal with it, and try to take some positive steps in the direction of a freer society, so that others would not have to undergo what he had.

I have no doubt that some medical marijuana patients have succumbed to bitterness and resentment toward government officials who have worked to frustrate them, perhaps arguably to persecute them, even after the people of California changed the laws. But few of those I've met have done so, preferring to reserve their energy for something more positive. They have worked to educate themselves and others and striven to see the bright side. Most don't want anything for themselves except the right to use, without undue hassle, medication they and their doctors believe works for them.

When he was in prison, Marvin Chavez reported to sick call every day. Every day he requested that the doctors furnish him marijuana and every day was refused. But he kept doing it because it gave him an opportunity to speak with doctors and other health-care workers—and with patients and prisoners—about how marijuana worked for him. He came out of prison undaunted and ready to begin work again.

As this book goes to print the trial of Michele and Steve Kubby is underway in Auburn, the county seat of Placer County, between Sacramento and Lake Tahoe. After delays having to do with availability of attorneys who had other cases, the trial began in September 2000, with the deputy district attorney prosecuting for Placer County and famed San Francisco attorney J. Tony Serra as lead defense attorney, along with San Francisco attorney J. David Nick as cocounsel. Due to Steve Kubby's medical condition the trial has been on a limited two-day-a-week schedule and should conclude in early December 2000. The prosecution has presented its case and the defense began in late October. The Kubbys are upbeat and optimistic, full of praise for the skills of their attorneys, but predicting the outcome of a jury trial is difficult for seasoned attorneys, let alone occasional observers.

As his criminal trial was in the preliminary phases, Steve Kubby, through the American Medical Marijuana Association, filed civil suits, for false arrest and other violations, against Placer County law enforcement personnel and the officials who authorized their activities. In early November 2000, the Placer County grand jury decided it could not sensibly consider these charges until the Kubbys' criminal trial had concluded. It did not commit to considering the charges in the civil suits but strongly implied that it would do so. Steve is convinced that local officials in places like Placer County will not begin to cooperate with patients and to implement Section 11362.5 in good faith unless they understand that there is a price to be paid if they don't. Few local officials pay at the ballot box for using the courts to determine whether a patient's medical claim is valid or not, and many are convinced that they will do so if they appear to be cooperating too closely with patients. Steve Kubby is urging other patients, with his own complaint as a model, to file similar lawsuits. But lawsuits take enormous attention and concentration and a certain amount of money. They are not for everybody.

On August 18, 2000, the U.S. Justice Department asked the U.S. Supreme Court to block Oakland federal judge Charles Breyer's modified order allowing the Oakland Cannabis Cooperative to set up a system to distribute cannabis to patients with a demonstrated medical necessity (see p. 129). Within two weeks the U.S. Supreme Court, by a 7–1 vote (Justice Stephen Breyer is Judge Charles Breyer's brother, so he recused himself) issued a temporary stay. The only dissenter was Justice John Paul Stevens, a Ford appointee generally viewed as part of the "liberal" wing of the Court. "Because the applicant [the federal government] in this case has failed to demonstrate that the denial of necessary medicine to seriously ill and dying patients will advance the public interest," Justice Stevens wrote, "or that the failure to enjoin the distribution of medicine will impair the orderly enforcement of federal criminal statutes, whereas respondents have demonstrated that the entry of a stay will cause them irreparable harm, I am persuaded that a fair assessment of that balance favors the denial of the extraordinary relief that the government seeks." But he was the only justice who thought so. Several news stories implied or even said that this decision by the U.S. Supreme Court signaled that the court was prepared to invalidate Proposition 215 and possibly similar initiative-created statutes in other states. It was not because the high court did not have a case before it that would have permitted it to do so. The civil suit against the Oakland cooperative was brought under federal law, not state law, and Proposition 215 (Section 11362.5) has not been challenged in court as being in conflict with either state or federal constitutions or for any other reason. Both Robert Raich and California Attorney General Bill Lockyer told me that the decision to grant the stay was procedural in nature and did not deal with the merits of the case.

On November 27, 2000, the Supreme Court announced that it would hear the Oakland Cannabis Cooperative case during the court's current session. This was not entirely expected. The high court generally takes cases out of the hands of a federal circuit court on an expedited basis, among other reasons, when it is presented with a situation in which two different circuit courts have delivered conflicting decisions on an issue and it is considered important to have the Supreme Court resolve the matter on a national basis. In this case the Ninth Circuit Court had made a decision and was ordered to revisit it. No other circuit court has ruled on the issue of a medical necessity defense against federal marijuana laws.

Robert Raich told me he thought the court took the case because the solicitor general requested it. "Ever since Bill Clinton said he didn't inhale," he said, "and especially with an alleged former recreational user running against an allegedly reformed former recreational user, the Clinton-Gore administration has gone out of its way to prove it is tough on drugs. If its rhetoric has to be fed with the pain, the suffering, or even with the death of sick people, those in power don't seem especially concerned."

The Supreme Court should find that the controversy over medical marijuana will present it with some potentially ticklish issues. The concept of "necessity" as a defense in criminal cases has deep roots in the common law, although the concept of "medical necessity," while fairly well established, is a modern variant. In recent years the Rehnquist court has signaled, in the *Lopez* decision and others, that it is in the midst of a large-scale reconsideration of the powers of the national government in a federalist system. Will it choose the issue of medical marijuana to strengthen federal supremacy, or will it see it as an opportunity to strengthen the concept of states' rights and a federalist system with a central government of limited and enumerated powers? Finally, the Gettman petition to have marijuana rescheduled under federal law might be decided before a judicial proceeding becomes "ripe" for the Supreme Court. Oral arguments are expected in April 2001, with a decision by the end of June.

In the November 2000 national election seven initiatives related to drug policy were on state ballots. Five passed by healthy margins. A proposal in Alaska to decriminalize possession of marijuana for personal use, authorize the commercial growing of hemp, and grant amnesty to those with certain previous drug convictions was defeated by a 60–40 margin. Question 8 in Massachusetts, which would have provided for probation and treatment for certain nonviolent drug offenders, reformed the asset forfeiture laws, and redirected money from seizures into drug treatment, lost by a 53–47 margin in the wake of an active campaign against it from law enforcement associations.

In Mendocino County in northern California, voters approved by a 58–42 margin an advisory initiative put on the ballot by local activists (without significant help from outsiders) in favor of legalizing the cultivation of up to 25 marijuana plants for personal use. The initiative does not change state or federal laws on marijuana possession, but it does direct the county sheriff's department to make marijuana law enforcement its very lowest priority. Whether it will have a real impact on the way laws are enforced or the way marijuana prohibition is viewed elsewhere is unknown at this time.

In Colorado, Amendment 20, the measure that had been passed in 1998 but not implemented because of questions as to whether it had properly qualified for the ballot, passed again, by a 55–45 margin. In Nevada, Question 9, the medical marijuana constitutional amendment that had passed by a 59–41 margin in 1998, was on the ballot again because Nevada requires constitutional amendments to be approved in two successive elections to take effect. It passed by a 66–34 margin the second time.

In Oregon and Utah the Campaign for a Sensible Drug Policy, the organization that evolved out of Americans for Medical Rights, with Bill Zimmerman and Dave Fratello operating an office in California funded in large part by George Soros, Peter Lewis of Cleveland's Progressive Insurance, and John Sperling of Phoenix University, sponsored measures to reform state asset-forfeiture laws. In Utah, Initiative B places the burden of proof on the government to prove that property was used in the commission of a crime or was the fruit of criminal activity rather than requiring the property owner to prove otherwise. It also directs proceeds from seizures to education rather than to the police agencies performing the seizures. It passed by a 68.9–31.1 margin. In Oregon, Measure 3 bars the completion of a seizure until the property owner is actually convicted of a crime and directs proceeds from seizures to drug education programs rather than to the police department. It passed by a 66–34 margin.

In California, the same group sponsored Proposition 36, which provides that those convicted of a nonviolent drug possession offense the first or second time be given probation and required to undergo drug treatment of a type approved and directed by the court and appropriates $120 million a year to expand treatment capacity. The

California Drug Court Association opposed the measure, arguing that the measure did not pay for drug testing and did not allow the judge the option of overnight "snap incarceration" when an offender in a treatment situation tests positive. The initiative passed by a 61–39 margin. In a conference call with reporters on Thursday November 9, Bill Zimmerman said the initiative victories were "a turning point" for the drug reform movement. In the same call Ethan Nadelmann, executive director of the Lindesmith Center/Drug Policy Foundation, noted that "Since 1996, we have won 17 of 19 drug reform initiatives. The momentum is clearly on our side."

Zimmerman and Nadelmann said they would focus on implementation of the initiatives passed before deciding where to sponsor initiatives next but left the strong impression that both initiatives and efforts to persuade state legislatures to deal with medical marijuana and other drug policies would be undertaken in the near future.

Much more remains to unfold on this issue. This book catches the story midstream, and several episodes are unresolved. But whatever the twists and turns, it is likely that the day is not far off when marijuana will be recognized, legally accepted, and widely used as medicine in the United States. It will probably be regulated and controlled more heavily than most advocates would prefer but more lightly than many current opponents would prefer. But the evidence (though sometimes anecdotal) and the advocacy (though sometimes ineffectual) are too pervasive for continued prohibition of marijuana as a Schedule I drug to seem likely.

Notes

Chapter 1: The Voters Speak

1. Janet E. Joy, Stanley J. Watson Jr., and John A. Benson, eds., *Marijuana and Medicine: Assessing the Science Base* (Washington, D.C.: National Academy Press, 1999), 6.
2. Ibid., title page.
3. Ibid., 9.
4. Jack Herer, *The Emperor Wears No Clothes* (Los Angeles: Queen of Clubs Publishing, 1990), 9.
5. Joy, Watson, and Benson, *Marijuana and Medicine,* 6.
6. California Secretary of State, 1996 Voter's Handbook.

Chapter 2: How Medical Marijuana Prevailed

7. Dennis Peron, interview by author, telephone, 11 May 2000.
8. Scott Imler, interview by author, telephone, 10 May 2000.
9. John Entwhistle, interview by author, telephone, 11 May 2000.
10. Imler, interview, 10 May 2000.
11. Dave Fratello, interview by author, telephone, 12 May 2000.
12. Entwhistle, interview.
13. Imler, interview.
14. Fratello, interview.
15. No on 215 pamphlet, 1996.
16. Ibid. Cowan confirmed to the author that he had actually made the statement during the 1992 NORML convention.

17. Lester Grinspoon, M.D., and James B. Bakalar. *Marihuana: The Forbidden Medicine* (New Haven, Conn.: Yale University Press, 1993).

18. Fratello, interview.

19. Imler, interview.

20. Letters to the Editor, *San Francisco Chronicle*, 26 September 1996.

21. Garry Trudeau, "A Hypocritical Generation," *Time*, 16 September 1996.

22. Fratello, interview.

23. Imler, interview.

24. Alan Bock, "Is Prop. 215 a Plea for Compassion or a Smoke Screen!" *Orange County Register*, 3 November 1996, Commentary section.

25. Imler, interview.

Chapter 3: Were the Voters Duped?

26. "Pot Proposition Takes Lungren Aback," *Los Angeles Times*, 7 November 1996.

27. Hendrik Hertzberg, "The Pot Perplex," *The New Yorker*, 6 January 1997, 4.

28. Robert L. Maginnis, *Medical Marijuana*, Insight IS97A1 (Washington, D.C.: Family Research Council, 1997).

29. Senate Committee on the Judiciary, hearings on medical marijuana, 2 December 1996.

30. Joy, Watson, and Benson, *Marijuana and Medicine*, 13.

31. Ibid.

32. Ibid.

33. Ibid.

34. Ibid., 14.

35. Ibid.

36. Ibid.

37. Ibid.

38. Ibid.

39. Ibid.

40. Ibid., 15. It is possibly of interest that the question of whether there really is "great risk of harm," objectively speaking—for 12–17-year-olds or for anybody—in using marijuana once or twice a week is not addressed in

this survey. The survey is intended to measure "perceived risk," and the government seems to think it's good if people 12–17 perceive great risk, whether the perception is warranted or not.

41. Ibid.
42. Ibid., 8.
43. Ibid.
44. Ibid., 100.
45. Ibid.
46. Ibid., 11.
47. Ibid., 12.

Chapter 4: Implementation: The Lungren Interlude

48. *Encarta Encyclopedia Deluxe 2000* [CD-ROM] (Seattle: Microsoft Corporation, 1999).
49. Wo/Men's Alliance for Medical Marijuana incorporation papers, 7 November 1996.
50. Californians for Medical Rights news release, 2 December 1996.
51. "Oakland Cannabis Club Steps Up Activity," *Oakland Tribune*, 22 November 1996.
52. Michael Fielding, "Sheriff Gates Still Attacking Prop. 215," *Orange County Register*, 15 November 1996.
53. S. Clarke Smith, M.D., interview by author, Irvine, Calif., 22 October 1999.
54. MedEx, Santa Cruz, flyer, 1996.
55. Carolyn Skorneck, "Opponents of State Medical Marijuana Laws Want Federal Laws Enforced," Associated Press, 3 December 1996.
56. "Lungren Gives Prop. 215 Interpretation," *Orange County Register*, 4 December 1996.
57. Proposition 215 Chronology, www.drugsense.org, accesssed 18 May 2000.
58. Robert Rankin, "Administration Adamant That Marijuana Is and Will Remain Illegal," Knight-Ridder News Service, 30 December 1996.
59. Robert Trautman, "U.S. Says It Will Fight New State Marijuana Laws," Reuters News Service, 30 December 1996.
60. Ulysses Torassa, "Judge to Let Pot Clubs Reopen," *San Francisco Examiner*, 9 January 1997.

61. Chronology, www.drugsense.org.

62. California Medical Association, news release, 27 February 1997.

63. Bob Egelko, "Judge's Order Seen As Victory for Prop. 215," *Orange County Register*, 12 April 1997.

64. Jerome Kassirer, M.D., "Federal Foolishness and Marijuana," *New England Journal of Medicine*, 30 January 1997.

65. Carolyn Skorneck, Associated Press, 7 February 1997.

66. Peter Larsen, "Medical Pot: Legal Fight Keeps the Doctor Away," *Orange County Register*, 9 February 1997, A-1.

67. California Department of Justice, Information Bulletin No. 97-BNE-01, 24 February 1997.

68. Ibid.

69. "White House: Doctors Can Discuss Pot with Patients," Associated Press, 2 March 1997.

70. Durk Pearson, interview by author, telephone, 7 March 1997; *Durk Pearson and Sandy Shaw et al. v Barry McCaffrey et al.*, 97-CV-00462 (WBB), U.S. District Court for the District of Columbia. On the Web at www.emord.com.complain.htm.

71. "San Jose OKs Pot Club," Associated Press, 26 March 1997.

72. Chronology, www.drugsense.org.

73. Chronology, www.drugsense.com.

74. Tony Bizjak, "AIDS Patient Wants Sacramento Marijuana Club," Scripps-McClatchy Western Service, 6 April 1997.

75. Robert Harris, Sacramento Patients Access Clinic news release and memorandum, 8 May 1997; Robert Harris, interview by author, telephone, 6 May 1997.

76. The NORML Foundation, Washington, D.C., news release, 24 April 1997.

77. Robert E. Klein, M.D., Associate Executive Director, Permanente Medical Group, Oakland, Calif., interoffice memorandum, 8 May 1997.

78. Ibid.

79. "Medical Marijuana Patients Arrested in Prop. 215 Test Cases," *California NORML Reports*, October 1997.

80. Michael Fleeman, "Mansion Houses Marijuana Treasure," *Orange County Register*, 31 July 1997.

81. Todd McCormick, interview by author, Santa Ana, Calif., 11 September 1997.
82. *People v Trippett,* A073484, 14 August 1997.
83. "Peron Pot Case Postponed," Associated Press, 21 August 1997.
84. "Hung Jury in Petaluma Pot Case," Associated Press, 23 August 1997.
85. Rand Martin, Chief of Staff for Senator John Vasconcellos, interviews by author, telephone, August 1997.
86. Imler, interview.
87. Ibid.
88. Ibid.
89. "Pot Siezures Up in California," Associated Press, 29 November 1997.
90. "Marijuana Arrests Up," Associated Press, 14 October 1997.
91. Bob Egelko, "Peron Pot Case Moved," Associated Press, 13 December 1997.
92. State of California, Office of the Attorney General, Dan Lungren to "All California District Attorneys," memorandum, 15 December 1997.
93. Imler, interview.
94. *People v Peron,* A077630, First Appellate District, Division 5, 1997.
95. Peter Larsen, "Panel Probes Medical Marijuana at UC Irvine," *Orange County Register,* 16 December 1997, A-1; Peter Larsen, "Medical Pot Panel Hears Patients," *Orange County Register,* 17 December 1997, A-1.
96. John Gettman, unpublished research report, May 2000.
97. Bob Egelko, "Government Moves to Close Marijuana Clubs," *Orange County Register,* 10 January 1998.
98. Americans for Medical Rights, news release, 9 January 1998.
99. Senator John Vasconcellos, news release, 12 January 1998.
100. Tiffany Montgomery, *Orange County Register,* 15 January 1998, B-1; Marvin Chavez, interview by author, Santa Ana, Calif., 14 July 1998; prosecution *in limine* brief, 19 July 1998.
101. Ordinance No. 1276, City of Arcata, Title V, Chapter 16.
102. James Silva, interview by author, Westminster, Calif., 11 November 1998.
103. Chronology, www.drugsense.com.
104. Ellen Komp, "San Jose Cannabis Center Raided," *215 Reporter* (Frazier Park, Calif.) May–June 1998.

105. "Bel Air Pot Grower Sought," Associated Press, 3 April 1998; Peter
      McWilliams, interview by author, telephone, 15 April 1998.

106. Mark Sauer, "Medical Pot Law May Face Local Court Test," *San Diego
      Union Tribune*, 7 January 1999; Steve McWilliams, interview by author,
      Santa Ana, Calif., 14 August 1998.

107. Phil Garlington, "Pot Grower Insists Others' Medical Needs Let Him
      Flaunt Weed," *Orange County Register*, 11 May 1997; Thomas J.
      Ballanco (Smith's attorney), interviews by author, 15 May and 4 August
      1999.

108. Bob Egelko, "Feds Move to Close Down Medical Marijuana Clubs,"
      Associated Press, 24 March 1998; Bob Egelko, "Judge Will Close
      Medical Marijuana Clubs," Associated Press, 14 May 1998.

109. Steve Kubby, interview by author, Santa Ana, Calif., 18 October 1998.

110. California Senate Committee on Public Safety, news release, 27 May
      1998.

111. Jeff Jones, interview by author, Oakland, Calif., 30 May 1999; Oakland
      City Council Minutes, 14 May 1998; Report of City of Oakland Task
      Force, 1 May 1998.

112. "Songwriter Arrested on Pot Charges," Associated Press, 14 September
      1998.

113. Michael Baldwin, interview by author, telephone, 14 October 1998.

114. "Marijuana Clubs Gain Face Closure," Reuters, 15 October 1998;
      "Medical Marijuana Advocates Say They Will Appeal Shutdown
      Ruling," Associated Press, 15 October 1998.

115. Editorial, *Orange County Register,* 17 September 1998.

116. Marvin Chavez, interview by author, Santa Ana, Calif., 24 September
      1999.

117. Orange County Patient, Doctor, Nurse Support Group, informational
      brochure, n.d.

118. Alan Bock, "Cast of Characters in Chavez Trial," *Orange County
      Register,* 13 November 1998, Op-Ed page.

119. Bob Egelko, "Lake County Men Not Guilty on Medical Marijuana
      Charge," Associated Press, 11 December 1998.

120. *"Medical Marijuana Defendant to Stand Trial," Sacramento Bee,* 19
      December 1998.

121. Dan Weintraub, "Lockyer Has Ambitious Agenda," *Orange County Register*, 29 December 1998, A-5.

Chapter 5: Implementation: The Lockyer Years

122. "Lockyer Outlines Plans," *San Francisco Chronicle*, 4 January 1999, A-1.

123. Dennis Peron, interview by author, telephone, 23 January 1999; Legislative Counsel's Digest 13583, RN9903646, 2 February 1999.

124. Chronology, www.drugsense.org.

125. Peter King, "Kubby Arrest Not about Marijuana," *Orange County Register*, 11 February 1999, A-3.

126. Editorial, "Outrage in Law," *Orange County Register*, 21 January 1999.

127. Steve Kubby, interview by author, telephone from jail, Auburn, Calif., 20 January 1999, and several subsequent interviews; Investigator Michael Lyle, North Tahoe Task Force (NTTF), interview by author, telephone, 20 January 1999; copies of NTTF press release and summary of charges, 20 January 1999.

128. Carl Armbrust, J. David Nick, and James Silva, interviews by author, Westminster, Calif., 29 January 1999.

129. Senator John Vasconcellos, "Listen Up, Washington, the People Have Spoken," *Los Angeles Times,* 25 February, 1999, Op-Ed page.

130. Vincent DeQuattro, M.D., Judge of Superior Court, Tahoe City, Calif., 4 February 1999.

131. Steve Kubby, medical records, released with patient's and doctor's permission: Diagnostic Battery I (plasma biochemistry, urine biochemistry, octreotide scan, stress echocardiogram, history, MRI chest, MRI abdomen, MIBG scan) conducted by USC Clinical Laboratories, 8–12 March 1999; Diagnostic Battery II (hair samples, blood samples, urine samples, 24-hour blood pressure monitor, neuropsychological evaluation by Dorothy Weiss, Ph.D.) conducted 14–15 April 1999; pulmonary function tests conducted 28 June 1999.

132. Joy, Watson, and Benson, *Marijuana and Medicine*, 3.

133. Editorial, "Science and Medical Marijuana," *Orange County Register,* 18 March 1999.

134. Teri Sforza, "Report: Marijuana Has Some Benefits," *Orange County Register,* 18 March 1999, A-1.

135. California Attorney General's Office, news release, 18 March 1999.

136. "McCaffrey and Reno Rebuff Lockyer," *Sacramento Bee,* 29 March 1999.

137. Editorial, "Medical Marijuana Stalls," *Orange County Register,* 2 April 1999.

138. Calif. Const., Art. V, sec. 13.

139. Alan Gathright, "Panel Ponders Medical Marijuana," *San Jose Mercury News,* 28 April 1999.

140. *San Francisco Examiner,* 13 July 1999.

141. Noah Isackson, "White House Takes Issue with Medical Marijuana Legislation," Associated Press, 21 July 1999.

142. Joy, Watson, and Benson, *Marijuana and Medicine,* 25–27.

143. *U.S. v Oakland Cannabis Buyers Cooperative et al.* 98-16950, 190 Fed. 3d 1109 (9th Circuit 1999).

144. *U.S. v Oakland Cannabis Buyers Cooperative* appeal, Justice Department brief (February 29, 2000), 9th Circuit issued order denying petition en banc.

145. Teri Sforza, "Medical Pot Advocates Appeal to Supervisors," *Orange County Register,* 19 March 1999.

146. Chronology, www.drugsense.com.

147. Ibid.

148. Richard Cowan, "Is Lockyer Turning into 'Lungren Lite'?" MarijuanaNews.com, 15 September 1999.

149. Entwhistle, interview.

150. "Joint Venture Bed and Breakfast," *Los Angeles Times,* 3 April 2000.

151. Ucilia Wang, "Mendocino Pot Initiative May Reach Ballot," Press Democrat News Services, 24 April 2000; "Mendocino Voters to Weigh in on Recreational Marijuana Legalization," Associated Press, 26 April 2000.

152. "Medical Marijuana," *Orange County Register,* 18 July 2000.

153. Robert Raich, interview by author, telephone, 17 July 2000.

154. Donald J. Abrams, M.D., interview by author, telephone, 21 July 2000.

155. Entwhistle, interview.

Chapter 6: Is Marijuana a Medicine?

156. Lynn Zimmer, Ph.D., and John P. Morgan, M.D., *Marijuana Myths, Marijuana Facts: A Review of the Scientific Evidence* (New York and San Francisco: The Lindesmith Center, 1997), 17.

157. Joy, Watson, and Benson, *Marijuana and Medicine,* 29.

158. Ibid., 31.

159. Ibid., 35.

160. Ibid.

161. Ibid., 37.

162. Ibid., 22–23.

163. Ibid., 27.

164. Zimmer and Morgan, *Marijuana Myths, Marijuana Facts,* 18.

165. Ibid., 19–20.

166. Ibid., 20–21.

167. Steve Kubby, interview by author, Laguna Beach, Calif., 18 June 1999.

168. Robert Schmidt, interview by author, Orange, Calif., 2 March 2000.

169. Robert Schmidt, interview by author, Petaluma, Calif., 23 March 2000.

170. Ibid.

171. Ibid.

172. Zimmer and Morgan, *Marijuana Myths, Marijuana Facts,* 24.

Chapter 7: It Didn't Start with George Soros's Checkbook

173. Jack Herer, *The Emperor Wears No Clothes,* 39.

174. Edward M. Brecher, and the Editors of Consumer Reports, *Licit and Illicit Drugs* (Boston: Little Brown, 1972), 424.

175. Zimmer and Morgan, *Marijuana Myths, Marijuana Facts,* 11.

176. Ibid., 12–13.

177. Dan Baum, *Smoke and Mirrors: The War on Drugs and the Politics of Failure* (Boston: Back Bay Books; Little, Brown, 1996), 20–21. Much of this summary is based on Baum's book and on Mike Gray's *Drug Crazy* (New York: Random House, 1998).

178. Baum, *Smoke and Mirrors,* 90.

179. Ibid., 91.

180. *Congressional Record,* 10 November 1981, Vol. 127, no. 164.

181. Zimmer and Morgan, *Marijuana Myths, Marijuana Facts,* 24–25.

182. Cited in Baum, *Smoke and Mirrors,* 222–223.

183. Alan Bock, "Crimping Progress by Banning Hemp," *Orange County Register,* 30 October 1988.

184. California Hemp Initiative, 1991.

185. Melvyn B. Krauss and Edward P. Lazear, eds., *Searching for Alternatives: Drug-Control Policy in the United States* (Stanford, Calif.: Hoover Institution Press, 1991), 379.

186. Ibid., 385.

187. Proposition P, 1991.

188. Dennis Peron and Mary Rathbun, *Brownie Mary's Cookbook and Dennis Peron's Recipe for Social Change,* (San Francisco: Trail of Smoke Publishing, 1996).

189. Ibid., 39.

190. Peron and Rathbun, *Brownie Mary's Cookbook,* 40.

191. Senator Henry Mello, letter to HHS Secretary Donna Shalala, 23 September 1993.

192. "Pot Smoking Acceptable at S.F. Club," Associated Press, 23 May 1995.

193. Dennis Peron, interview by author, telephone, 10 May 2000.

194. Imler, interview.

Chapter 8: Before Prohibition: Medical Marijuana's History

195. Brecher, *Licit and Illicit Drugs,* 397–398.

196. Tod H. Mikuriya, M.D., ed., Marijuana Medical Papers (Oakland, Calif.: Medi-Comp Press, 1973), 118.

197. Ibid., xiv.

198. Ibid., 3–33.

199. Ibid., 134.

200. Brecher, *Licit and Illicit Drugs,* 405.

201. Ibid.

202. Ibid., 406.

203. Ibid.

204. Mikuriya, *Marijuana Medical Papers,* xix.

205. Ibid.

206. Ibid.

Chapter 9: No Compromise—Why Is Opposition to Medical Marijuana So Fierce?

207. Baum, *Smoke and Mirrors,* 331–332.

208. Ibid., 339.

209. Gray, *Drug Crazy,* 198.

210. Gallup Poll, 19–21 March 1991, 73 percent were for "making marijuana legally available for doctors to prescribe." Lake Research poll, 5–9 February 1997, 60 percent said yes to "Should doctors be able to prescribe marijuana for medical purposes to seriously or terminally ill patients?" CNN Internet poll, 12 March 1998, of 25,000 respondents (self-selected, not a random sample) 96 percent said they "support the use of marijuana for medical purposes." ABC News/Discovery News poll, 29 May 1997, 69 percent said doctors should be allowed to prescribe marijuana, while 75 percent opposed decriminalization for recreational use.

211. Ronald Hamowy, ed., *Dealing with Drugs* (San Francisco: Pacific Research Institute for Public Policy; Lexington, Mass.: Lexington Books, 1987) 183–184.

212. Ibid., 184.

213. Ibid., 185.

214. Krauss and Lazear, *Searching for Alternatives,* 27.

215. Hamowy, *Dealing with Drugs,* 328.

216. Ibid.

217. Ibid., 329.

Chapter 10: Taking It National

218. www.levellers.org, accessed 16 May 2000.

219. Ibid.

220. The main source for much of this section is James Sterngold, "Turned on by Politics: Meet Arizona's Happiest Taxpayers," New York Times News Service, 7 October 1996.

221. Ibid.

222. Ibid.

223. Ibid.

224. Ibid.

225. Louis Sahagun, "Arizona Launches a Drug War Revolt," *Los Angeles Times,* 10 December 1996, A-1.
226. Ibid.
227. Ibid.
228. Ibid.
229. David Schwartz, "Arizona Deals Hard Blow to Medical Marijuana," Reuters News Service, 17 April 1997.
230. Ibid.
231. Fratello, interview.
232. Ibid.
233. The source for information on the various initiatives is Drug Policy Foundation, "Election '98," September 1998.
234. "U.S. Officials Issue Medical Marijuana Warning," Associated Press, 13 December 1996.
235. Fratello, interview.
236. "McCaffrey: U.S. Public to Decide on Medical Marijuana," Reuters, 2 October 1997.
237. Roger Pilon, "The Medical Marihuana Referenda Movement in America: Federalism Implications," testimony before Crime Subcommittee of House Judiciary Committee, 1 October 1997.
238. All excerpts from state legislation taken from NORML, "Medical Marijuana Legislation," 29 January 1998.
239. Reuters, 18 June 1998.
240. *Congressional Record,* 6 August 1998.
241. Editorial, "A Nonsense Resolution," *Orange County Register,* 17 September 1998.
242. Associated Press, 19 October 1998.
243. Reuters, 19 October 1998.
244. Barry McCaffrey, "Science, Not Politics, Should Govern Medical Marijuana," *Los Angeles Times,* 22 October 1998.
245. Chronology, www.drugsense.org.
246. "More Work Ahead, Say Pot Proponents," Associated Press, 4 November 1998.
247. "Uncertainty Haunts Medical Marijuana Patients," *Grants Pass Daily Courier,* 19 January 1999.
248. "Hawaii Governor Pushes Medical Marijuana," Associated Press, 4 December 1998.

249. "Gallup: Majorities for Medical Marijuana," Associated Press, 26 March 1999.

Chapter 11: What Does Federal Law Really Say?
250. Francis L. Young, "In the Matter of Marijuana Rescheduling Petition," Opinion and Recommended Ruling, Docket No. 86-22, 8 September 1988, 27.
251. Scheduling definitions in this chapter are from Joy, Watson, and Benson, *Marijuana and Medicine,* appendix C.
252. Young, "Opinion," 68.
253. Ibid., 1, 8.
254. Ibid., 27.
255. Ibid., 28–29.
256. Ibid., 32.
257. Ibid., 38.
258. Ibid., 56–58.
259. Joy, Watson, and Benson, *Marijuana and Medicine*, 196.
260. Young, "Opinion," 31.
261. Joy, Watson, and Benson, *Marijuana and Medicine*, 202.
262. Ibid., 205.
263. Ibid., 203.
264. Ibid.
265. Ibid., 205.
266. John Gettman, interview by author, telephone, 12 May 2000.
267. Ibid.
268. Harry F. Rosenthal, "Feds Say Doctors Can't Prescribe for Illness," Associated Press, 30 December 1996.
269. Donna Shalala, "Marijuana Legalization Not the Answer," *Wall Street Journal*, 18 August 1995, op-ed page.
270. Joy, Watson, and Benson, *Marijuana and Medicine*, 200.

Chapter 12: Frontier Journeys
271. All quotes in this section are from Dr. Tod Mikuriya, interview by author, Berkeley, Calif., 22 March 2000.
272. John Entwhistle and Dennis Person, interview by author, Lake County, Calif., 24 June 1999.

273. Entwhistle, interview, 11 May 2000.
274. Ibid.
275. Peron, interview, 11 May 2000.
276. All quotes in this section are from Schmidt, interview, 23 May 2000.

Note: Some sources of information are stories directly from a wire service rather than from a newspaper. All wire services (and many major newspapers) now have searchable archives available at http://search.news.yahoo.com/search/news/options.

Index